BOBBY JOHNSTONE

THE PASSING OF AN AGE

BOBBY JOHNSTONE

THE PASSING OF AN AGE

JOHN LEIGH

First published in Great Britain in 2007 by

The Breedon Books Publishing Company Limited

Breedon House, 3 The Parker Centre, Derby, DE21 4SZ.

This paperback edition published in Great Britain in 2013 by DB Publishing,

an imprint of JMD Media Ltd

ISBN   978-1-78091-293-6

Printed and bound in the UK by Copytech (UK) Ltd Peterborough

CONTENTS

Acknowledgements and Dedication

I am grateful to many people who have assisted with the material in this book, among them several individuals and organisations whose contributions have been partly driven by their own inclination to see the career of Bobby Johnstone permanently recorded. I could not have made progress without the assistance of the clubs that Bobby Johnstone played for, and, in this respect, the support of Selkirk FC, Hibernian FC and Manchester City FC has been total. The secretary of Manchester City **Bernard Halford** has given much of his time, and he has brokered my access to several individuals who have made contributions that I hope put this work into better context. The official historian of Manchester City **Gary James** has given freely of his time and advice; his experience means there can be no better source of guidance for someone in my position, as I am undertaking this task for the first and only time. Next, I owe a very large debt of gratitude to Hibernian FC, and would particularly like to thank the club director and secretary **Garry O'Hagan**, who has been most hospitable and allowed me access to the club's historical information. I also had the opportunity to conduct research alongside the club historian **Tom Wright**, who is now beginning to despair of ever seeing Hibernian reclaim the Scottish Cup, which Hibs last won over a century ago. In the absence of that Tom, it's my round! I was further privileged to interview two genuine legends of the Scottish game in **Eddie Turnbull** and **Lawrie Reilly**, the latter in his home, and I am grateful to **Mrs Reilly**, too, for her patience and hospitality.

The MCFC **Former Players' Association** have given great support. In particular, two ex-playing colleagues and long-time friends of the subject, **Ken Barnes** and **Bert Lister**, provided illuminating remarks during interviews. In Scotland, Selkirk FC have been wholeheartedly supportive, and I record my thanks to the club chairman, **Craig Douglas**, his wife **Judith** and their family. It has been a privilege to visit the town of Selkirk and meet with people who grew up with Bobby Johnstone and played alongside him in schoolyards, fields and, later, organised matches – and not just football matches. Their hospitality to a Sassenach is to their great credit, and my affection for the town, it's folk, and its football club will endure, hopefully for many years yet. I must single out **Graham Bateman**, a gentleman now approaching his 90s, and his wonderful wife **Nancy**. Having played football as a goalkeeper behind Bobby's father in the early 1930s, Graham wrote *A Century of Soccer in Selkirk* in 1980, a pivotal reference for this work. He remained a friend of Bobby's until the end and was entrusted with penning the eulogy that was read at his graveside; what a marvellous job he made of that task. A true gentleman, I shall treasure the time I have spent with him.

My brief time at Workington FC was of great interest, and the day spent in West Cumbria, as a guest of the inimitable **John Walsh** (BBC Radio Cumbria), was a pleasurable one. I left there with the fervent hope that the club can return to better days and repay the loyalty shown by the likes of **Peter Foley, Billy Watson** and **Steve Durham**. Their passion for their club will endure even if success doesn't come, and I thank them all for their important contributions here. Thanks also to club chairman **Dale Brotherton, Alan Clarke** and **Matt Henney** for a most entertaining afternoon, and the sense of connection with the action that best comes from standing on the terraces.

Beyond the auspices of the football clubs, many other individuals have helped me, sometimes simply by providing encouragement, and I hope they, too, enjoy reading the finished book. Thanks to **Steve Fleet, Roy Cheetham, Johnny Williamson** and **John Riley** (secretary), all members of the MCFC Former Players' Association, and **Mr and Mrs Johnny Hart** for their hospitality. Also **Ian Niven**, Bobby's fellow Scot, who happily provided a home for him and went on to provide sterling services to junior football supporters in the blue half of Manchester. Thanks to **Roy and Margaret Allison, John Gwynne, Jim Jeffrey, Jim Conway, Bob Bond, Dave and Sue Wallace** (*King of the Kippax*) and **Fred Eyre**, all of whom generously gave permission to use their material. My long-time friends **Ian McColl, Alan Course, Nigel Gregory** (my driver!), **Roy Conner** and **Phil Noble** all provided data and other information, and I know we will remain friends for many years to come. Finally, at the Manchester end, I am indebted to **Paul Hince** of the *Manchester Evening News*, Mr Halford's personal secretary **Rebecca Firth, Ed Garvey** and the archives of the **Manchester Central Library**.

In Selkirk, **Mr and Mrs Archie Smail, Louise Ovens, Mr and Mrs A. Millar** (thanks for the book, Alison), **Keith Anderson, David Knox, Alastair Watson, Davey Watkins** (Radio Borders), **Bill Stark, Walter Bateman**, the **Glen Hotel** and finally **Mr and Mrs Pratt** of **The Hawthorns**, near Galashiels.

Further thanks for support in researching the Oldham Athletic years is due to **Bill and Marjorie Spurdle, Dave Moore, Bob Davidson, Jimmy Frizzell, Chris Stuttard, Alan Hardy, Gordon Lawton,** and especially **Tony Bugby** and his colleagues at the *Oldham Evening Chronicle*.

In addition to Messrs **Gabriel, Becker** and **Fagan**, several people have offered practical support, often helping me cut through what seemed like major barriers at the time, many borne of my own naivety at what lay ahead. Besides **Steve Caron** and his colleagues at Breedon Books, I want to thank **Peter Williamson** (Witton), **Andy Betts, Bill Pennington** and especially **Jon Williams** for their help.

Members of Bobby's family have been of great assistance, especially his sister **Margaret Johnstone**, a lady who remains very active some time beyond her 80th birthday. I have attempted to describe Bobby's life without upsetting or harming anybody involved with his story, but almost inevitably there will be inaccuracies in the text, and this may lead to some frustrations after publication. Writing the story of a great footballer's life necessarily involves some reference to off-the-field activities and family matters, and I have tried to achieve this without exaggerating or sensationalising any aspect. To the extent that they have been both able and prepared to assist with that, I am grateful to Bobby's sister **Betty**, his nephew **Robbie**, niece **Jackie**, ex-wife **Heather Turnbull** and finally Bobby's daughter **Nicola Taylor**.

On a personal note, my immediate family will be delighted that this project is finished. I dedicate this book to my wife Pauline, while apologising for the major disruption this has caused during the last two-and-a-half years. There have been numerous occasions when I have put domestic and social routines to one side, and

I intend to try to make up some of the ground lost, especially to my four children and granddaughter, and resume our usual family life.

My son, Alexander, has covered many hundreds of miles with me in pursuit of this project, and early in 2005 he made a guest appearance for Selkirk FC's Under-14 side. The sight of him running muddied from the pitch and into the Bobby Johnstone Pavilion at Yarrow Park was an inspiring one for me. That autumn he visited Borough Park, Workington, one weekend, and Arsenal's Highbury the next, marvelling at each. I felt I'd instilled a proper sense of what football is about...

PREFACE

I didn't see Bobby Johnstone play, but as a young lad I was drawn inexorably towards Manchester City. Their appeal was instant and magnetic, drawing me in completely; I never wavered for one second. Their training ground was next to my primary school in Cheadle, Cheshire, and I stood on the fence there, while Malcolm Allison bawled instructions at the brilliant players of the late 1960s. On Saturdays I would go back to watch the A and B teams play, and early in my teens I progressed to first-team games at Maine Road as well as reading and collecting anything associated with the club. Later, I found out that City's reserve team had played against Bury at Gigg Lane on the day I was born: Tuesday 11 November 1958. That day was also the 40th anniversary of the ending of World War One and, less remarkably, nine months and five days after the Munich air disaster. My father, a United fan of sorts, had apparently been inconsolable for three days after the awful news from Germany.

After a long time searching, I finally tracked down and bought the team sheet for my birthday game, and so began what, to me, was the perfectly natural process of looking more deeply into the careers of the City players listed, chief among them Bobby Johnstone. The game finished in a 1–1 draw, and Bert Lister, a good friend of Bobby's, played alongside him.

In the autumn of 2001 I heard the news that Bobby Johnstone had died. Why would I feel a peculiar sense of loss? Here was a man that I'd never seen play; many of his greatest footballing achievements came before my parents met. Yet from the things I'd read and heard from those who had seen him play, I knew he was my kind of player. His story intrigued me. In 2003 Bobby's home-town club Selkirk FC, an East of Scotland League side, staged a match against a young Manchester City XI. The occasion celebrated the opening of the Bobby Johnstone Pavilion at Selkirk's beautiful new Yarrow Park ground, and at the game I met Bert Lister, who had travelled up to Scotland in honour of his mate. Bobby and Bert first played together at City but went their separate ways at the end of the 1950s, before several successful years together at Oldham Athletic.

Bobby was described that night as 'a genius with a football at his feet', and I felt his story was worth exploring. Late in his life Bobby had been asked about an autobiography, and his response was 'who would read it?' Perhaps he was right, but at least this book will provide a permanent record of the football career and life of a man still revered in at least three club boardrooms (that would be four, except that Selkirk FC don't have a boardroom). Bobby Johnstone and his contemporaries are remembered fondly by those interested in the game as it used to be, long before all-seater stadia, Sky Digital, and Bosman transfers, days when, after the match, everyone involved went home on the bus, and the players could aspire to £20 a week if they were lucky.

As part of the research required to complete the project, I had the privilege of meeting some wonderful people, including men who played football alongside Bobby at each stage of his footballing life. Archie Smail, now 83, still lives happily in a tiny cottage in Selkirk with his wife Eileen. Archie told me 'We kicked balls along the gutter in school days. My brother Davy played for Selkirk and Newtongrange, and he signed for Newtongrange with Bobby – it was junior football. I played behind Bobby at right-half for Selkirk, and when I passed the ball down the wing, he was supposed to be there...' Later, as Bobby was establishing himself at Hibernian, the legendary Eddie Turnbull, who became the first British player to score in European football, looked after him, and he related some wonderful tales about the 'three musketeers', a little grouping formed with Willie Ormond. In Manchester Ken Barnes was a close pal, and he too had some tales to tell about the player, whom he described as: 'on his day, the best I ever played with'.

Graham Bateman, now approaching his 90s, initially kept goal behind Bobby's father, a full-back for Selkirk in the 1930s, and he later played in the same team as Bobby. Graham recalls that Bobby came back to Selkirk each summer and enjoyed his cricket too... 'Bobby was still happy to whitewash the cricket screens when he came home to Selkirk; amazing, this big star in Manchester, who'd scored in two Cup Finals'.

This book tells how Bobby Johnstone played the game at the highest level, in front of some of the largest crowds in the history of the British game. His retirement from football in 1965 came just as the game embraced a new age, leaving Bobby and his ilk behind. It was the passing of an age.

FOREWORDS

Eddie Turnbull

Bobby was a key member of the Famous Five; when he came in it finished things off and we never looked back. Before then, we'd lacked Bobby's skills – he fitted in so well with Gordon Smith on the right wing. Willie Ormond and myself on the left were a bit harder, yes, but we couldn't really compare in terms of football skills. Later, Bobby, Willie and myself became great mates because we did a bit more socialising than Gordon and Lawrie Reilly. We had some fantastic times and got into one or two scrapes, such as the time at Aberdeen! I was a few years older than wee Bobby, and at first I used to look after him. You got players that tried to intimidate him in those days because he was so skilful. If anybody kicked Bobby on the field, I'd say 'OK son, I'll sort it out', and I would tell them 'you touch that boy...', and the wee man never forgot it. He was a lovely guy, a real character. Out on the pitch he got into the right place at the right time. I don't know how he did it; he wasn't a ball-watcher, he just seemed to drift this way, or that, and the ball came...

Ken Barnes

He was out of this world, bloody 'ell, what a player! On his day, he was quite simply the best I ever played with. His forte, I can still see it now, was the 'weighted' pass... just perfect, so that you don't break your stride when you're in full flight. Where I played, I often linked up with him as an attacking wing-half, I got to know the things he would do, taking players away with him... I'd run into the space he'd left, because it was on the cards that he'd back-heel it to me or something, as I overlapped. Off the park, he came across as quiet, unless you knew him well, but in time we became close mates, and we had some great times going about. There ain't any Bobby Johnstone's about in the game today, I can tell you. They don't try to beat players now... and, honestly, I don't think that Scotland have produced a player as good as Bobby in the whole of the time since his playing days.

CHAPTER 1

Bobby's Childhood and Schooling to 1946

'Hopey, your wee fitba' player's here...'

The message was for George Johnstone (who was known as Hopey); when he heard it he was thrilled. His wife, Elizabeth, had given birth to their first son Robert at their home in the Scottish border town of Selkirk. It was 7 September 1929; in those days, whenever a birth was imminent, it was quite usual for apprehensive fathers to find other matters to occupy their thoughts. There can be no doubt that Hopey's attention was suitably diverted – it was a Saturday, and he had been playing full-back for Selkirk Football Club. The message arrived at around 5pm, just about the time that the football scores were coming through on the wireless; Hopey and Liz had the result that they had wanted.

The Johnstones already had two daughters, but this time Hopey had mentioned to Liz that he would like a son. His wish was granted, and once the youngster, who was always called Bobby, was delivered safely into his mother's arms, a message was sent urgently on its way from No.11 Cannon Street to the nearby Ettrick Park football ground. The new arrival would achieve all of Hopey's sporting ambitions and more; wee Bobby Johnstone would go on to surpass the footballing achievements of anyone, not just from Selkirk but from the wider Borders area, too. In doing so, he would bring the name of this idyllic Scottish town to the attention of millions.

Family and Home
Bobby was the middle of five children, and the only boy. Margaret, the eldest, was born in 1925, and two years later Jenny arrived. After Bobby came two more girls: Betty in 1932 and Sheila in April 1935.

At home on Cannon Street, close to the banks of Ettrick Water, conditions were far from ideal. The Johnstone family home was dated even by the standards of the day, consisting of one bedroom, a living room and a small kitchen. As the bedroom accommodated just one bed, there were two more in the living room. Typically for the time, sanitary facilities were unsophisticated; the toilet was in a small outhouse to the rear of the property.

In 1934, when Bobby was just four, he contracted diphtheria. It is not clear how, although there was another case in the town at the same time, another young lad named Bailey. Although very rare in Britain these days, diphtheria is nonetheless a serious illness, most commonly affecting youngsters. It can sometimes cause permanent damage to the heart and nerves, and in Bobby's case its onset severely restricted his breathing. Fortunately, the emergency doctor happened to be at another house on Cannon Street and was quickly summoned. After examining Bobby, he ordered his immediate hospitalisation and was concerned enough to travel directly behind the ambulance as it sped to the Fever Hospital in Galashiels, some six miles away. There Bobby underwent a tracheotomy, one of the earliest uses of this technique in the Borders area. It must have been traumatic for one so young, and the ward sister sat with young Bobby all night, assuring him that he would be alright, that she would look after him, and that he wasn't going to die, as he feared.

The next day the family all came to see him and in subsequent years were able to recount how they'd seen his 'pale wee face up at the hospital window'. Bobby was then kept in strict isolation and confined to bed for around two months, but thanks to the quality of nursing care he made a full recovery. Subsequent events show that the illness had no long-term effects on his health, 'although he would carry the scar on his neck for the rest of his life. The main difficulty seemed to be that once he returned to his feet he had to practically re-learn to walk.

The 1930s saw a great deal of economic depression across Britain generally, and Selkirk was no different. Regular work was often hard to come by. In common with many other men of the town, Hopey often struggled to get a full week's work as a machine operator in the tweed mills. Walter Bateman, who also lived on Cannon Street, and Billy Stark, two of Bobby's school mates, recalled that 'There were very few fellows of Hopey's generation who didn't suffer from unemployment at some stage in their lives... the only yins that always kept their jobs steady were the engineers and such, skilled men, on maintenance, who were used to keep the machinery going.' Walter recalled that his father, a butcher, also had regular work: 'It was unbelievable how some managed, living on little or nothing. There were some who would come to the butcher's and get a bone, and make a large pan of soup. It never meant any the worse for us though; everyone was in the same boat, and there was no such thing as obesity!'

Sport offered the working classes an escape from the drudgery of working life, and Hopey had been playing football locally for many years. His football 'career' continued for some years after Bobby's birth, and a couple of Hopey's brothers were also good enough to play for Selkirk FC. Indeed, while Bobby was still a toddler, his father played in the Borders Cup-winning sides of 1931 and 1932. The Johnstones were quite a footballing family, and at this time the club was enjoying a spell of success. They even began to attract new supporters in what has invariably been rugby union territory, and on several occasions attendances actually topped the 1,000 mark. In one instance, against Vale of Leithen, the take at the gate had yielded in excess of £20![1]

Primary school was just a short stride along the banks of Ettrick Water for the Johnstone children, and they all attended Philiphaugh School until the age of 11 or 12. At that age, children moved up to the high school at Knowepark on Curror Street, meaning a walk to the other end of town. Bobby walked to school with his mates, kicking a tennis ball along, to avoid being seen in the street walking alongside his sisters. Archie Smail, a fellow Souter, who was a few years older than Bobby, recalled the schooling of the time: 'You went to school at four or five and stayed until 14; Bobby went to Philiphaugh as I was at Knowepark, up the hill, and you'd stay at the high school if your parents could afford it, if you didn't have to go to work. Most working people wanted their kids in work though; I started work at 14 on 5/- per week, then 7/6, then back to 5/- a week on an apprenticeship for 49 hours, including to 12 o'clock on Saturday morning. What you could buy for a penny, though!'

Outside of school, for Bobby and his mates it was sport, sport, sport, often football, but also cricket and rugby union. It was an environment in which children could indulge themselves; wide-open spaces and few cares about traffic or cantankerous neighbours to confine them. Walter Bateman, who was in the year above Bobby at Philiphaugh, recalled Bobby with his tennis ball: 'On the way to school, at dinner time, on the way home from school... it didn't matter what else he would have for school, he always had a tennis ball in his pocket, and he would dribble it up and down the road. He even used to kick a tennis ball about with his dad when they were out for a walk on a Sunday! There used to be a factory nearby, called Corby Lynn Mill, and we'd play there night after night. There was a wall for one goal post and a coat for the other. We played cricket there, too; any ball games, which Bobby loved, but he played Cowboys and Indians with us, and Robin Hood too, all down by the waterside, the Ettrick. We'd also play a game 'hoose baw' – they'd call it rounders now, where you run to a base. We'd play game after game at the back of the mill or at Victoria Park. That was our playground really, down by the mills. There were a lot of factories in Selkirk at the time, and we always knew what time it was for lunch and tea, because of the horns and the whistles blowing as the shifts ended.

'At the top of Bridge Street there was a wood, it belonged to Jack Harrison; we called it Harrison's wood. There were swings and everything. We used to play up there. I remember though, when we were playing football, when we used to pick teams, if you did nae get Bobby on your team, you were struggling. Bobby was always going to play for Hearts, like Tommy Walker, that was his ambition; everything he played, he was playing for Hearts.' Lex Millar, another contemporary, who would remain a close friend of Bobby's long into adulthood, remembered, 'Bobby would be kicking a ba' up against a wall, even if he didn't have anyone else to play with. Later, during the war, even when there were no organised fitba' and rugby, we would still practice.'

Bobby particularly loved ball sports, and his interest in football developed through his father, of course, and also his uncles, who gave him plenty of encouragement. He played when he was delivering newspapers and would trap and kick the ball as it came back to him at all angles from a slanted roof at home. Having developed his ball-control techniques, he found it so much easier when playing with a full-sized football, and, allied to an obvious natural ability, this made him appear so comfortable. 'There was no television or anything like that, so we used to go to the haugh a lot and just play match after match, night after night, and I think it was just mainly practice,' he said many years later, trying to explain his own apparently-effortless ability.

Even though he was a Heart of Midlothian supporter, with heroes like Tommy Walker, Andy Black, and Alec Massie, the top forwards of the day, there was little chance of Bobby being able to go into Edinburgh to see his idols. 'They were all brilliant players in their day, and they were the sort of players that I looked up to, but I didn't go and watch professional football because I played that much football myself.' Black later left Edinburgh for English League football in the North West with Manchester City, while Massie played for Bury. Instead of Hearts, Bobby was able to watch his father play for the local team, although his younger sister Betty recalled that she and her sisters never did: 'We never saw our father play football – but we knew he was a good player. My mother never went either; she had other things to do. Women didn't really go to the football then.'

The Johnstones had been closely linked with Selkirk FC since shortly after the club's inception in 1880, and several members of the family had served in various capacities. The lineage was started by Bobby's great-uncle, Geordie, a stalwart of the 1890s team that had collected Selkirk's first-ever football trophy; he actually scored in the 1895 Border Cup Final. Hopey, born in 1904, was a better player than Geordie had been – the best yet of the footballing Johnstones. At over six feet tall, he was among the tallest in the Border Amateur League and had an athletic frame. Hopey was invited to trials with the mighty Rangers at Ibrox Park, and many a good judge felt that, had he been so inclined, he could have made good progress in the game. However, Hopey was not so inclined, and en route to Glasgow he left the train journey at Galashiels, having apparently been persuaded that Peebles Rovers, offering £1 a week, was a better option.

Hopey was a wholehearted player, a 'tough as teak' full-back. To be more candid, he was ordered off every football ground in the Borders at one time or another, but invariably for over-enthusiastic rather than foul or dirty play. He was a great character, and Selkirk football folklore recalls a couple of instances in which he was heavily involved. The first occurred during a vital League match against Duns, when a penalty was awarded after an ill-judged tackle by Hopey. While the Duns players were deciding among themselves who might best take the penalty-kick, Hopey, frustrated at their prevarication, ran up and blasted the ball past his own 'keeper, into the net! He turned to face the referee, who promptly sent him off for ungentlemanly conduct. Walter Bateman was there: 'Hopey was not noted for his sense of humour when he was playing, and one day he was ordered off for fouling this guy, the ref just sent him straight off. The changing rooms were in a little hut by the side of the park, and I was at the bottom of the steps. As the teams came off the pitch and went in the hut door, this Duns guy came straight back out again, down the steps, head over heels!' Later, against Bo'ness in a Scottish Cup qualifying tie, an opposing player had to be taken from the pitch by stretcher after an over-zealous challenge by Hopey. There was some considerable pushing and shoving among the players after the incident (rather more than 'handbags' according to an eye-witness), after which Hopey fell to the ground. Another stretcher was then brought on to the pitch to cart Hopey off, although he was seen to be winking at his teammates as he was removed, somewhat diplomatically, from the fray.

Tough as he was, Hopey was skilful too, and Jimmy Douglas, a teammate (and later business partner) of Hopey's, told his grandson Craig that Hopey was one of the few players who could actually volley a ball correctly at that time. 'Volleying the ball was difficult, but Hopey could do it well, even when it was soaking wet.' The balls were heavier then, and would absorb water easily.

Amateur football brought no income, of course, and money was very tight, but the family managed to afford the occasional holiday, usually by the seaside at Portobello, on the east coast of Scotland. There, Bobby and his sisters played together on the beach and visited the funfair. Liz sometimes took the five children on holiday without Hopey; it seems that he didn't like to leave home too often, telling the children 'a day out of Selkirk is a day wasted'. A more likely explanation is that Hopey preferred to be on hand in Selkirk, ready to take up any opportunities for extra work that might arise.

Walter, who still resides in Selkirk, recalled how everything depended on wool: 'If the woollen industry was going great, then fine... they used to reckon that if every Co-op member in Scotland bought one bonnet, it would keep the Co-operative mill in Selkirk going for a year! A lot of times the work in the mills would be seasonal. I was a painter, and in the winter, there was no painting, so I was paid off, because of the weather. We used to get jobs in the mills, but it was up and down, anything could happen, and it was for very low pay; there wasn't much work outside Selkirk either. Often there seemed to be work at one mill or another, and people moved from job to job a lot, but during the 1930s it was very, very hard.' By the middle of the decade, Hopey was supplementing the family income by earning a few extra shillings as a partner in a rather clandestine, 'street-corner' bookmaking venture. Alongside Jimmy Douglas, a member of another prominent Selkirk football family, he used to accept horseracing bets, a risky business at the time, and not just in the financial sense. These activities had to be kept quiet so as to avoid attracting the attentions of the constabulary. It was one of the ways in which Hopey tried to provide for the family, but, of course, there was always the worry of being exposed to obligations that couldn't be met. Some time later, their business partnership split up, possibly acrimoniously, though Jimmy never spoke of a fall out. The two of them enjoyed arguing with each other on and off the pitch anyway, and Hopey probably decided not to continue, and so wanted his share of the 'book' – a split of about £30! Jimmy went on to make rather more of a success of the business in subsequent years and apparently owned a car, although curiously he never drove. Years later, a horse called Jean's Dream was a hot tip circulating in the town, and when it won at 14–1 it meant the end of Jimmy Douglas's bookmaking days too.

Margaret remembers how hard their early years were: 'My mother was so busy as a housewife, and father generally had three days work at the tweed mills, down by the station. The bookies was a sideline, but they had a fall-out, so that was that.' Significantly she also felt that the concerns of providing for the family weighed heavily upon Hopey, and, ultimately, were seriously detrimental to his health. Though she doesn't recall him making a sudden decision to finish playing football, by the start of the war in 1939 he was no longer able to play competitively. At that time, of course, all able-bodied men were required to go off to fight, but Hopey failed his medical, so he had to stay put and join the Home Guard. There were fewer men around, of course, but otherwise the impact of the war in this part of Scotland was not so great immediately, and for the youngsters life went on much as before.

Although young Bobby was recognised as an all-round sportsman, his quality as a footballer was obvious, and his mates recognised it. 'Davy Grieve was a good footballer too, but Bobby had something different. I don't know what is was, why you could say definitely he was better than anyone else... but whenever he got the ba' you thought something was going to happen.' Davy Grieve was a good friend of Bobby's for many years, and he later had a brief spell as a professional in England. Billy Stark, who also still resides in Selkirk, played football with Bobby during the short time that they both attended Knowepark in the early 1940s, and he remembers trying to tackle him: 'Whenever he came up to you with the ba' and you tried to tackle him, the next thing ye ken is the ba' has flashed by the side o' ye leg, before you could get yer leg oot, and Bobby was roond the other side... he was quick, and he was awful tricky. He and Davy were a great couple, because Bobby had a tremendous fitba' brain, and Davy was a real speedster, a winger, very fast, and it suited Bobby. He used to speak about running into space even then... you run into space and the ball'll be there. Even as a boy he would say that.'

Boys being boys, they were not slow to exploit Bobby's sleight of foot, and Walter and Billy recalled an hilarious incident from their childhood: 'Bobby was very accurate with a fitba', and during the Common Riding, there was a showground and a fair at Victoria Park, the haugh down by the river, and we got him into trouble. You know the wooden men with the loose heads? You kick a ba', and knock the head off? We gave Bobby our ha'penny, and he was guaranteed to get you a coconut with three shots, and the showman chased him off the ground!'

1943 was a formative year for Bobby, but it also saw great steps forward for the whole Johnstone family when they moved to a new home, at No.2 Linglie Road. Newly-built, the house was not far from their previous home in Cannon Street, and they had been able to keep an eye on its construction, which had started before the war. By the housing standards of the day, it was a substantial structure, semi-detached, and with much more living space. There were gardens to the front and rear, and, most importantly, a bathroom and toilet inside the house! Understandably, the Johnstones were not sorry to leave the Cannon Street terraces, which amazingly survived another 50 years before being demolished in the mid-1990s. Walter can remember the new houses being built, probably because it meant the loss of one of their best playgrounds... 'The houses that Bobby and his family moved into had been started before the war. When I was a boy, there was just a field with old buildings there, and the guy that had the chip cart kept his horse on that land. Alec Dixon was his name, and he came round with a horse and cart selling fish and chips. He had a big black horse called Jimmy and a fire on the back of the cart. I used to help him peel the potatoes, about four pails. I pushed the potatoes through a chipper, and he'd put them on the cart, then about four o'clock he lit a fire on the back and set out around the streets.'

Now approaching his 14th birthday, Bobby's schooling was coming to an end; continuing with an education was not an option for most working-class children. Even Bobby's eldest sister, a very bright girl, had left school a few years before. She was blessed with good, all-round intelligence and had won several prizes. The headmaster at Knowepark, Mr Gemmell, had tried hard to persuade her to stay on at school beyond 14, but to no avail. The needs of the family had to come first, and so she went out to work. Bobby did fairly well at school. His best subject was English, for which he won a prize, but he too left at 14, with no clear idea of what he wanted to do. His choice of trade might have been influenced a couple of years earlier, when, along with his sisters, he had helped decorate the Railway Mission Hall, where the local Sunday school was held. Shortly after leaving school, he found employment as an apprentice painter and decorator with a local firm, Nicol, where he started earning 7s 6d per week.

Walter Bateman had also left school and begun a painting apprenticeship, but Lex Millar, who left school the year before, started in the mills. These were the types of careers that were open to the youngsters of Selkirk, and even at this point Bobby had no notion of taking up football professionally. He didn't believe he was as useful a player as his father had been, and didn't think he could be good enough. Although he didn't particularly like painting and decorating, it was a job, and so he simply knuckled down to his four-year apprenticeship.

Bobby's social life at this time centred around the local café, where he and his friends would spend their free time, with trips to the Selkirk Picture House when work and sporting commitments would allow. On Sundays, after church, walks on Selkirk hill were a favoured pastime for Bobby and the rest of the crowd. His favourite girl was Louise McEwen, and she still recalls those innocent days: 'Bobby and I paired up within the gang, as young ones do; we went to dances together, and we'd go for walks. Bobby always had a wee ba' with him.' As the boys got older, their sport became more organised, and Bobby started to play in outdoor five-a-side football competitions, which were quite popular in Scotland. They enjoyed success in tournaments at Peebles and also the Ettrickbridge (or, more colloquially, 'Bridgend') Fives, around five miles away. This was always a well-attended day of sport and socialising and an annual event. Although Hopey's competitive football days had ended some time before the war, events such as these allowed him to play some veterans' football, while Bobby lined up with teammates Tom Simpson and Graham Bateman, among others, in the open-age events. Graham, a goalkeeper now in his mid-20s had kept goal behind Hopey before the war, and he also knew the older Johnstone brothers too. Tom had introduced him to young Bobby a couple of years earlier, and Graham was impressed. 'It was at Ettrick Park, when we used to go down in the mornings prior to a game. The groundsman was preparing the field, putting sawdust down for the lines, and we'd have a kick-around, and I recall Tom Simpson, who was a very good player himself, saying "Graham, watch this wee fella kick a ba'." Tom placed a full-sized ball on the penalty spot, a real football, heavy, leather panelling and stitched, and suddenly this little chap, wearing the heavy-type boots that we all had then, stepped forward and banged the ball straight into the back of the net. I'd expected, with the size of the little chap and the weight of the ball, that it'd trickle to the goalline, but it didn't, it flew straight into the net – and that was my introduction to Bobby Johnstone.'

Bobby began to gain valuable experience around this time playing for local team Parkvale Rovers, and then further afield with army cadet sides and Newtongrange Bluebell and Newtongrange Star with Davie Smail, the elder of the Smail brothers. Trips to the mining town of Newtongrange were a considerable journey for the young lads, as it lies around 30 miles from Selkirk, on the southern outskirts of Edinburgh. It was a long way, and with no car they usually travelled on the bus. His sisters got tired of Bobby, always the focus of attention and always on the last minute: 'there was always a mad rush, all round him, all of us had to help get this ready for him, get that ready for him'. But there was pride too – Bobby was making good progress in sport, and Graham Bateman's view, given in a radio interview during the 1980s, was that Bobby could have excelled at any sport he chose: 'he was the type of chap, he was so well balanced and had such an excellent temperament, that no matter what sport Bobby had've tried, he would have been a success. For instance, as a little lad at Philiphaugh School he teamed up with one of the famous Cowan rugby-playing brothers in Selkirk, Jack Cowan. Bobby was scrum-half, and I'm quite sure that had he taken to rugby, he would have played rugby scrum-half for Scotland as well.' Bobby also continued to enjoy his cricket, and later in life would excel at billiards, snooker, running, golf and bowls, playing at a very competitive standard. He was a natural.

As organised football recommenced at the end of hostilities, he began to play open-age football for his home-town club, following a family tradition that now went back over half a century. Bobby was three years into his apprenticeship and was coming up to his 17th birthday.

It was September 1946.

Note
1. This equates to 1,200 people paying 4d admission.

CHAPTER 2

Developing a Football Career

Sixteen members of the Selkirk Football Club lost their lives during World War One, and World War Two also took a toll on the club's strength, with several members of the late 1930s team now either lost or incapacitated. Among the group capable of resuming their amateur football were the Smail brothers, Davie and Archie, Tom Simpson and Eck Piercy, and to add to those names were some new ones, including Bobby Johnstone and his mate Davie Grieve, who had already represented Scotland as a junior. Bobby was now giving every indication that he too would turn into a decent player, although he was hardly a chip off the old block. It was clear that he was not going to grow into a six-footer, like his father, and his football technique was entirely different. He relied upon speed of thought, coupled with a rare ability to pass the ball with just the right amount of weight.

During the short time that Bobby Johnstone played for Selkirk FC, they had some success, and on one occasion, in October 1946, a crowd of 1,500 saw them deservedly overcome Queen of the South. The forward line that day was Davie Grieve, Bobby, Davie Smail, Tom Simpson and Bobby Miller, and since then a side from the Borders has seldom, if ever, matched the quality of football that attacking line up could produce. The team went all the way to the Final of the East of Scotland Cup, where they lost 2–5 to the semi-professional outfit, and perennial local rivals, Gala Fairydean.

This was open-age football, of course, and Bobby recalled 'That was a good season, we'd a very good team at Selkirk, all local players, all good footballers, you know. Nearly everybody could play the game well at that time.' By now 17, and still serving his apprenticeship, Bobby was still not thinking about a full-time career in the game – the possibilities hadn't occurred to him. As with most local players, he worked a five-and-a-half day week, around 50 hours, and played football on Saturday afternoons purely as a leisure pursuit. Archie Smail, by now 24, well remembers the difficulties of playing for an amateur club in that post-war period: 'I'd work 'til 12 on Saturdays, and have to race home, and might have to get ready for travelling to an away match – and we never got paid anything by Selkirk of course.'

Bobby Johnstone had been playing for Selkirk FC for only seven or eight weeks when, along with teammate, centre-half Eck Piercy, he attracted the interest of the mighty Hibernian Football Club, based around 40 miles away in the capital, Edinburgh. While it is capricious to imagine an efficient scouting network suddenly discovering Bobby's raw talent, the fact is that he had been a decent prospect for a few years anyway. At the time, Hibernian ran a junior team in the same League as Selkirk, and they usually played their 'home' games in Peebles; it is more plausible that Bobby's advance into the more competitive arena of Border League football had been noted. Hibs were still one of the major attractions of the Scottish game, although they hadn't collected any major honours for over 40 years. Bobby picked up the story: 'I'd been playing in five-a-sides, at Peebles, and there was a photographer there called Alec Pyre, an ex-professional player for an English club, who'd come up and played for Hibernian. He approached me and asked if I would consider going to Hibernian myself. I got hold of my father and Bob Lindsay, who was organising our football club at that time, and we all went through to Edinburgh on a Sunday morning, and I signed for Hibs on £4 a week.' The manager of Hibs, an acknowledged gentleman named Willie McCartney, was very progressive, and he signed many outstanding youngsters around this time, although, as far as Bobby ever knew, McCartney never actually saw him play. Nonetheless, the manager's visionary recruitment policies would pay off handsomely, though there is some evidence that he had work to do in persuading Bobby that he was good enough to become a footballer. Those wages certainly helped though – they represented untold riches, in fact a ten-fold increase in income for Bobby – and were more than enough to get any young lad to think seriously about a career in fitba'.

Betty told Margaret, who by now had left home to start her nursing studies, the exciting news – his signing for Hibs came as quite a surprise to her: 'He always wanted to play for Hearts, but they wouldn't sign him, saying he was too young. My dad took him to Edinburgh, and he signed for Hibs... he was only 17.' Bobby had told Louise about Hibs' interest, and that he hoped he might be going to play for them. 'Then one night he came to the dance at the Victoria Halls and told me that he had signed for Hibs. He had some papers in his pocket, and he showed me his new tie from the club.' Years later, in a radio interview, Bobby recalled the excitement he had felt: 'I'd never even thought of signing professional, but when it came, it seemed to just come out of the blue, and, after all said and done, I was only just over 17. It was nice that a club really wanted me at that time, and... the other attraction was getting £4 a week.'

The Hibernian club had a long and proud history, though they had not won the Scottish League Championship since way back in 1902–03. The club had been formed in 1875, during a meeting of the Young Men's Catholic Association, though Bobby's signing was certainly not related to his religion – the Johnstone family were not Roman Catholics. These early Irish links led to Hibs' first application to join the Scottish FA being refused, the response being that the 'Association was formed for Scotchmen'. This matter was soon resolved though, and Hibs quickly established themselves among the leading clubs in the Scottish game. In 1887 they became the first Edinburgh side to win the Scottish Cup, and the same year they defeated the Preston North End side that would shortly gain renown as the Old Invincibles when they won the first-ever double in England. These successes gained popular appeal, and Hibs' success was a factor leading to the formation of another side over in Glasgow: Celtic FC.

The late 1940s saw Hibernian enter their golden age, and in the seven years following World War Two they would go on to reach the Scottish Cup quarter-finals five times. There would be a titanic battle with Rangers for supremacy within the Scottish football sphere, and Hibernian would more than hold their own, finishing outside of the top two in the League just once in that period. Further, by the mid-1950s they would be able to reflect on having collected the game's major honour, the Scottish League Championship flag. To this day, they have not been able to reproduce that feat. Bobby Johnstone was to play a major role in that success. While the rise in Hibernian's fortunes cannot be attributed exclusively to the emergence of any one player, it is fair to say that Bobby Johnstone was the final piece of the jigsaw – he was the last to join the world-renowned Famous Five forward line, and, as we shall see later, the first to depart.

* * * * *

From November 1946 Bobby began travelling daily to training at Easter Road in Edinburgh, usually by bus, although he often took the train. At the time, a single railway track ran between Selkirk and nearby Galashiels. There, Bobby would change trains and join a Carlisle to Edinburgh service for the run into the city. The morning train left Selkirk at 8.20, taking 15 minutes to reach Galashiels, and Bobby would be on Edinburgh Waverley station, for the short journey up to Hibernian's ground in Leith, before 10 o'clock. The bus journey took considerably longer, but for one spell there was a luxury option, as Margaret, who travelled into Edinburgh for her training, drove a car. In any event, the key here is that Bobby did not entertain thoughts of moving to Edinburgh; he carried on living at home with the rest of the family, where he felt happiest. Margaret recalled 'The Selkirk to Gala train was called the coffee pot, it was only one carriage, but it was quite well used. The guard on the Gala to Edinburgh train used to shout "Herr-iott", and if I was taking Bobby through to Edinburgh in the car he would shout it too, as we drove by the station there on the A7.' Bobby also took the train on the days when he had to go for massages with the rest of the team, usually at Portobello baths. This happened most weeks, but Bobby was seldom properly prepared – he was always on the last minute, a disorganised young man. One day he got off the train at Galashiels on his way to work, and when he was asked for his ticket he then discovered that he'd lost his wallet! He'd been at Portobello baths the day before, where luckily his wallet had been found and handed in.

Selkirk and Hibernian had agreed, on the basis of a 'gentlemen's promise', to play a friendly match as part of Bobby's transfer deal – an opportunity for the host club to realise some much-welcomed revenue. Around a year after Bobby's transfer, in October 1947, Hibernian honoured that pledge by coming to the Royal Burgh to defeat Selkirk FC by 11–2 in front of a crowd of around 2,000 at Ettrick Park. Bobby, still some 18 months short of his first-team debut for Hibernian, was granted permission to turn out for his old club. By this time, he was 18 years old, and he had now moved to Edinburgh, but not into club 'digs' provided by his employer. A blot on Bobby's landscape, and indeed that of all 'fit and able-bodied' young men, was the obligation to complete national service on attaining the age of 18.

Bobby soon found himself housed in quarters that were fit for a king, though it is unlikely that he considered himself fortunate to move into Edinburgh Castle! National service came as rather an inconvenience for a young man trying to carve out a career as a professional footballer, and this was why he was forced to leave Selkirk for the first time. His service actually commenced in September 1947, the month before the Selkirk friendly game, with an initial posting to Yeovil, Somerset, down in the south of England. As had been the case during the war years, sportsmen enjoyed favourable treatment during their national service. The army's policy was to support all sporting activity because it encouraged 'fitness, teamwork, and inspirational leadership'. Sportsmen, especially those professionals in serious training, were all but excluded from most military duty, and this was the privileged position in which Bobby found himself, although the basic pay for a private, £1 8s (£1.40p) per week, was no attraction. Soon after his posting to Yeovil, he was moved back north to Edinburgh Castle, where he joined the Royal Army Service Corps. Conveniently, this was less than two miles away from Easter Road, and, though it is not certain whether Hibs were able to exert any influence, Bobby's lot was much better than that of many of his contemporaries. Once posted to the castle, his main function seems to have been to act as chauffeur to a senior officer, a general, and he acknowledged his luck: 'He was only put back to Edinburgh Castle because they wanted him for Hibs,' recalled Betty, but, even so, the family back home in Selkirk hardly saw him during his two-year spell of duty.

One fellow Souter that Bobby did bump into was Walter Bateman. 'I'd left school the year before Bobby, and I took a painting and decorating apprenticeship too, though not with the same firm. I was allowed to finish my apprenticeship before being conscripted, and went into the army before him. I saw him play for the army at Easter Road, and I also saw him a couple of times around at the castle. I was a bugler in the King's Own Scottish Borderers, and we used to guard there…' While Bobby got on with his national service, and a conspicuous career in army football, Hibs were starting to become a force within the Scottish game, and the 1947–48 season was their breakthrough year. At this time, Hibernian ran just two senior sides, and, with a playing strength of around 84, many players, including Bobby, were at best merely watching and learning on Saturdays, kicking only their heels – there was little chance of a game. The first team had overcome a start that had seen them lose three times to city rivals Hearts, and things were now going extremely well. Indeed, Hibs topped the League table in November, but before glory arrived tragedy would strike the club.

* * * *

Willie McCartney is recognised as the individual who was key to laying the foundations for Hibs' sustained spell of success, not least by his signing of numerous top-quality youngsters such as Bobby Johnstone, Eddie Turnbull, Lawrie Reilly and their contemporaries. A large man, he had no background as a footballer, although he was born into the profession, having followed his father as manager of Heart of Midlothian in 1919. Always a flamboyant figure, he dressed immaculately, invariably being seen wearing a three-piece suit complete with buttonhole carnation. Outdoors, an expensive Crombie-style overcoat and a bowler hat usually completed the ensemble. He resigned suddenly from Hearts in 1935 and some months later was quietly approached by Hibs chairman Harry Swan, and he agreed to take up similar office at Easter Road during the 1936 close season. He was to remain in that post for the last 12 years of his life.

Commanding both instant respect and devotion from his players, legend has it that his appearance in the mouth of the tunnel during matches at Easter Road was guaranteed to galvanise the players into extra labours. Harry Swan, meanwhile, was a more abrupt man, who made enemies quite readily within the game, including, much later, Bobby Johnstone. However, he was undoubtedly a visionary, and on the appointment of Willie McCartney he had promised that Hibs would be great again within 10 years. For a club with only one Championship flag in its 61-year history, this was some claim, and, if one discounts the years lost to World War Two, one that would be fully realised.

In January 1948 McCartney fell ill during a first-round Scottish Cup tie at the Cliftonhill home of Albion Rovers in Coatbridge. Hibs won the tie, but that detail later paled into insignificance as, some hours after being taken home, news emerged that McCartney had not recovered as initially thought, but had died at his West Edinburgh home during the evening. In a newspaper interview three days prior to his demise, McCartney had stated tellingly: 'give me two more years, and Hibernian will be more than a challenge to Rangers'.

There were significant high points in this tragic season, and, indeed, a few weeks after McCartney's death a crowd of 143,570, a record for any Hibernian game, saw the Scottish Cup semi-final at Hampden Park, Glasgow, which Rangers won 1–0. More importantly, Hibernian created a club record undefeated run of 17 games and went on to take the Scottish League Championship for only the second time in their history, which now stretched back well over 70 years. In doing so, they became only the second side outside of Glasgow's Old Firm to win the Scottish League since 1904. They collected an impressive 48 points over the 30-game season, two points more than Rangers, who were runners-up. Significantly, at least in terms of the style for which Hibernian would become renowned in future years, they scored 86 goals – 22 more than Rangers. It seemed that this was just the beginning. Over 1½ million spectators had watched Hibs during the season, and the club had posted profits of over £16,000, a figure that, according to the *Daily Worker's Football Annual*, topped anything that had gone before in Scotland. The chairman, Harry Swan, said 'The directors, manager Hugh Shaw and the players are all very anxious that the team which has won us the honours should be kept together. We are all confident that since we have learned to win the premier glory, the League Championship of Division A, further honours will come our way.'

In addition to his army commitments, including much football, Bobby had been playing in Hibs' reserve side, who were, if anything, even more dominant than the first team. When Scottish League football resumed after the war, it had done so on a re-organised basis, with the former Divisions One and Two being replaced with Divisions A and B. A new feeder C Division included some of the leading clubs' reserve sides, though these were ineligible for promotion to the main League. Hibernian's reserve side, featuring Bobby Johnstone, played in the wholly separate Reserves League, and they had won their League even more impressively than the first team had, losing just two and drawing one of their 30 games. Often playing in front of five-figure crowds, particularly at home, they finished 16 points clear of Hearts' second string. The Jambos managed an impressive 69 goals in their 30 games. Hibernian scored 119.

The following season, 1948–49, Bobby Johnstone continued to pick up searing reviews for his performances in the reserves, and once again the side walked away with their Championship. By this time, people were writing regularly to the newspapers, and indeed directly to Hugh Shaw, the new manager, urging him to include young Johnstone in the first team. In one case, Shaw received a written report from a supporter, who, when describing the little inside-forward, said 'the boy is something special – full of football'. Eventually, and after what must have seemed a long apprenticeship, almost three seasons in fact, Bobby's first-team breakthrough came.

CHAPTER 3

Hibernian and the Famous Five – Reaching the Top

By late March 1949 Hibernian's hopes of retaining the Scottish League Championship title had almost completely evaporated, and as the season faded out manager Hugh Shaw took the opportunity to blood two or three youngsters. On Saturday 2 April 1949 Bobby Johnstone made his full first-team debut in a Scottish League Division A game at Love Street, Paisley, the home of St Mirren FC. Though Bobby made a promising start, the 0–2 defeat saw Hibs' Championship challenge finally extinguished.

Opinion varies around this key point: many sources state that Bobby's debut was against Partick Thistle, assertions probably founded upon newspaper reports of the time. One report states that in the next match (against Thistle) Hibernian had 'played two new faces, one being the fearless goalkeeper Tommy Younger'. While this was true, there were two new faces as far as the Easter Road spectators were concerned, it has led some to conclude, incorrectly, that this latter game saw Bobby's debut.[1]

Bobby Johnstone now became the last to join what would soon become renowned as the Famous Five forward line, although in this match Gordon Smith was missing through injury, with Bobby having replaced the usual inside-forward, Cuthbertson. It was three weeks later, on 21 April 1949, that the Famous Five first played together, in a friendly game against Nithsdale Wanderers at Sanquar. The game was won 8–1, with Lawrie Reilly, Willie Ormond, and Eddie Turnbull each scoring twice, while Gordon Smith and Mick Gallagher managed one each – thus Bobby was the only member of the forward line not to score. However, he did not have long to wait for his first goal in a Hibs shirt. On Wednesday 4 May the Five played together again in another friendly, against an Irish Football League XI at Windsor Park, Belfast, in aid of the Northern Ireland War Memorial Building Fund. Hibs won 4–0, and along with Smith and Turnbull, who scored one each, Bobby Johnstone scored twice.

The League season ended disappointingly for Hibs though, with main rivals Rangers finishing a point clear of Dundee and becoming the first side ever to win the domestic treble of the Scottish League, Scottish and League Cups. Hibernian finished in third place, having scored 75 goals, 12 more than the Champions. This pattern of high goalscoring by the Hibs team, and the forwards in particular, would be repeated relentlessly over the next few seasons, quite irrespective of where the silverware went.

Bobby had finally made the breakthrough to first-team professional football. He finished the season, having made just those two League appearances, but he was now on the point of making himself a permanent fixture in the side, though he had yet to complete his national service. It didn't take long for the Hibernian supporters to take the wee Souter to their hearts. A distinctive yet diminutive figure, he had a lock of black hair flopping over his eyes, creating the impression of a boy in a man's world. While he lacked any obvious physical 'presence', and wasn't the fastest over the ground, his speed of thought and reactions were remarkable, his passing was sublime, and one newspaper described him as 'looking as if he has eyes in the back of his head, and with a shot like a shell'. His teammates, and primarily the full-back Jimmy Cairns, soon coined a nickname for Bobby, linking him with a famous cartoon strip that appeared each week in a Scottish newspaper, the *Sunday Post*. The hero of the cartoon series, Black Bob, led to an obvious connection given the colour of Bobby's hair, but that character had a pet dog, a border (or 'Selkirk') collie named Nicker, and it was this name that stuck, a seemingly ideal choice for this rather slight young fellow from the Borders. Incidentally, Bobby's breakthrough caused quite a ripple back in Selkirk too, the pride felt within the town being almost tangible. Graham Bateman, who was by now working at the *Southern Reporter*, recalled his manager telling him 'it's just wonderful to go into Edinburgh and see this wee Selkirk lad out there with all of those big names'. That was how everybody in the town felt, and it was noted too that the style of Hibs' play was familiar to Bobby – the first post-war Selkirk FC team had played with an abandon similar to that now employed by Hibs, a game focused essentially upon an attacking approach.

It is probably judicious at this point to expand upon the phrase 'The Famous Five', the name that refers to the all-international forward line that played for Hibernian during their golden years, each of whom were capped for Scotland. Besides Bobby, the others were Gordon Smith, Lawrie Reilly, Eddie ('Ned') Turnbull and Willie Ormond. All five scored at least 100 League goals for Hibs, and Reilly and Smith hold club goalscoring records that stand to this day. Alongside Bobby, the other individuals were as follows:

Gordon Smith

Many regard Gordon Smith as the greatest player ever to play for Hibernian. He was born in Montrose in May 1924, represented Scotland at Schoolboy international level, and as a junior played for Dundee North End. In April 1941, aged 16, he played in a Scottish 'Junior' Select team against a combined Hibs/Hearts select team. This was ironic because Gordon supported Hearts as a boy and had desperately hoped to sign for them. He scored a hat-trick in that game, a 3–2 win, and the next day one daily paper announced that he had signed for Hearts, who were certainly interested. Everyone reckoned without the formidable Willie McCartney though, because while Hearts deliberated, offering Gordon just a trial, McCartney rang the lemonade factory next to Smith's house, got the youngster to the phone, and arranged to meet him in Arbroath. There it was explained that Hibernian saw no need for a trial, and they were prepared to give him a deal straight away. Thus, Hibs took the plunge, signing the first member of the Famous Five for £10. It seems barely credible today, but after signing Smith travelled straight over to Tynecastle for a wartime League game against Hearts, arriving without any boots. He scored a hat-trick in a borrowed pair and enjoyed a derby debut that finished in a 5–3 victory. Smith's fellow debutant, Bobby Combe, scored too, and to complete a memorable day all round Smith will have been pleased that his hero, Tommy Walker, scored all three of Hearts' goals.

Gordon benefitted hugely from his experience of wartime soccer and the opportunities to play alongside some of the great names that guested for Hibs during that period, men such as Matt Busby and Everton's Jimmy Caskie. Once football resumed after the war, it wasn't long before Hibs gained the Scottish League Championship flag for only the second time in their history; one of that season's most notable feats came against Third Lanark, when Gordon scored five times. This was the first of three seasons in which Smith was the club's highest scorer, prior to the emergence of Lawrie Reilly.

In the early 50s, he was deservedly made club captain, and in 1951 he was acclaimed Scotland's Player of the Year. The following year, in September 1952, Smith received his benefit match, which was granted by the board of directors following what by then was 11 years' service. The game was a classic encounter, played at Easter Road against the English League Champions Manchester United. In fact, Hibs would have preferred a fixture against Arsenal, but at Smith's insistence they contacted his former colleague Matt Busby to arrange the clash. Inspired by 'Gay' Gordon at his most devastating, Hibs turned a 2–3 half-time deficit into a 7–3 victory. Notably, Smith was the only one of the Five to enjoy a testimonial, and the whole subject of these awards generated considerable ill feeling among other members of the Five, and beyond, during succeeding years.

His forte was running at defenders with pace, carrying the ball past them with an elegance that was effective but also pleasing on the eye. He combined this skill with the ability to take chances with a powerful shot, and it seems unlikely that another winger will ever surpass his phenomenal number of career goals. The quiet one of the Five, he didn't enjoy the limelight in the same way as the others and seldom socialised to the same extent. He was recognised as a gentlemen of his time, noticeably more diplomatic in his statements and dealings with club officials than others. His exemplary disciplinary record was a credit to him, in spite of receiving 'close attention' from the hardy full-backs of the day. As a key supplier he was further marked out for some ferocious tackles over the years, yet he was booked only three times throughout his entire career. He did accept having retaliated on one occasion in a match against Rangers, but the other two he considered to have been unfair!

Smith gained 18 Scotland caps in total, spanning 13 years. He captained the international side twice in 1955, firstly against Austria, when he scored in a 4–1 win, and then later against Hungary. In 1959, after over 500 Scottish League games for Hibs and 364 goals, including 17 hat-tricks, he joined Hearts on a free transfer. Amazingly, he collected another Scottish League Championship medal in his first season with Hearts, and then yet another with Dundee in 1961–62 when, by now aged almost 38, he created numerous chances for the young Alan Gilzean. He is the only man to collect Scottish League Championship medals with three different clubs, each outside of Glasgow's Old Firm. Remarkably, he also played in the European Cup with each club, reaching the semi-finals with Dundee in 1962–63 and losing only to eventual winners AC Milan.

After leaving Dundee, Gordon played briefly for Greenock Morton and then Drumcondra in Ireland. He finally hung up his boots in 1964, having been a professional footballer for 23 years, and only a week before his 40th birthday. He remarked later that after leaving Hibs 'I played on for another five years, and always felt that I could have given those years to Hibs, but it wasn't to be'. In retirement, he continued to live at his home on the coast at North Berwick. He seldom visited Easter Road thereafter, although he took part in the honouring of the Famous Five with the naming of the new stand there in 1998. In August 2004, and following a long illness, he died, aged 80, at a North Berwick nursing home.

Lawrie Reilly

Born in Edinburgh in October 1928, Lawrie was unique among the Five in that he was actually a boyhood Hibs fan. As a youngster, his father, a railwayman, took him all over Scotland to watch the team play – 'I've been to see Hibs on nearly every ground in Scotland, and it never cost us a penny. We travelled either beside the driver or the guard's van at the back. They wouldn't let you do that now!' In 1941, as Gordon Smith left Tynecastle on foot, having scored a hat-trick on his debut, he was approached by the star-struck 12-year-old as he passed near to the Reilly family home. Young Lawrie invited him in for a cup of tea as Smith left the ground, and many years later laughed that 'Gordon must have thought I was just a daft young laddie – and he was probably right'. Little more than four years later, Smith and Reilly were playing in the same forward line together, and Gordon took up that earlier offer many times!

Lawrie began playing for North Merchiston and then Edinburgh Thistle before signing for his favourites in 1945. As with other members of the Famous Five, he too was invited to attend trials with Hearts, but again this was their mistake. Lawrie mentioned the approach to Harry Reading, who ran the Thistle team but was also Hibs' groundsman. He warned his employers, who quickly came in to sign him for £20. Lawrie initially joined Hibs as a right-winger, while Smith was usually centre- forward. He quickly broke into the first team, but as a replacement on the left wing for Willie Ormond, who had broken his leg. Initially, Reilly admits that he was over-awed playing alongside his hero, Smith, looking to pass to him constantly, but he progressed very quickly in the professional game, could play in any position in the forward line, and did sufficiently well to earn a place in the Scotland team. He was actually on his way to Easter Road to play in a testimonial for Willie McCartney's widow when a Hibs fan in the bus queue told him that he had received his international call-up. Later, he moved to centre-forward, where he stayed for the remainder of his career. In 1950–51 he scored 23 League goals, and so began a sequence in which he was the club's leading League goalscorer in each of the next seven seasons.

Popularly known as 'Last-minute Reilly', he earned that nickname when famously scoring a very late goal to earn Scotland a draw against England at Wembley in 1953. He is most proud of the fact that he was victorious in his first 12 full internationals and went on to earn a Hibs record total of 38 international caps at a time when internationals were few and far between. His strike rate of 22 goals gives him a superior goals per game ratio than more recent heroes Denis Law and Kenny Dalglish, and by the end of his career he had scored five times in as many games at Wembley.

At the start of the 1953–54 season, Lawrie nearly left Hibernian after refusing to sign a new contract. He had discovered that the club had no intention of granting him a benefit match, and so he went on to the transfer list and did not play for four months. He later patched up his differences, chiefly because he did not want to play for another club. He was not the usual type of bustling centre-forward, although he did score a good number of headed goals. He was quite short, at 5ft 7in, and always gave the credit to other members of the Five who delivered telling crosses and passes. But his own fearless bravery and sense of timing were key factors too, and he was a genuine 90-minute player, remembered for continuing to try for goals at all times during a game and not giving up when the game might appear lost – he didn't mind pulling one back, consolation or not. Reilly's career lasted until he was 29, thus he was both the first and youngest of the Five to quit the game, largely due to knee problems, something he shared with Bobby Johnstone. He had undergone knee surgery in May 1957 but continued to play, though the 1957–58 season was his last. He kept going until late April, and in his last game, almost inevitably, he scored in a Monday night victory against Rangers. The following Saturday, Hibs lost the Scottish Cup Final against Clyde without Lawrie, and from then on the legendary Joe Baker assumed his mantle. In total he had scored 234 goals[2] for Hibs at first-class level, and he remains their all-time leading goalscorer.

Throughout the latter part of his subsequent working life, he catered for the thirst of Hibs fans, running a pub in Leith, though he is an absolute teetotaller himself – he has never had an alcoholic drink. He continued to visit Easter Road, although he initially declined the opportunity to sit in the director's box, preferring to sit in his own reserved seat. He was particularly disparaging of the way that segregated crowds had affected the atmosphere at games. Now in his late 70s, he has mellowed and attends most Hibs games in the manner befitting a hero, often with his friend Eddie Turnbull – but he still has problems with his left knee!

Eddie Turnbull

Born in April 1923 at Carronshore, a small mining village around two miles from Falkirk, 'Ned' Turnbull is the oldest of the Five and the most natural leader. Following his Royal Navy demobilisation in 1946, and just one game for Grangemouth side Forth Rangers, he signed for Hibernian. 'I was woken in my bed and told I had to report to Easter Road the following night in a taxi they were sending.' Willie McCartney had arranged to get Eddie and his elder brother to Easter Road, though they were under instruction from their father to sign nothing. Once there, the ever-impressive McCartney spoke with Eddie and kept his brother supplied with a few nips. By the end of the meeting McCartney's personality had won Eddie over, and the whisky had seen to his brother, so the deal was sealed. He recalled 'I played one game for Forth Rangers and signed for Hibs in August; I was in the first team by September, so it was all very quick. Then my first game here was against Spartak Prague.' Eddie made an immediate and dramatic impact in Hibs' first team, and within a few months he played in front of 82,000 fans in the Scottish Cup Final against Aberdeen at Hampden Park, although he collected a runners'-up medal.

In 1948 Eddie was deputed to travel back to Edinburgh with Willie McCartney after the boss had been taken ill at the Cup tie against Albion Rovers, and he was devastated when he discovered later that night, from the newspaper vendors, that the boss had died at home. As usual, Ned had been out dancing. He became particularly close to Willie Ormond, whom he often roomed with on away trips, and Bobby Johnstone, and the three of them were renowned for enjoying the social life, often accompanied by a wee half.

Although not the most skilful of players, Eddie Turnbull was known for his powerful shooting, which earned him the nickname Thunderball. He had a great brain for the game, and he was the man who galvanised others when things were not going so well. He took on the role of protector to the likes of Bobby Johnstone and Gordon Smith, who were frequently the victims of rash tackles. He played 482 games for Hibernian, scoring 199 goals in his 12-year career, including a notable hat-trick of penalties within his four goals against Celtic in February 1950. Appointed club captain in 1954, the following year he became the first British player to score in European competition when he netted against Rot-Weiss Essen in the inaugural European Cup competition.

Eddie gained nine caps (and not eight, as many records indicate), making his debut in 1948 in a 2–0 victory against Belgium at Hampden Park – the only time he played in a victorious Scotland team on home soil. His fourth cap came in the disastrous home defeat to Austria in December 1950, Scotland's first-ever home defeat against foreign opposition. He then spent some eight years in the international wilderness, making him the only one of the Five never to appear alongside Bobby for the national side. He picked up a further five caps around the time of the 1958 World Cup but surprisingly failed to score for his country. His opinions, which he made freely available, sometimes got him into trouble, and a good example came during a game on the pre-season club tour of Germany in 1950. Willie Ormond had made an innocuous challenge, and Eddie laughingly suggested that the referee ought to send him off, at which Willie was ordered from the field! It is well known that the peculiar eight-year gap in his international career followed a 'fall-out' with the selectors. A member of the panel told him quite plainly 'as long as I am chairman of this selection committee, you won't play for Scotland again'. Fall-outs with others demonstrably affected his chances of moving as a player to England.

By 1959 Eddie had arranged to move to Falkirk on a free transfer, but Hibs were reluctant to let him go and offered him the post of trainer instead, which he accepted. Later, he moved to Queen's Park and then progressed to the manager's role with Aberdeen in 1965 with great success, winning the Scottish Cup in 1969–70. He returned to Hibs in 1971, where he furthered his reputation as a volatile manager, who could be especially harsh on under-performing players. He fell out serially with some, usually those who believed that their own ideas were worth hearing. Yet he produced what is regarded as Hibs' best side since the halcyon days of the early 1950s, a team revered in their own right as 'Turnbull's Tornadoes'. That side collected the Scottish League Cup in 1972, beating Celtic in the Final (a tremendous achievement as the Hoops dominated Scottish football at the time), and they immortalised themselves by winning 7–0 at Tynecastle on New Year's Day, 1973. There was a final trip to Hampden Park in 1979, when Hibs lost the Scottish Cup Final to Rangers after two replays. Later, Eddie quit somewhat prematurely, in 1980, after 34 years in the game.

Having spent his entire playing career at Hibs, and having managed them too, he can be described as having made the greatest individual contribution to the club. His service gives him the distinction of being the club's longest-serving employee, and, now in his 80s, he continues to live near the ground in Edinburgh. In recent years, as Honorary President of the Former Players' Association, and a 'Club Champion', he enjoys attending as many Hibs games as he can.

Willie Ormond

Born in Falkirk in February 1927, Willie Ormond was unique among the Five in that he actually cost Hibernian a transfer fee (of £1,200) when he came from Stenhousemuir in November 1946. He went straight into the first team and had scored his first goal for the club by Christmas. He generally played on the left wing and for a few years had Eddie Turnbull alongside him at inside-left. He was very unlucky with injuries: he suffered a broken leg three times, broke an arm and suffered a serious ligament injury during his career. Willie was left-footed, fast and very direct. Bobby Johnstone described him as 'having a good left foot, one of the best I ever saw, it was deadly, but his right was just for standing on'. Even the diplomat Gordon Smith referred to his right foot as 'suspect'.

Willie gained six caps in an international career that started with five games in 1954, when he was the only Hibernian player to go on the disastrous trip to the World Cup Finals. He then waited five years for one further cap, against England at Wembley. By the time he left Hibernian, after 15 years, he had played 350 games, scored 188 goals and collected many of the Scottish game's major honours.

In August 1961 Willie became the last playing member of the Five to leave Easter Road when he signed for his home-town club, Falkirk. It was while at Brockville Park that Willie made the transition into management, becoming Falkirk's assistant trainer. In March 1967 he moved to Perth to manage St Johnstone for a six-year spell. The Perth club have never won a major honour, but for a short while they were at least competing with the best in Scotland, and under his stewardship they reached the Scottish League Cup Final in 1969, losing to Celtic. They also finished third in the League in 1970–71 and qualified for Europe for the first time in their history. St Johnstone fans remember him fondly for having led them to their greatest achievements. In 1973 he was appointed manager of the Scotland national team, whom he steered through their 1974 World Cup Finals campaign in West Germany. Popularly regarded as their greatest-ever national side, that Scotland team came home as the only undefeated team in the tournament, and during the tournament Willie awarded a final cap to one of the Scottish all-time greats, Denis Law.

Having enjoyed a distinguished football career as both manager and player, Willie was awarded the OBE in 1975. He left the Scotland job, and, after a spell as manager of Hearts, returned to Easter Road for a short spell working under Eddie Turnbull in 1980, before he briefly succeeded Eddie by taking over the manager's role. Illness forced him to retire from active involvement in football shortly after. Sadly, Willie was the first member of the Five to pass away, on 4 May 1984, aged only 57.

To summarise, the Famous Five were leading lights in Hibernian's only truly great side. All of them could score goals, but their ability to interchange was the key feature of their play and the aspect that most confounded opponents; they were all capable of doing the job of all of the others. If Lawrie Reilly found himself out on the left wing he was quite able to cross the ball, and if Bobby Johnstone was running through the middle he could put in a good header. Each man had his own special merits, and it is Eddie Turnbull's view that Bobby Johnstone became the brains of the Five. 'The Famous Five were unique because they had all the required attributes gelled into one, but the best brain was Bobby's. I brought something else… I played outside-left, inside-forward, centre-forward, before dropping back into the half-back line. Och, I played about six or seven positions for Hibs, but Bobby had the brains.'

* * * * *

The 1949–50 season began with Bobby largely on the sidelines as Hibernian qualified easily from the early stages of the League Cup, winning five of their six group games. In the quarter-final they faced Partick Thistle at Firhill, and it was here, on 17 September, that Bobby, having now been demobbed from the RASC, got his next chance for senior action. He replaced the injured Gordon Smith on the right wing, and though the game ended in a 2–4 defeat, Bobby Johnstone scored his first goal for Hibernian in a full first-team fixture. Back at Easter Road, he was dropped again for the second leg, but the deficit was cleared within the first 10 minutes of the game, and Hibernian eased into the semi-final with a 4–0 win. The semi-final was scheduled for neutral Tynecastle, the home of city rivals Hearts, and a place where Hibs often fared poorly – indeed they had suffered their only League defeat of the season there. Hibs fans might well have harboured some trepidation about the venue, but surely not their opponents – Dunfermline Athletic. Hibernian were the obvious favourites to win the tie, not least because Dunfermline were a B Division side and hardly an outstanding one at that – they were destined to finish the season outside of the promotion places, and by a good margin.

But football is a funny game. The Hibs midfield trio had struggled to assert themselves since the start of the season, even though numerous permutations had been tried out. With the season now around a dozen games old, the Dunfermline match resulted in a humiliating defeat, and a watershed for the Hibees. There were no excuses, but there was recognition that certain players had displayed an unwarranted complacency. One story that emerged later was that Eddie Turnbull, not renowned as a gambler, had gone to Falkirk dog track with his brother on the Thursday night before the semi-final and lost his anticipated 'win bonus' at the greyhound races. Turnbull apparently thought long and hard about his approach in future, having lost both his money and his chance of a medal. Chairman Harry Swan could do nothing but wish Dunfermline all the best in the Final, which they promptly lost 0–3 to East Fife.

Hugh Shaw's response was a revolutionary one, and following thinly-veiled criticism of aspects of the team's defending the entire half-back line was dropped for the next game, which was against Queen of the South at Easter Road. On 15 October Bobby Combe was eased back into midfield, permanently as it turned out, to become a replacement wing-half. This created a space in the forward line, which Bobby Johnstone took, and thus the Famous Five appeared together in a full first-team fixture. Naturally, attention was mainly focused on the new arrangements in the middle of the park, so few of the 25,000 witnesses will have appreciated that further up the pitch new partnerships were being formed that would soon be seen as ground-breaking. Gordon Smith and Eddie Turnbull scored in a 2–0 win, and Bobby's place in the forward line became almost automatic during the next five years, a period in which he missed only four League games. Lawrie Reilly feels the focus upon the Famous Five became rather unfair from this point forward, especially to those he refers to as the Super Six – the defence! 'Bobby Combe dropped back to allow wee Bobby into the forward line, and Combe settled very well at wing-half. He was a strong lad too, and had scored four goals from inside-forward against Rangers when Hibs beat them 8–1 in 1941.'

The following month Bobby scored his first League goal against Motherwell at Fir Park, and 19 November brought his first goal at Easter Road. As usual, many of his friends were in the crowd to see him play against East Fife that day, and among them was Louise Ovens (née McEwen), who had married the previous week and was honeymooning in Edinburgh. Her husband took her along to the game: 'Everyone liked to follow him and see how he was getting on. The town was so proud of him, lots of us would try to watch the games.' Billy Stark recalled the excitement too: 'busloads of the supporters' club from Selkirk would go into Easter Road to see Bobby play'. The match programme for that red-letter day does include one item of news designed to raise a smile… centre-half Johnny (Jock) Paterson had just knocked Hibs' billiards title-holder out of the club Championship – and in the first round, too! Paterson apparently insisted on maximum publicity for his defeat of the lad whom teammates had nicknamed Billiards Bobby.

With the new-look formation settling well, the team went right through to the New Year dropping only one point, and that was when Celtic equalised in the last minute at Parkhead. Given the coincidence of Hibs' devastating run of form and Bobby's establishment in the side, the new decade might well have come as a shock to him, as there was very early evidence that Hibs were not going to win every week. On New Year's Day, Hearts, already winners of the first 'derby' of the season in September, now inflicted Hibs' second League defeat, this time at Easter Road. To be fair, Hearts, too, were in good form, and they came from behind to record their 11th consecutive win. An Edinburgh record attendance of 65,850 witnessed the game. Later in the month, Hibs went out of the Scottish Cup, in a 0–1 home defeat to Partick Thistle, before normal service was restored with a 4–1 win against Celtic at Easter Road. Eddie Turnbull scored all four goals against the Bhoys that day, including a hat-trick of successfully taken penalties; an extremely rare feat.

Eddie Turnbull recalls that Bobby settled well. He had become an established first-team player, and along with Willie Ormond they were becoming good friends off the park too. 'Bobby was close friends with Jimmy Cairns as well, the left-back in the early days. I was very close with the other three of them because I made up the four for the card school when we travelled anywhere. They were great lads and great company.' After two months without a goal, Bobby scored in a 1–1 draw at East Fife, and the following week came a surprise defeat to the only other side that managed to lower Hibs' colours during the whole season, Third Lanark. A subsequent run of five wins meant that Hibs travelled to Ibrox Park for their last fixture, and Bobby knew that a win against Rangers would earn him a Championship medal. Hopey was in the crowd with some of his mates, but back home in Selkirk Bobby's mother and sisters, who seldom saw him play, couldn't bear the tension. They normally listened to the wireless, trying to keep up with events, but on this occasion Liz couldn't even manage that. Betty, who only ever saw Bobby play twice as a professional, still recalls the strains of that titanic match: 'it was on the radio, but our mother wouldn't listen'. In the event, Hibs managed only a 0–0 draw, in front of a crowd of 101,000, though Bobby was left with indelible memories of Willie Ormond shaving the post with a last-minute effort. Hibs left Ibrox still on top of the League table, on goal average, but having completed their fixtures, while Rangers still had a game to play. The 'Gers knew that a point would do against Third Lanark. The Glasgow side did earn that, but they were grateful that Thirds missed a penalty late in that game, with the scores level. So Hibernian finished as runners-up again, in spite of only losing three League games and earning 49 points, sufficient to win the title in almost any other season. Further, they had scored 86 League goals, while Rangers, who had achieved the League and Cup double, had needed fewer goals to collect both major trophies! For the third season running, Gordon Smith was Hibs' top scorer, with 25 League goals. Bobby, not in the side for the first three League games, had thereafter missed just one, and he had scored nine times, including a brace at home to East Fife and one in the return at Bayview Park.

As was now usual, the new season began with the League Cup, and Bobby scored against all three opponents in the group stage, including two at St Mirren in a 6–0 win. There was a thriller at Brockville Park, where Falkirk scored three times without reply in the first 18 minutes, only to lose 4–5 after a Gordon Smith hat-trick had initially levelled the tie at 3–3. Bobby scored in the home games against both Dundee and Falkirk, but the most peculiar aspect of this phase occurred in the away tie at Dens Park, Dundee. The match was abandoned due to torrential rain, with Hibs leading 2–0, and as it was clear that Dundee couldn't catch Hibs in any event, the replay was simply never played!

Gordon Smith was now captaining the side, although his approach was more measured than many of his counterparts. Lawrie Reilly thought that his style was to lead by example: 'he certainly did nae shout any encouragement, if we we're on the park, you know, come on then lads! – There was none of that urgency with Gordon. You were just left to do your own thing, but generally we didn't think any the worse of him for that.' Lawrie feels that Eddie Turnbull might have seen that particular side of Gordon as quite a significant weakness though – Eddie seemed much more cut out to be a leader: 'Eddie probably would have made a better leader, and he would have been in a better position. I don't think the captain should be a winger – I don't think the captain should be a goalkeeper either – that's my opinion.'

Nonetheless, Gordon had led the team on to the quarter-final of the League Cup, where they faced Aberdeen, and it was a remarkable Cup tie by any standards: one that Bobby would recall for the rest of his life. He gave Hibs the lead at Pittodrie, but with Smith out Hibs still lost the first leg by 1–4. A massive crowd packed Easter Road for the second leg the following Wednesday, more in hope than any realistic anticipation that Hibs could do it. Remarkably, Bobby scored on the hour as Hibs surged into a 3–0 lead, taking the game into extra-time. When Lawrie Reilly scored, it looked as if he had secured a win for Hibs, only for the Dons to force the game into a replay as the darkness descended.

Hibs then played two League games, at home to Hearts and away to Aberdeen, losing both, before the League Cup tie with Aberdeen was replayed at Ibrox Park. This match was drawn 1–1, and Aberdeen will not have bothered to travel home, because the second replay was the following night at another neutral Glasgow venue, Hampden Park. Here Aberdeen had no answer to Hibs, and Bobby netted twice in windy conditions, helping his side to overwhelm the Dons by 5–1. For a man not given to overstating the importance of footballers and footballing matters generally, Bobby's recollection of this tie is remarkable and testament to its quality; the detail was still almost crystal clear in the 1980s when he was asked in a radio interview to recall his favourite games. 'Oh, I've got lots, a lot of memories from Hibs, aye, some marvellous matches. I remember a game against Aberdeen; we went there in the League Cup. In the old days it was a two-legged affair, and we lost 4–1 at Aberdeen, and everybody wrote us off. We came to Easter Road on a Wednesday night, played Aberdeen again, and it was three-nothing at 90 minutes, so we had to play extra-time, and then we scored, that made it 4–0, so we were in front, and in the last minute of extra-time Aberdeen scored so that made it five each! On the Monday we had to go to Ibrox, and play a replay against Aberdeen, which finished up two-each[3], after extra-time. Then the next night we had to go to Hampden, for another replay, and luckily enough we came out on top, winning 5–0 at the finish. You know, these four games were marvellous games to play in. If these games had been televised, they'd be showing them yet because some of the goals were absolutely brilliant, and, of course, it was exciting because of the amount of goals that were scored.'

Good League Cup form had carried Hibs into the semi-final, where Eddie Turnbull took the plaudits with a hat-trick as they eased past Queen of the South 3–1, despite going a goal down at neutral Tynecastle. Hibs were to face Motherwell, and coincidentally the two also met at Fir Park in the last League game prior to the Final. Hibs warmed up by thrashing the 'Well 6–2 in what was only their fourth League game of the season. Bobby scored twice that day, including a goal that he later reflected on as perhaps the best goal he ever scored: 'it was against Motherwell early in my career. I beat three or four players and walked the ball into the net. You don't see players beating opponents and dribbling like they did at that time.' These goals, alongside the eight goals from the 10 League Cup ties, took his season total to 10, and now there was a real chance for Bobby to earn his first major trophy.

Given the result the week before, Hibs were clear favourites for the Final, which was played at Hampden Park in front of over 64,000 spectators. For an hour it looked as if they would overwhelm their opponents for the second week running, but with Turnbull missing this game the pace slackened later, and Motherwell nicked two quick goals and then a third from a goalkeeping error. Bobby's first honour at senior level was a runners'-up medal. His disappointment was enormous, but he had scored lots of goals during the run, played in the memorable four-match extravaganza against Aberdeen – and he sensed that this was only the start.

Having lost two League games already, Hibs now needed to firm up their challenge for the title, and this they did in earnest. Following the League Cup disappointment, only Rangers were able to claim a point from the Hibees in the nine League games that remained before the end of the year. The Christmas period is a busy time for footballers, and this year saw a fantastic win at Brockville against Falkirk, but Lawrie Reilly's outstanding memory of that day was Bobby, Willie and Eddie turning up at Waverley station for the train out, 'I remember one game, when the three comedians turned up to take the train to Falkirk. The carriage smelled like a brewery, and those three looked really rough, but we still went out and won 5–1.' Bobby scored that day, but not on New Year's Day, which saw Hearts, as usual, winning the traditional derby match at Tynecastle. Happily, it seems that an active social life wasn't too badly impacted by a demanding fixture list. Eddie Turnbull obviously relished these carefree days, and he and his mates were enjoying it to the full: 'We used to play New Year's Day, of course, and you'd play the next day as well. New Year's Day we lost to Hearts, and at night, Ormond, Nicker and I, we're down at Portobello, at a hotel, where there's a wee dance going on. And this bookie we all knew, big Bill Upton, a lovely man, but he was a Hearts supporter! Bobby says to big Upton, what'll you give me if I score two goals tomorrow? [against Aberdeen]. Upton says, "you think you'll score two tomorrow, the state o' you? I'll give you 10–1"… Anyway, we all had two pounds on at 10–1. How many did he get? He got two, you look back in the record books and see the goals Johnstone scored that day, it's true, the day after New Year's Day.'

Hibernian's Scottish Cup exploits to some extent mirrored their experience in the League Cup. As before, Hibs needed a replay to overcome first-round opponents, this time St Mirren, but again they did so emphatically, and again Bobby netted two in a five-goal romp. There was also a key game at Ibrox Park, but this time it was against Rangers, their perennial main rivals for the League. A crowd of 106,000 watched the second-round tie, with Hibs twice coming from behind. This was another in the series of games that seemingly centred on Rangers' renowned defence and the Famous Five, and it looked for all the world as if Hibs had forced a creditable 2–2 draw. Eddie Turnbull even recalls shouting to his mate, Rangers defender Sammy Cox, 'see you Wednesday' in the last few minutes. As the clock ran down, Hibs gained a free-kick, outside of the box, on the 'keeper's left-hand side. It was Turnbull territory, and the Rangers wall lined-up to face the inevitable thunderbolt. Bobby positioned himself on the right-hand side of the defensive wall and was not expecting what happened next. Ned Turnbull rolled the ball into Bobby, who had his back to goal. He collected the pass, teed the ball up as he squirmed among the Rangers defenders, and as he got towards the centre of the box, he hit it with his right foot into 'keeper Bobby Brown's top left-hand corner. Johnstone recalled 'as soon as I hit it, I knew it was in'. The Rangers players were floored, completely surprised. The Hibs players were merely quite surprised! While it appeared that the move had come from the training ground, it was in fact completely off the cuff, and a sign of the confidence within the team. This was a side on the top of its game; seemingly a side that were going to achieve real glory –

and soon. That was the first time that Lex Millar had seen Bobby in the first team, and he had watched the game in comparative luxury. 'Bobby got me a ticket. When he got tickets, they were usually for the stand. Or the enclosure, so we didn't have to stand up.' He was lucky. There were hundreds of Hibernian supporters locked out of this game, many of them huddled around wirelesses in the adjacent coach park. They were blessed with more room than those inside the ground to celebrate the news – 'Nicker' Johnstone had nicked it. The occasion must have been incredible to play in, but Bobby revelled in it. 'This was one of the greatest games I ever played in, we used to go to Ibrox and Parkhead thinking we would win in those days – and the size of the crowd helps a player, it raises his game.'

Having received a bye in the third round of the Scottish Cup, the team were now making great progress on two fronts, and March opened with two successive games at Broomfield Park against Airdrieonians. The first, a League game, saw Bobby score Hibs' only goal in a 1–2 loss, which proved to be a fourth and final League defeat of the season. The following week, Hibs were back, but this time they triumphed 3–0 in a Scottish Cup quarter-final tie, earning the right to face their League Cup conquerors Motherwell once again. Hearts, incidentally, who had a free afternoon having been knocked out of the Cup by Celtic, entertained Manchester City in a friendly match, although Bobby's boyhood hero Andy Black had moved on from City the previous August to nearby Stockport County, the town where he would live for the rest of his days.

On the last day of the month, that Scottish Cup semi-final against Motherwell at Tynecastle saw Hibs suffer incredible bad luck. At a goal down after just 20 seconds, due to a slip-up by John Paterson, literally, Hibs then found themselves chasing the game with 10 men when John Ogilvie broke his leg after 15 minutes. Bobby Johnstone had to drop into a deeper position as part of the rearrangements, but after hanging-in tenaciously, and the game in the melting pot at 2–3, Willie Ormond was carried off with ruptured ligaments, ending any hopes of a Cup Final double. Some Pathé News film footage of the game has survived, and it shows Lawrie Reilly equalising after Ogilvie had become the first stretcher case, and then later pulling the score back to 2–3 after Kelly and McCleod had scored for Motherwell. This was a tremendous blow to Hibs, and it rankled with the players that luck seemed to desert them whenever Cup glory came within striking distance. League results continued in the same vein as before though, and Hibs claimed the Scottish Championship flag with four games to spare when they went to Shawfield Park for a Wednesday night match in the middle of April. There they clobbered Clyde by 4–0, though Bobby and Lawrie Reilly did not play. There is little sense that the players celebrated their Championship flag in the public manner that would be expected today. In those days, of course, there was much less sports news generally, and almost no media 'hype' as such. For the players' part, they almost expected to be in the shake-up for the title anyway, and if anything it was the Scottish Cup that was seen as the more glamorous competition. Further, the season hadn't ended, and Bobby and Lawrie had reported to the Scotland camp, where Bobby was to make his debut against England at Wembley, the home of the Auld Enemy, in a Home International Championship match.

Described in the match programme as looking even younger than his years, the

England fans didn't know too much about Bobby Johnstone at this time. They learned that he had initially come to prominence while playing in army teams, he had been instrumental for Hibs that season, and that he was still just 21. There was no mention of the fact that Bobby and Lawrie had both now gained their first Scottish League Championship medals – clearly the notes had been compiled before the Championship denouement. On the Saturday after earning a first major domestic honour, Bobby Johnstone received his international cap just two years after his League debut. He represented Scotland against England in front of a crowd of 98,000 at Wembley Stadium, though approximately a third of that number came from north of the border. It was something of a transitional time for the Scotland international team, as their previous international fixture, in December 1950, had been an undistinguished one. There they had conceded their unbeaten home record against foreign opposition. For a nation with an early international soccer history, reaching back to 1870, this was something of a blow, although closer inspection of the records reveals that it wasn't until 1933 that a foreign side actually threatened the record by stepping on to Scottish soil!

Newspaper reports from the time imply that Scotland were taking something of a gamble by including wee Bobby, the concerns centring on his experience and readiness for a match that did in fact prove eventful. England struggled after losing Wilf Mannion, who was carried off on a stretcher after fracturing his cheekbone in a collision on the edge of the box. Film footage shows Mannion being stretchered off the park after only 15 minutes with blood staining to his shirt, yet England still took the lead. Then Bobby, described by the commentator as 'Hibs wonder boy', broke through, but he was foiled by 'keeper Bert Williams, who cleared the ball. Soon after, Bobby equalised, bursting on to a pass from Lawrie Reilly, and crashing it home from eight yards. From there the game went the way of the Scots, who took the lead early in the second half when Bobby returned the favour for Reilly to score. Later, Bert Williams, the over-worked England goalkeeper, who had been having an excellent match, fumbled, allowing Billy Liddell to put Scotland 3–1 up. It seemed to be all over. Yet England made a good fight of it, Tom Finney pulled one back, and they also actually had a good chance to equalise, with Mortenson shooting wide of the post. Billy Liddell, who scored Scotland's third goal that day, played alongside Bobby for Scotland on six occasions in total, and he features in Bobby's story much more controversially, when they were on opposing sides about five years after this game.

Bobby was asked many times about his international debut. He was just a wee lad from the Borders, the youngest player on the pitch, relatively inexperienced, and facing the might of England at a packed Empire Stadium. England featured world-renowned names such as Matthews, Mortenson, Finney and the captain, Billy Wright, yet Bobby always claimed that it hadn't fazed him one bit. He'd scored a goal against the Auld Enemy at Wembley, helping Scotland win the Home International Championship outright, yet his own recollections centred only around the game itself, and in particular around some missed early chances. 'Yes, that was a sort of funny game to tell you the truth. It was a good experience, and I played with Willie Waddell outside-right, and he was a real gentleman Willie Waddell, he made me feel right at home, right from the beginning. Course in those days we didn't have three and four days together before an international; we went down on the Friday and stayed at Oatlands Park hotel and played on the Saturday. I was a bit disappointed with my first game, because I should have scored about three times in the first 20 minutes. Every chance seemed to fall to me that day, which was a funny experience because normally I wasn't a great goalscorer, but every chance seemed to fall to me, and I missed two or three reasonable chances. England had scored through Harold Hassall, and Harold and I'd been in the army together. We went up the other end, and I scored, so that made it one each. I think it was 1–1 at half-time, and Reilly was playing which made me feel a bit happier with the position, because I got on very well with Lawrie Reilly, he was an easy player to play with, and in the second half we got on top and ran out winners 3–2 at the finish up, but we were always in charge after I'd equalised. I was back in Selkirk the following Wednesday night, watching it on the Pathé News, so that was a bit of a coup for me.'

While Bobby's modesty does him credit, the press were far more effusive. Jack Harkness, the famed journalist and former Scottish goalkeeper, described how Bobby's brilliance had matched that of England's Matthews, '...cute, perky, confident and devastating, he was Scotland's star'. Soon after the game, and in a gesture typical both of Bobby's generosity and his passion for rugby (as a youngster he had displayed considerable potential as a scrum-half and had played for Selkirk's junior rugby teams), he donated his first international jersey to the local rugby club, and to this day, on high-days and holidays, it is displayed in the Selkirk Rugby Football club pavilion at Philiphaugh.

After the excitement had died down, the completion of the League programme might have seemed rather mundane for Bobby. The last four League fixtures were completed in a spell of just 10 days before the end of April, with both members of the Old Firm succumbing to Hibs in the last two games. During this busy spell, Hibs also found time to play a friendly against Tottenham Hotspur, themselves only days away from securing their position as Champions of the Football League. That game was drawn 0–0, but Bobby's goal in the 4–1 win against Rangers was his 12th League goal of the season, which, when added to his 11 Cup goals, gave him a total of 23. In the final analysis, Hibernian had dropped just 12 points, winning the League with 48 points, 10 clear of runners-up Rangers. They had lost both games to city rivals Hearts for the second season running, though – seemingly Champions of Scotland, but not Champions of Edinburgh! Partick Thistle were the only other side to leave Easter Road with so much as a point, and they also escaped defeat in the 0–0 draw at Firhill Park.

For the first time, season 1950–51 saw Lawrie Reilly take Gordon Smith's mantle as Hibs' leading scorer. He scored at least 22 League goals (although other authoritative sources record him as scoring 23) which, added to his Cup goals, gave him a total of 36 (or 37). Within a couple of weeks of the end of the season, Bobby quickly earned his second and third caps when Scotland played international challenge games (friendlies, essentially) against Denmark and France. Both were victories for the Scots, in front of crowds of around 76,000 at Hampden Park. The latter game caused Bobby to miss the celebrations at the East of Scotland Shield match against Hearts, played at Easter Road the previous evening. In both international games Bobby was again flanked on the right by Willie Waddell, with the only significant change to the forward line being the replacement of left-winger Billy Liddell with another player whom Bobby would face in a future high-profile encounter – Bobby Mitchell, who had just collected an FA Cup-winners' medal with Newcastle United. While Lawrie Reilly managed a goal in each game, Scotland fans were left waiting for Bobby's first international goal on home soil. The squad then left for a couple of games on the continent, against Belgium and Austria, but they travelled without Bobby Johnstone, who was not selected for the trip.

But Bobby was not idle. That same month, the May of 1951, Hibernian undertook an end-of-season trip to France, where they played two games before returning home to further action in a Festival of Britain match against Rapide Wien. There was little time for a close season as such, because in mid-June the team flew north for a friendly against Inverness Thistle, and so there was little time to catch breath before the pre-season Festival Trophy, also known as the St Mungo Cup competition, started. The 1951 Festival of Britain celebrated the centenary of the Great Exhibition, with many social and cultural events held throughout Britain, football being well to the fore. One of the main elements, the Industrial Power Exhibition, took place in Glasgow, and the St Mungo Cup ran concurrently, being funded by Glasgow Corporation and organised jointly with the SFA. Essentially, all Scottish Division A clubs competed, although Clyde and Queen's Park, being Glasgow clubs, were included at the expense of Airdrieonians and newly-promoted Stirling Albion. The main tournament started on 14 July, with a parallel competition running for the excluded (mostly B Division) sides. In the opening round Hibs, one of eight teams drawn to play at home, defeated Third Lanark 3–1, with Bobby scoring twice in five minutes. Now the competition moved to Glasgow, and in their second-round game, played at Celtic Park, Hibs overcame Motherwell by the same score, with Bobby's 61st-minute goal being preceded by two others from Turnbull and Souness during a devastating eight-minute spell early in the second half. Hibs drew the semi-final 1–1 with Aberdeen at the same venue, and this obviously caused something of an organisational headache, because the replay was played at Pittodrie, Aberdeen, some 150 miles from the hub of the competition! With home advantage, the Dons won the semi-final and were later 2–0 up against Celtic in the Final at Hampden Park, before succumbing 3–2 in front of a crowd of over 80,000.

The tournament was a success; a rare example of a successful tournament being sponsored by a local authority. There had been some trepidation at likely gates for summer football, especially as the tournament coincided with the Glasgow industrial holidays, but attendances were good, even though Rangers played only one game (and that in Aberdeen). Queen of the South's three games were the only ones to attract crowds of less than 10,000, and over 97,000 spectators saw Hibs' four games, so the clubs made good money. Bobby had scored three goals, and, as with all players, he received £10 appearance money for each game played and an inscribed commemorative pewter tankard, though he would no doubt have preferred the solid silver versions presented to the winners.

The season proper began in mid-August, and Hibs' main target was to retain the Championship flag; thus far, no club outside of the Old Firm had ever successfully defended the title. All concerned with Hibs will have hoped that the form shown in the early stages of the League Cup was no indicator, because a 2–4 defeat at Partick was swiftly followed by a crushing 0–4 defeat by Motherwell, and at Easter Road. While things improved slightly from there, with Bobby himself scoring three goals in the other homes ties – easy wins against Stirling and Partick – the six group games garnered a mere five points, and to put it graciously, in the context of a serious assault on the Scottish League Championship, that was one distraction out of the way.

Early in the September, Bobby's travel options were disrupted when the railway line between Selkirk and Galashiels was closed to passengers. This meant that travellers from the Selkirk area now had to take a bus service to Galashiels or Melrose in order to connect with the capital, but whatever the effect on Bobby's routines he made a great start when the League fixtures began, scoring in a 2–0 win at the Kirkcaldy home of Raith Rovers. Then he added two more in the 4–4 draw with Aberdeen the following week. The all-Edinburgh fixture, so problematical in recent times, was negotiated next: a 1–1 draw at Tynecastle brought a welcome point, and the month was rounded-off satisfactorily for Bobby when he netted twice more in the 5–2 win against Third Lanark, bringing his total to five in the first four League games.

October began in a similar vein, with Bobby receiving his fourth cap against Northern Ireland at Windsor Park, Belfast. A crowd of 57,000 saw the Scots run out fairly easy winners, with two goals from Bobby, though this was to be their only win of that season's Home International Championship, which was played over a six-month period. Further representative honours came when Bobby was once again selected to represent the Scottish Football League in their 50th International League match. In a team dominated, at least numerically, by the seven players from Old Firm clubs, including the entire defence, they faced the Football League at Hillsborough, Sheffield, though Lawrie Reilly did accompany Bobby once again in a 1–2 defeat.

Back at Hibs, Bobby and his teammates continued to play well, though there was a three-game spell in which Bobby failed to score, and only two points were collected. In the middle of November, Bobby got back on scoring form as Hibs defeated East Fife and replaced them at the head of the League table. Hibs now hit a purple patch that saw six consecutive wins in the lead-up to Christmas – this was turning into a habit. By this point, Bobby had scored 17 times in the 16 League matches Hibs had played, though the festive period (not for the first time) cost Hibs dearly. The last game of the year was lost 1–3 at Motherwell, though Bobby scored yet again, and then the Ne'er Day derby rang in the old: Hibernian 2 Hearts 3.

The following day, Thirds were thrashed 5–0 on their own ground in an inexplicably brilliant performance, and by now Bobby was on his way to a career-best goal total, having already scored 19 times in 19 League games and at least once in eight of the last nine. The Hearts curse was getting beyond a joke, though... Bobby had yet to score against his boyhood team, and they had now won three years running at Easter Road, with Hibs managing just one solitary point in the six League meetings since Bobby had come into the team. In late January there was an epic Scottish Cup tie against Raith Rovers, with Hibs drawn to play at Starks Park, where they attracted what was then a record crowd. Again, film footage of the match has survived, and Bobby can be quite easily identified, playing his accustomed role behind the main strikers. The match ended 0–0, as did the replay at Easter Road, and only at the third attempt did Raith overcome the Hibees, by 1–4. Hibs were still at the top of the League table at this point, although their main rivals, the ubiquitous Rangers, had games in hand. There was no time to wallow in disappointment after the Cup exit, as the next game was at Ibrox, and the 2–2 draw was reckoned to be a good point on balance, though it was plain that the reigning Champions were not as often the force that they had been the previous term. Defeats at East Fife and then, more worryingly, Queen of the South (by 2–5) caused trepidation, but thankfully Rangers were not setting the world alight either, and with only two fixtures left Hibs enjoyed a short break from the demands of League fixtures. They left Rangers, who faced four away games, to play catch-up and attempt to close the three-point gap.

As Hibs seldom lost games to the weather, they had found themselves with just three League fixtures to complete after 1 March, and this presented the opportunity to arrange a series of friendly fixtures against English sides. The week before the Queen of the South defeat, Hibs had travelled to Manchester to play City at Maine Road in a high-profile friendly. City supporters knew that Hibs were reigning Scottish League Champions, reckoned to be the fittest team in Scotland, and they were warned to expect the attackers to 'switch their positions; as such the numbers on their backs should be seen as incidental'. Bobby was described as 'full of tricks and twists, and the leading scorer, with seven caps'[4] and it was noted that Hibs had already scored 84 League goals. Perhaps some of the Manchester City players also caught sight of this information, because they were bamboozled as the match finished 4–1 to Hibs. Outside-right Jimmy Souness played in Gordon Smith's place, with the usual winger absent with a knee injury. Souness, a late replacement who had to be summoned down from his job in Edinburgh, scored all four of Hibs' goals in a 34-minute spell, though three of them were deemed to have been 'handed to him on a plate' by poor defending. Don Revie pulled one back after the third, and the crowd of 35,000 went home thinking that they had seen football from another planet. In the *Maine Road Gossip* column for City's next home match, Hibs were congratulated on their grand football, alongside the admission that City were a well-beaten side, long before the finish. They had been 'yards slower than their opponents, and one of the few redeeming features had been the saves of Bert Trautmann from Johnstone, Ormond and Souness'. Hibs' apparently superior fitness had been noticeable in this clash between the two Leagues, although one wonders what training the Manchester City players did to leave them lagging behind this regime, described by Bobby some years later: 'On Mondays we had a road run around Arthur's seat, and down to Portobello. Tuesday was golf. We didn't have many midweek games, and if we did they were generally on a Monday, so it was golf at North Berwick or Longniddry, or somewhere down the coast. Wednesday/Thursday was fairly hard training. Hugh Shaw was a hard trainer, so it was mainly exercise, and into the sweat box underneath the stand. Friday was the easiest day; we just got spikes on and did a few laps and sprints. Then we'd have a meeting about what we would do on the pitch the next day, but it more or less never happened because you can't plan a fitba' match, so we didn't end up planning very much. He (Hugh Shaw) told us to go out and enjoy the game, and we did. We could all do each other's jobs'. Lawrie Reilly and Eddie Turnbull were critical of the fact that little of the training involved interaction with a football. 'The only black mark was that we were never allowed the ball in training.' Lawrie complained, while Eddie never accepted what the players were often told: 'If you don't get the ball in training during the week, you're hungry for it on a Saturday.'

In the first week of April, Bobby gained his fifth cap when he faced England once again, this time at Hampden Park. Three of the Five played, with Gordon Smith playing alongside Bobby for the first time at international level, but this was not a great day for the Scots, as England won 2–1, with two goals from Stan Pearson, who was playing alongside his Manchester United teammate Jack Rowley. Jack would play a larger role in Bobby's football life almost a decade on, but the story of this match finished when Lawrie Reilly pulled back a goal for Scotland with a few minutes left.

A few days later, when Hibs beat Dundee at Easter Road, they knew that once again the Championship was theirs. Hibs pipped Rangers by four points and scored 92 goals in their 30 League games – over three per game! Lawrie Reilly got 27 as Hibs earned a third Championship in five years. Rangers' challenge had fizzled out quite unexpectedly in the latter stages, and once again they were well behind Hibs in the goalscoring stakes, managing 'just' 61. Bobby Johnstone scored 23, the only time he managed to exceed 20 League goals during his career, and three League Cup goals, giving him a total of 26.

Notes

1. To add to the lack of clarity, Bobby himself is quoted in an Oldham Athletic match programme (albeit some 51 years after the event) talking about various issues, including the start of his football career. On the subject of his first-team debut, he is recorded as stating 'It was for Hibs in a League-Cup tie at Partick Thistle, and we lost: I was 17 at the time, and it was quite an ordeal as the side had so many big-name players in it.' If Bobby was quoted accurately, then his memory was playing tricks, because in this 1948–49 season Hibernian's League Cup section opponents had been Clyde, Rangers and Celtic. As was usual at the time, games in the initial stage of the League Cup were played on a home and away basis, in a mini-League format, at the beginning of the season. Hibernian had not progressed beyond the group stages, so there was no League Cup game against Partick Thistle that season, and further, by this time, Bobby was now 19 years of age. It may be that the confusion centres on the fact that Bobby's first senior goal for Hibs came (later) against Partick Thistle, in a League Cup tie.
2. Gordon Smith's total includes wartime games.
3. In fact, the score was 1–1, and following a more substantial break in between than Bobby implies, although the two replays were indeed played on consecutive nights in Glasgow. The slight confusion probably stems from the fact that the two replays were on the Monday and Tuesday after the League game at Pittodrie. The final League Cup match ended 5–1, not 5–0.
4. At this stage of Bobby's career, he had received four 'full' international caps, and gained further representative honours when playing for the Scottish League on three occasions.

CHAPTER 4

The Glamour Profession?

During the summer of 1952, Bobby underwent a fairly minor operation at the Western General Hospital in Edinburgh, where some repairs were carried out on the cartilage in his left knee. This meant that he wasn't quite fully fit and ready for the start of the new season, which was a disappointment to him as he wasn't used to being affected by injuries and so seldom missed games. (He missed only three throughout the whole of the previous season.) With Bobby now unavailable for several of the early-season League Cup ties, Hibs ploughed on without him, qualifying comfortably with four wins from their six group games. Injuries are part of the game, of course, and this was Bobby's first taste of an occupational hazard that would regularly interrupt his career from this point onwards.

Around the same time, Hopey's health, which had been poor for some time, deteriorated to a point where it began to give the family serious cause for concern. Bobby's father had been quite ill since the previous autumn, and, though it hadn't been diagnosed at that time, it later transpired that he was suffering from a stomach ulcer. Later, this perforated, requiring an operation, and during that procedure a tumour was found, also in the stomach. Having failed to be admitted to the forces at the outbreak of war because of his physical condition, a few years after the war his poor health meant that he had to stop working in the mills, and this had worried him greatly. He also developed epilepsy, and it is also possible that he was suffering the effects of a knock to the head from his own football days, although this could never be proved. Margaret, Bobby's eldest sister, believes that their father's wide-ranging health problems were directly attributable to the years of constant worry caused by trying to obtain work in the tweed mills so as to provide for the family.

In late August Hopey required another operation, and the family were told that his time was limited. By this time Margaret had completed her training in Arbroath, passed her final examinations, and she was able to secure a move to the East Fortune Hospital in the east of Edinburgh. Now much nearer to Selkirk, she could nurse Hopey, and he was able to spend the last three weeks of his life at home. In spite of Margaret's wonderful care, Hopey passed away on 6 September, aged just 48. He had remained lucid to the end, and was able to wish each of his children the best of futures. 'It was a big break in the family, even though we all knew he was dying,' Margaret recalled. Bobby was devastated, too. Although Hopey had been present at many of his son's greatest moments in the game, Bobby guessed that his father would miss out on many more. 'The last time my father saw Bobby play was against Rangers when he got the winning goal. Dad went with Erys Grieve and Tammie Leech. The excitement of that game was terrific, I still remember reading all about it in the newspapers.' Bobby would refer to his father often in later years, and he told his friends that he honestly believed his father had been a better player than he was. Lawrie Reilly also remembers Bobby's little joke about Hopey: 'My dad was a waster' he used to say, before going on to explain about one of the jobs that he had done. Hopey had taken employment collecting the waste from around the looms in a large woollen mill, work that involved collecting up the surplus material and removing it for off-site disposal.

On the day that Hopey died, Hibs' challenge for a hat-trick of League Championship flags got off to a poor start with a home defeat against Queen of the South, though Bobby's mind was understandably elsewhere. He soon scored twice in both legs of the League Cup quarter-final against Morton, but those two games sandwiched a truly significant event as Gordon Smith received the benefit match that had been approved in 1951, on his completion of 10 years' service with Hibernian. Their opponents were the highly-attractive Football League Champions Manchester United, and the occasion brought a crowd of around 28,000 to Easter Road. It was a fantastic match, full of incident, and later described by Lawrie Reilly as the best game he ever played in. Hibs famously turned around a 2–3 half-time deficit to win 7–3, with all members of the Five apart from Bobby finding the net. One newspaper declared that fans had seen 'perhaps the finest exhibition of football artistry ever witnessed', and besides the 10 goals actually scored, there were a further three disallowed, a penalty missed (by Manchester United) and numerous near things at both ends. The *Edinburgh Evening News* declared 'the home side proceeded to reach the heights of football perfection and pugnacity'. It was a match that would not be forgotten, not least by the other members of the Famous Five, as the benefit match issue became the root of much ill-feeling over succeeding years; it can readily be argued that this match sowed the seeds that would lead to the break-up of the Five.

Two days after that game, Morton came to Easter Road for the second leg of the League Cup tie, and, as in the first leg, Hibernian helped themselves to six goals. The following Saturday Reilly scored three against Hearts, and it meant that Hibs had scored '22 goals in a week, a feat most unlikely to be repeated', according to *The Scotsman*. Best of all, it seemed that the derby bogey was laid to rest, and with Hibs now into the semi-final of the League Cup it was all smiles and on to Motherwell, a 7–3 League win in which Bobby scored twice. October proved fruitful, too, though Hibs' defence was more than charitable when they were defeated 1–7 by Arsenal in a floodlit match played at Highbury. The match, attended by the Duke of Edinburgh, was a fundraiser for the National Playing Fields Association and unfortunately the first time that Hibs were shown live on television. By November Hibs had taken 10 points from the five League games since the opening day disaster against Queen of the South, and Rangers had already lost three times. League Cup hopes disappeared though, with Bobby's hopes of a second Cup medal fading at neutral Tynecastle against Dundee, in spite of the fact that Reilly gave them the lead.

It was a busy life, and Bobby was enjoying it to the full. During his afternoons off, he enjoyed plenty of golf, or the odd trip to the races. He played snooker and billiards with his teammates in Edinburgh and also at the Selkirk Institute, where his mates gave him a handicap of -60 for the club tournament! 'That puts me right out of it' Bobby said, but he still had strong hopes of retaining his Easter Road crown in Hibs' club Christmas Handicap. Golf formed an important part of sporting life generally for young men with time on their hands, and the Hibs players would get out for at least one round of golf each week. An article in a match programme from this time tells of the club's trainers, Jimmy McColl and Sammy Kean, celebrating a win on the golf course over Eddie Turnbull and Bobby, but only after persuading them to concede six strokes! 'Large cigars were the order of the day' as the trainers unexpectedly won 3&2. These sorts of sporting events were of great value for team-building purposes, and the impression is that team spirit was extraordinarily high at Easter Road.

After the weekend games, there was time to socialise with his pals, some of whom used to travel into Edinburgh with Bobby to watch him play. Lex Millar was one: 'He sometimes met us in a hotel on George Street, and afterwards most of the Hibs players were there, Reilly and that, but Gordon Smith didn't come out because he didn't drink.' Back in Selkirk, Bobby would take his turn to watch his mates play rugby, and there would be dances locally. For some time Bobby had been spending his evenings with a young lady, Heather Roden, who had moved to Selkirk at the age of four and had spent her first nine months living in Canada. Walter Bateman recalled 'He used to go out with Heather, to the dancing and that, every Saturday, but on a Friday you'd not see them because he'd be sitting in before the game, but we knew he was seeing Heather.'

According to Lex Millar, 'These were good days. We went to dances with bands at the Victoria Hall. Of course, Bobby was a good lad to know, he was a good pal. One time one of our mates, Ronnie Turner, came home on leave. he was in the Cameronians (Scottish Rifles). He wasn't demobbed, but we got him a ticket for the dance, and everyone in the place was buying him a nip, and he ended up flat out. I went and got Bobby, and he said "right, we'll away and get him, the car's in the square," and we got the car and saw Ronnie home. He wouldn't drive normally, but we needed to get Ronnie home, and that was the kind of chap he was.'

After the League Cup exit, results turned the season into something of a curate's egg, with a mixed run through to the New Year. As the festive period approached this was epitomised by a 4–5 reverse at Partick, being immediately followed by a 7–2 win at Queen of the South. The ship was steadied with a 2–1 win at Hearts on New Year's Day, and two days later Motherwell suffered their second seven-goal mauling of the season. The Scottish Cup campaign began with an 8–1 hammering of Stenhousemuir (notably, Bobby managed a goal in that game), and there were big wins against Clyde and Airdrie, the latter going down 7–3 at the end of February. Bobby must have been relieved to score twice in the latter match as he had managed just one League goal since October. This most barren run of his career started, perhaps coincidentally, shortly after the loss of his father. Hopes of Scottish Cup success were initially raised by two more big wins but were yet again extinguished, this time by an Aberdeen side that first gave a brave performance in a draw at Easter Road and then battled through 2–0 at Pittodrie in the replay the following Wednesday night.

Once again, the disappointment was palpable, and Eddie Turnbull took it badly. 'We were beaten in the Aberdeen Cup tie. Afterwards I got Ormond and Johnstone – we were the three musketeers, we nipped about together – and said "I don't know about you two, but I'm not going on that train tonight." It was a four-hour train journey in them days, and we left Pittodrie, and I said "If you want me, I'll be across in the wee boozer." They were umming and arghing, while I was in there having a wee half-pint, and who walks in? Johnstone and Ormond! Anyway, we stayed in a hotel, got the milk train home, and went straight to the ground the next morning. I'm just taking my jacket off, and the trainer says "The boss wants to see you – upstairs."

'Hugh Shaw told him off. "You know the rules, we travel together as a team, we all travel as a unit." I told him I was upset, I thought one or two of them hadn't pulled their weight. And he blamed me for Johnstone and Ormond too! Me... I'd been away five years in the bloody war! He was a wonderful guy though, Hugh Shaw, and I knew I'd let him down. I knew I was going to be punished. He said "I'll tell you what I'm going to do – I'll write to your mother!"' Eddie was the senior man, of course, but as the train had headed south to the capital the other two had been worried, too, knowing they would have to face the music. The three of them had comforted themselves with the conclusion 'if he drops one, he'll have to drop all three of us'.

Following that Cup defeat, Hibernian found themselves at the top of the League, and, what is more, they would remain unbeaten to the end of the season. Three of the next four games were drawn though, and even Bobby's two-goal salvo in the other game, a 3–1 win at Parkhead, was insufficient to prevent the initiative shifting towards Rangers. In early April, as pressure grew in the race for the title, Hibs accepted another invitation to play Selkirk, where Bobby still lived, of course, but on this occasion it was a reserve side that overwhelmed the Souters, and by 7–0, in front of a healthy Easter Monday afternoon crowd. Gordon Smith sent some remarks apologising for the fact that he was unable to play, adding that, with Hibernian now out of the Scottish Cup, they were making 'an all-out effort to win the League title for the third successive year'. In fact, none of Hibs' first team played, but Bobby did attend the Bank Holiday fixture with one or two of his colleagues at what for him was a very busy time professionally.

Later in the month, Bobby played for his country once again, earning his sixth cap and his third against the Auld Enemy. In fact, he had missed the previous five Scottish international games and had not played in the year since the previous England game. He loved these games, of course, believing that the large crowds helped a player to raise his game, and it is true that England respected Bobby. England manager Walter Winterbottom called him 'the most complete inside-forward in the home countries'. This match ended famously, for the Scots at least, in an exciting 2–2 draw at Wembley. Newsreel film of the match shows Ivor Broadis giving England the lead in the early stages, before Bobby hit the bar, allowing Reilly to barge the ball over the line for an equaliser. Later, Sammy Cox of Rangers picked up a serious injury while attempting to tackle Tom Finney, but the Preston man still managed to cross the ball from the left, and Broadis made it 2–1. The highlight for the Scots came almost at the end of the game, with just a few seconds left, when Johnstone and Reilly combined to save Scotland.

Interviewed in 2005, Lawrie Reilly could still recall the details: 'The last person to touch the ball before me was Bobby. The next was the goalie picking it out! The ball came through from the defence to me, and I flicked with my right foot to Bobby, turned, and Bobby chipped it through. Luckily it was off the ground, a bouncing ball, which went past the centre-half. Gil Merrick came out, and really I lobbed him. He was a big lad Gil Merrick, and I've got of a photograph of him trying to get it, but the ball was way up here you know, and luckily it cleared him. It wasn't a shot, it was a lob, and fortunately for me Bobby's pass through was bouncing, otherwise I wouldn't have been able to lob it, but I just carried it on – on the up, I just carried it on, over the 'keeper and into the net. The newspapers did the 'last-minute Reilly' thing... later on I worked for the papers, and they asked how many goals I'd scored in the last minute... it ran to about 19 or something – I'd probably scored 20 goals in the 48th minute, but the press weren't bothered about that.'

Sadly, Hopey never got to see Bobby at Wembley, but Margaret did travel to London for the game with her mother Liz. 'We went down on the train overnight. I still have a photograph of a group of us leaving from Selkirk. It was just a few months after Dad had died, and the excitement... Bobby passed to Lawrie Reilly in injury time, and there was the fuss with the 'last-minute Reilly' thing, it was terrific at the end. I was nursing, training in Edinburgh, and I had such a rush to get back there.'

Hibernian now faced three home games, and they needed to win them all to force Rangers into collecting at least three points from their remaining two games. In the first, Hibs effectively killed off the challenge by the interlopers from Methil, East Fife, with Bobby scoring in a keenly-fought 2–1 win, just two days after the England game. It was now a straight, two-way fight. The following Saturday, Bobby scored the first hat-trick of his senior career, against Third Lanark, who were shot down 7–1, with four of the Five scoring. Just four days later, in the final game of the season, Bobby scored twice more in the 4–1 win against Raith Rovers, and so Hibernian finished the season with 43 points.

Rangers beat Dundee 3–1 and then headed for Dumfries, where they then earned the required point against Queen of the South through Willie Waddell, who equalised with just a quarter of an hour to go. Rangers had their three points and claimed the Scottish League flag on goal average. The modern goal-difference system would have seen Hibernian collect a third consecutive title. The runners-up had scored a record 93 League goals, and of these the Famous Five had scored 85, with former inside-forward Bobby Combe chipping in another six on the odd occasion he got a game in the forward line. With such a fine margin between the two sides at the end of the season, statistics seem to suggest that Hibs had the more compelling case than the eventual winners – ignoring the final League table of course! In the 'head-to-head' against Rangers, Hibs had dropped a solitary point in the 1–1 draw at Easter Road. Further, Hibs had won their home and away games against each of the sides finishing in third, fourth and fifth places in the League and scored a total of 20 goals in these six key games. Sixth-placed St Mirren had been the highest-placed side to beat Hibs, when they secured a surprise win at Easter Road in late November.

Looking back to the war, the seven seasons since had seen Hibs win the title three times, and Rangers four – only Dundee had otherwise managed the runners'-up spot. Yet Hibs habitually scored more goals than the 'Gers, and had actually accumulated four more points than their rivals over the seven-year period. Of the 14 League fixtures between the two leading clubs, Hibs had managed six wins and six draws, conceding just 14 goals. They had scored more than any other club in the Scottish Division A for the sixth consecutive year, and it is this feature that makes the Famous Five era stand out – put simply, Hibs scored more goals than any other side in the League, even where that wasn't sufficient to claim the title.

Bobby Johnstone got 16 goals in the League, in spite of that barren spell, among his total of 22 for the season. Eddie Turnbull scored 11 (out of his 14) penalties, but it was Lawrie Reilly who led the goalscoring charts with a phenomenal 44 in all, plus a further three in the end of season Coronation Cup. Reilly scored 30 in just 28 League appearances, including seven hat-tricks and seven in two games against Motherwell! A further nine came in the League Cup and five in the Scottish Cup, yet amazingly the following season Bobby Johnstone would be Hibs' top scorer, as Lawrie Reilly's off-the-field story moved to the centre of the stage. At the end of another successful season, there was no silverware at senior level, though the third team, where Bobby had played early in his Hibs career, won the East of Scotland League title yet again, in this, the final year that they competed in that competition. Bobby had little time to dwell on failure, if indeed he saw it as such. In early May he gained another cap, his seventh, in the friendly fixture against Sweden at Hampden. Watched by almost 84,000, Bobby scored Scotland's only goal – his first for his country on home soil – but it was only a consolation in the 1–2 defeat.

Hibs now embarked upon a series of high-profile post-season games. The prestigious Coronation Cup was an invitational event, planned as part of the celebrations for the forthcoming coronation of Queen Elizabeth II. The top four sides in England were invited, as were the top three sides in Scotland, plus Celtic. Hibernian needed a replay to overcome the first hurdle, Tottenham Hotspur, but they then easily overwhelmed Newcastle United 4–0 at Ibrox Park, with Bobby Johnstone scoring against his old mate Ronnie Simpson. The Final was at Hampden Park, and Hibs faced Celtic in front of a crowd of over 107,000. An all-Scotland Final to this prestigious tournament was quite a fillip to the Scottish game given that the best teams from England had been despatched. During that match Celtic held the lead for a long time but were under tremendous pressure in a titanic struggle, and very late on it seemed that Bobby's header would mean extra-time, but Bonnar made a great save, and from there Celtic went up to the other end of the pitch and put matters beyond Hibs with a second goal.

At the start of June, Bobby set out as part of Hibs' 20-man squad for the mammoth journey to Brazil for their close-season tour. Both the Brazilian and Argentinean FAs had invited the club to South America, but they chose Brazil, where they were guaranteed a minimum of three games. Plans were laid to stay in Rio de Janeiro for a fortnight, with the option to extend the stay should they progress in the tournament. The first flight was to London, a place that sensible planning would have avoided given that this was 2 June, Coronation Day. Bobby and his colleagues watched the events live on television while waiting to fly out of Heathrow, but many flights were badly disrupted by the unparalleled demand for air travel on that day. The party eventually left London at around 9pm, arriving in Rio at midnight the following day – undoubtedly the longest journey Bobby ever undertook.

Hibernian had done much to spread their popularity within the British Isles and were among the pioneers in travelling abroad long before the concept of foreign club tours was widespread. Lawrie Reilly recalls club officials planning trips abroad with relish and certain aspects being taken care of with meticulous detail: 'When we went abroad, the management used to take plenty o' drink fer themselves, and they were very close with 'KG4', King George IV whisky. They always took a case of whisky abroad, but they needed the things carried, so 12 players all got a bottle each – we went on tour every year, and we all got a bottle of whisky to pack in our case, to give to them when we got over. The manager would come to us, on the first night, "bring your bottle to Room Five, or whatever." I was glad to get rid. I didn't want to be carrying a bottle of whisky I didn't want. This one time, there were the usual 12 bottles, but they only got nine back. Three of them got "broken in transit," although nobody ever saw any broken glass! You can guess the three who'd lost theirs. They were a hell of a bunch, Turnbull, Ormond and Bobby, a real gang they were. We had some great times together abroad. The harmony in the club at the time I was there, it was just great, and some of the defenders were right into it as well, you know Jock Govan, Hugh Howie and that. Gordon Smith didn't take a drink either, and his closest friend was Bobby Combe, who had moved back into the middle; they were close, Bobby Combe and Gordon. We all thoroughly enjoyed their company, although I never took a drink with them.'

Hibs drew their first game, thanks to a last-minute Reilly goal against Champions Vasco da Gama, and many years later Lawrie recalled the adventure. 'After that horrendous journey, we played the Brazilian Champions in the Maracana and the most amazing thing is that we managed to get a 2–2 draw, and there were about 30,000 locked out!' Subsequently, the games against Botafogo and Fluminense were both lost, and the team returned home after a marathon journey, having been away from home for over three weeks. No doubt the club's officials had learnt many lessons for the future, and it had been an eye-opener too for the players. In the 1980s Gordon Smith gave an interview that revealed just how much they had seen. 'I heard later that Vasco da Gama, the Brazilian Champions, were interested in buying me and Bobby. Going abroad, you learned a lot of things, especially how old-fashioned our football could be. Our press blamed the ball, or the state of the pitches abroad for British teams losing, but the footballs we played with were too hard. You couldn't squeeze your thumbs into them. The balls they used abroad were undoubtedly superior, as was the footwear. On one tour, Adidas supplied us with boots with moulded soles, not the usual studs. They were a real godsend. The difference was like night and day. How could you dribble on frosty grounds in Scotland with studs? That's why I used to wear basketball shoes.' In spite of the results, the tour was a success, and Bobby Johnstone brought home at least one memento, having been awarded a golden matador figurine by the Scottish football writers, who voted him the best Hibs player on the tour. There was just time for a few days holiday, and Bobby and several of his teammates watched the Open Championship at Carnoustie. The golfing tips that Bobby picked up there evidently stood him in good stead, because just before the season kicked off he teamed up with centre-half Hugh Howie and won a few pounds in a players competition played at Kilspindie, out on the East Lothian coast.

Prior to the start of the 1953–54 season, Lawrie Reilly had asked Hibs to provide him with a guarantee that he would get a benefit match once he had completed 10 years' service, but the club refused, and in doing so they almost broke up the Famous Five. Chairman Harry Swan pointed out that Willie McCartney, the previous manager, had approved Gordon Smith's game, and since Hugh Shaw supposedly did not agree with such games, the club's policy had changed. In any event, Reilly was told there were claimants with better title. It is thought that other players, particularly members of the Famous Five, made similar noises, but gradually they had all been picked off. Eventually they accepted 'new' terms – essentially the same terms! Lawrie Reilly was determined though, would not re-sign, and he was placed on to the 'available for transfer' list. 'I fell out with Hibs because I wanted them to give it to me in writing that they would play me a testimonial; if they had done I would have signed. Turnbull, Ormond, Johnstone and I, we said, well why do we not get a testimonial when we're due? So that's what the four of us were to hang out for. But I was let down – and Bobby was one of them… the other three let me down and they re-signed. I was the only one that took a pig-headed stand; I'm sticking it out, so they started the season without me.'

In the end, Reilly did not play football for four months, and during this period there was intense press speculation about where he might end up. There were stories that he flew to Manchester to talk to United among others, although he flatly denies this. In mid-August Manchester City made public that they had offered £30,000 for him, but he never knew anything about it, and it would not have mattered if he had… he is adamant to this day that he never had any intention of joining an English club. 'I didn't want to leave Scotland, truthfully. I was a Hibee, and I only ever wanted to play for the Hibs, and I did nae want to leave even when Glasgow Rangers were interested. That came about mainly because there were five Rangers lads in the Scotland team, and I was very friendly with those five, in fact I used to stay with one or other of them when we were playing there. I've stayed with Ian McColl, and Willie Waddell when I was through in Glasgow, and after the game we all went out together for the night with our wives. I was pretty close to the Rangers lads, and they were keen to get me to Ibrox when I'd fallen out with the Hibs. But I always wanted to play for the Hibs. I did nae want to play for Rangers.'

During his absence from football, Lawrie got employment as a representative for a motor vehicle tyre and paint company, and ironically he reckons to have made as much from newspaper articles discussing the issue as he could have earned from actually playing the game. As time passed without a resolution, the Scottish Football Association became increasingly involved because of their mounting concerns about how Reilly's international position would be affected – and there was a World Cup imminent. Initially, Lawrie went back to football on a part-time basis, but he continued to work away, often in London, so Hibs arranged for him to train with Arsenal. Eventually, matters came to a head. 'The SFA came to the Hibs and said, look you'd better get Lawrie Reilly sorted out, because we want him to play for us, for Scotland, so you better get him re-signed. So George Graham, the secretary of the SFA, told Harry Swan [who became President of the SFA himself later] to get me re-signed. When he said something to them, they did it.

Graham was absolutely the head man, and he told Hibs that he would even supply the opposition, if Hibs agreed, and so it was a Scottish Select that played in my testimonial.'[1]

The whole issue caused alarm both to those running football clubs and the administrators of the game. There was increasing agitation against the 'retain and transfer' system, with the players setting out to see it (and south of the border, the maximum wage) abolished, though that achievement was still a decade away. There was very little difference in what clubs paid the top players, and in Lawrie Reilly's case they were fortunate that he simply didn't want to move clubs. Elsewhere within the Famous Five, Bobby Johnstone's position was different. He had accepted the usual terms, but undoubtedly harboured resentment that Hibs wouldn't offer him and his colleagues more, particularly given the recent achievements of the club. His view was that if Hibs aren't prepared to do more for me than, say, St Mirren, why would I stay here? The issue would not go away.

Meanwhile, Hibs started their season in some style, with 17 goals in the six group League Cup games. The match programme for Hibs' first game of the season, the tie against Falkirk, contained an editorial piece in place of the usual notes from Hugh Shaw (who, it was pointed out, had had little time to call his own during the foreshortened close season – there was no pity evident for the poor players). The article refers to the 'good deal of publicity that Hibernians had endured of late', but points out that the matter is purely one for management. The programme editor does opine that 'the interests of the Hibernian club, both now and in the future, will dictate the policy to be followed by the management,' and he concedes that they had received a number of letters, yet, incredibly, he goes on to claim that 'most club supporters are perfectly content to leave any decisions in the responsible hands of the manager and his board of directors'! Chairman Harry Swan missed the opening fixtures as he was away on a driving holiday in the south of England, and not, as many Hibs fans might have imagined, because he was busy dealing with the Reilly issue. In fact, there is no mention of the words Lawrie or Reilly anywhere in the match programme.

Two weeks later, the Falkirk programme editor was bold enough to mention that Hibernian would be appearing without Reilly, but a greater focus was placed upon Gordon Smith '...the international selectors' problem child. Week after week he turns on brilliant performances for his club, and yet on numerous appearances in the Scottish colours he has never quite set the heather on fire.' Hibs won the match 2–1, and having qualified for the next stage with five wins and a draw they thumped eight past Third Lanark over the two legs in the quarter-final. With Lawrie Reilly out of the picture, Bobby Johnstone took the opportunity to establish himself at the head of the goalscoring charts, scoring eight of the 25 goals thus far, including another hat-trick against Third Lanark.

In contrast, the League flag campaign started very poorly, with the opening two games both being 0–4 away defeats at Raith Rovers, and worse, Hearts. It was only around the end of September, just as Lawrie Reilly was beginning to mend his fences, that Hibs managed to secure some points, with Bobby scoring twice in a 4–1 win over Hamilton Academical. Around that time another chance of Cup glory went begging when Hibs lost 2–3 to eventual League Cup winners East Fife in mid-October.

The Selkirk Common Riding is an annual pageant that co[...]
when the King repaid the gallant Selkirk folk for their s[...]
granting them land, and to this day the boundaries of the R[...]
on horseback in a symbolic spectacle. The Riding, one of [...]
events in Europe, is held in June each year and forms the cer[...]
of celebration. The greatest honour that can be bestowed on [...]
the standard bearer at the Riding, and, as a true Souter Bobb[...]
honour can only be bestowed upon a competent horseman, [...]
within the burgh boundaries. Further, convention holds tha[...]
honour aspirants perform the role of attendant to the stand[...]
part of the mounted cavalcade supporting him on at least t[...]
As a child, Bobby had not learned how to ride, and initiall[...]
some question too over his address – Linglie Road lies o[...]
Ettrick Water and technically outside of the town boundary[...]

After the war, Bobby did begin horse riding. In 1951, [...]
riding gear (riding hat, jodhpurs, knee-length boots with r[...]
proudly taken his place as an attendant during that year's [...]
for Bobby though, that was the height of his achievement in [...]
of Hibs' subsequent summer tours clashed with the Riding[...]
Shaw put a stop to Bobby's riding activities in case he fel[...]
Bobby would never achieve the ambition of all Selkirk me[...]
miss the Common Riding. Unfortunately the 1954 event, [...]
and all other years, coincided with football's World Cup[...]
Beattie quit, the minds of Bobby and the folk of Selkirk we[...]
their festival began, as usual, in the very early hours. By th[...]
hours after celebrations had begun in earnest, many burgh[...]
to accurately compute the seven goals that Uruguay [...]
countrymen.

Coincidentally, Bobby's interest in the Common Riding [...]
usual, because his close friend Davie Grieve had enter[...]
Games sprint. Bobby had helped train his mate, taking h[...]
him on Selkirk Hill. They were both delighted when Da[...]
that realised at least one Selkirk schoolboy's dream. Da[...]
great friends since those days, and strangely it was Davie [...]
the way to a professional football career. Unlike Bobby, he [...]
in both Boy and Junior level internationals, and after leavi[...]
to enjoy a modest career as a professional footballer in the [...]
for Reading, Crystal Palace (where he was signed by the g[...]
League Worcester City. Both lads also excelled at cri[...]
together playing for Selkirk Cricket Club. Graham Batem[...]
with a cricket bat: 'he was an exceptionally fine cricke[...]
Philiphaugh still talk about the running between the wic[...]
was almost as fond of cricket as he was of football, and [...]
of 1954 demonstrate that passion. 'Oh, I loved cricket, a[...]
best games we ever played I think; once you're out in th[...]
on your own, it's up to yourself. We'd all played as boy[...]

football in his life! He was only about 4ft 11, I'm not exaggerating, a wee, wee man, and he had funny turned-up toes when he walked. He used to come in, and I used to think what a load of crap, you know... how could you tell us what to do, you've never played in your life! Well, he wrote to my Dad and said I'd given him a mouthful – I was a bit cheeky, but Christ – a five foot guy telling me how to play, and he's never, ever kicked a ba' in his life?'

To summarise, Bobby could not control his own wages, he did not reckon much to the contractual benefits on offer, and he was not getting a discretionary benefit match. For their part, Hibernian could legitimately point out that it wasn't quite as simple as paying Bobby Johnstone and the others more, but the use of that argument left the clubs exposed. Why were the clubs themselves not working to establish a right to negotiate directly with players over the length of playing contracts? Did Hibernian, or Rangers, or Clyde, for example, not want the opportunity to offer a package that put them in a position to attract the best? What does this say about clubs who were evidently happy with the status quo?

Bobby and his ilk had limited options. Another was to opt out of professional football altogether, find a job and a non-League club, and leave Hibs holding a worthless registration. While this was practical to a greater extent in England, where some non-League clubs could pay good 'expenses', there was not the same non-League infrastructure in Scotland. A Scots player would have to leave his family, find accommodation (at a time of severe post-war housing shortage) and try to make his way in the English non-League game. Another option was to move clubs, perhaps take an illegal signing-on fee, or negotiate a more lucrative set of 'personal terms'. Many years later, Bobby said resentfully, 'If you did 10 years, you were supposed to get a benefit in those days, we all wanted it, but the chairman wouldn't guarantee it. I made my mind up then that if they're not going to give me a benefit, there was no point in my staying.' Bobby had decided that he was better off moving to a club that would try to meet his requirements.

Fifty years later, Eddie Turnbull provided his recollections of this whole issue. Eddie hadn't fallen out with the club as some of the others had; perhaps he was a more committed Hibs man? He didn't think so, but revealed that 'Regarding the benefit... I got £750, less tax, probably about £500. I didn't get a game... just the £750. Later, I could have gone to Manchester United. Busby wanted to sign me three times, but I refused three times, because they weren't making it worth my while.' As the last part of that sentence was spoken, Eddie, an open and forthright man, rubbed his fingers together, indicating that there was at least the potential for unofficial additions. Apparently Manchester United were not prepared to pay them, and so Eddie stayed put. But Bobby was looking to move.

* * * *

Back in April, before the England defeat, the Scottish selectors had nominated 18 players, and it was intended that this pool would serve for the World Cup warm-up matches and then go into the Finals themselves. A couple of weeks after the 1953–54 season finished, Bobby's 10th cap came in one of those warm-up games against Norway at Hampden on 5 May. Only three players managed to survive the

cull that followed the England match, and Bobby himsel
right to outside-right in a largely experimental affair. A cr
up to see their heroes off to Berne, an early indication o
Cup at this time, though the team did oblige with a 1–0
there was a return match in Oslo, but Willie Ormond an
this game, for reasons that seem unbelievable in this day a
squad assembled to prepare for the game in Oslo, neith
considered for selection as they were playing against Boc
a club tour! Both men missed a national team training
Cup preparations, due to what Hibernian club officials c
Harry Swan, who rather bullishly declared himself ha
admitted this. The following week Willie and Bobby
available to play in the last warm-up game against Fin
scored in the 2–1 win. Amazingly, this proved to be the
played an international fixture outside of the Home Co

The selectors now announced that they would take j
two of which were goalkeepers. The obvious captain
Young of Rangers, was excluded because he had been i
was selected, though he was probably more accuratel
country dispute, with Rangers having decided to play
days prior to the England international. Then came the
Johnstone too was injured and unable to participate
replaced, and Aberdeen's George Hamilton was the lu
no bones about his preference to stay at home and play
called upon. One might readily conclude that Bobby
likely to be shambolic, had decided that a summer on
baize of Selkirk held greater appeal. The travelling pa
Gordon Smith and Lawrie Reilly, of course, and Eddie
year spell in the international wilderness. Further, the
the tour dates for Germany might be interpreted as inc
club versus country debate at that time – ambivalence
was the only Hibs man with the fortune to represent h
Cup. The tournament did indeed turn out to
embarrassment to one of the world's oldest footballi
against Austria, Scotland suffered a 0–1 defeat. Two
Uruguay fixture, the manager, Andy Beattie, quit, alth
had done so before flying out to Switzerland! The fol
There were no training bibs, no pennants to exchange
though perhaps Scotland could consider themselves
but subsequently the 'luck of the draw', which had th
go on to finish third and fourth in the tournament
before Scotland properly sorted out their managerial
to international football. The prevailing air of
superiority was to cost them dear, and Eddie Turr
crystal clear: 'A lot of blame lies with the SFA. Th
merchants running a game they knew nothing about

that went to the cricket club at that time were very keen. Then, there was no television, so you used to have to get up to the club by about six o'clock, or it was impossible to even get a go in the nets.'

The 1954–55 season began with Eddie Turnbull taking over from wing-half Bobby Combe as captain of the side and Gordon Smith back fit. But Lawrie Reilly was still recovering from the illness that had kept him out since January, and there was a disappointing failure to qualify from the League Cup section. Bobby also missed two of those games through injury, though he did manage to score twice in the final group match, a 5–3 victory at Queen of the South. The League programme got off to a tough start once again, and a promising point at Ibrox was followed by a home defeat to Hearts and a 1–3 defeat at Aberdeen, who would be crowned Scottish League Champions for the first time later in the season. Bobby scored in the latter two games, and he did so again the following Wednesday, when Hibs inflicted a first-ever floodlit defeat on Leeds United at Elland Road. Gordon Smith and Bobby played really well on the right, treating the crowd to their array of tricks, and Bobby scored a goal from an oblique angle, which completely bamboozled Leeds 'keeper Scott and indeed most of the crowd. Gordon Smith also scored twice in that 3–1 win, but the best news of the night was probably back in Edinburgh, where Lawrie Reilly, clearly not yet ready for first-team duty, returned in a reserve-team game against Hearts at Tynecastle. The following Saturday, as the season entered October, Raith Rovers won at Easter Road for the second year running, and so it was not until the fifth game that a League victory was secured, a second win in Dumfries.

Bobby now had his own car, but as he wasn't allowed to drive on the day of a match, he would either get the bus or the train, or take a lift into Edinburgh. Lex Millar remembers one trip, probably not quite the mode of transport the club had in mind: 'Someone had to drive him in, but one day Selkirk were at home in the morning, and Bobby wanted to watch the game. He had arranged for a baker's driver to pick us all up in Selkirk, and take us into Edinburgh, to a place near the top of Leith Walk, Littlejohn's, where we all had lunch. All the players met there for lunch, it was good for fish and such, Harry Swan's place I think it was. Anyway, we had a lovely meal with Bobby and his teammates, and then we all went off to Murrayfield for the rugby! And Bobby would have come with us too, if he could have.' Whenever his playing commitments allowed, Bobby would arrange to go with whoever fancied a trip to Murrayfield for rugby, or Musselburgh for the horse racing. In October the Hibs boys took part in an annual golf pro/am tournament that was sponsored by the *Daily Record* and played at Cawder. Hibs' team was Bobby, Eddie Turnbull, Lawrie Reilly, John Paterson and Willie MacFarlane, with the best three rounds counting. Bobby was playing well at the time, and at one stage had got his handicap down to eight, but some of his teammates, especially Lawrie, were even better than that. Golf was one of the few ball sports where they stood a reasonable chance of extracting a couple of shillings from Bobby's pocket.

Back with the football, in mid-October Hibs unveiled their own floodlighting, mounted on 100-foot pylons. The system was reckoned to be the best in Britain, yet while Hibs claimed to be 'leading lights' just off the pitch, on it their city rivals Hearts won the inaugural friendly, Hibs suffering a 0–2 defeat that saw gloom football in his life! He was only about 4ft 11, I'm not exaggerating, a wee, wee man, and he had funny turned-up toes when he walked. He used to come in, and I used to think what a load of crap, you know... how could you tell us what to do, you've never played in your life! Well, he wrote to my Dad and said I'd given him a mouthful – I was a bit cheeky, but Christ – a five foot guy telling me how to play, and he's never, ever kicked a ba' in his life?'

To summarise, Bobby could not control his own wages, he did not reckon much to the contractual benefits on offer, and he was not getting a discretionary benefit match. For their part, Hibernian could legitimately point out that it wasn't quite as simple as paying Bobby Johnstone and the others more, but the use of that argument left the clubs exposed. Why were the clubs themselves not working to establish a right to negotiate directly with players over the length of playing contracts? Did Hibernian, or Rangers, or Clyde, for example, not want the opportunity to offer a package that put them in a position to attract the best? What does this say about clubs who were evidently happy with the status quo?

Bobby and his ilk had limited options. Another was to opt out of professional football altogether, find a job and a non-League club, and leave Hibs holding a worthless registration. While this was practical to a greater extent in England, where some non-League clubs could pay good 'expenses', there was not the same non-League infrastructure in Scotland. A Scots player would have to leave his family, find accommodation (at a time of severe post-war housing shortage) and try to make his way in the English non-League game. Another option was to move clubs, perhaps take an illegal signing-on fee, or negotiate a more lucrative set of 'personal terms'. Many years later, Bobby said resentfully, 'If you did 10 years, you were supposed to get a benefit in those days, we all wanted it, but the chairman wouldn't guarantee it. I made my mind up then that if they're not going to give me a benefit, there was no point in my staying.' Bobby had decided that he was better off moving to a club that would try to meet his requirements.

Fifty years later, Eddie Turnbull provided his recollections of this whole issue. Eddie hadn't fallen out with the club as some of the others had; perhaps he was a more committed Hibs man? He didn't think so, but revealed that 'Regarding the benefit... I got £750, less tax, probably about £500. I didn't get a game... just the £750. Later, I could have gone to Manchester United. Busby wanted to sign me three times, but I refused three times, because they weren't making it worth my while.' As the last part of that sentence was spoken, Eddie, an open and forthright man, rubbed his fingers together, indicating that there was at least the potential for unofficial additions. Apparently Manchester United were not prepared to pay them, and so Eddie stayed put. But Bobby was looking to move.

* * * *

Back in April, before the England defeat, the Scottish selectors had nominated 18 players, and it was intended that this pool would serve for the World Cup warm-up matches and then go into the Finals themselves. A couple of weeks after the 1953–54 season finished, Bobby's 10th cap came in one of those warm-up games against Norway at Hampden on 5 May. Only three players managed to survive the cull that followed the England match, and Bobby himself was moved from inside-right to outside-right in a largely experimental affair. A crowd of just 25,897 turned up to see their heroes off to Berne, an early indication of the profile of the World Cup at this time, though the team did oblige with a 1–0 victory. Two weeks later there was a return match in Oslo, but Willie Ormond and Bobby were dropped for this game, for reasons that seem unbelievable in this day and age: when the Scotland squad assembled to prepare for the game in Oslo, neither Bobby nor Willie were considered for selection as they were playing against Bochum in Germany while on a club tour! Both men missed a national team training session, part of the World Cup preparations, due to what Hibernian club officials called a 'mix up with dates'. Harry Swan, who rather bullishly declared himself happy to take responsibility, admitted this. The following week Willie and Bobby were back in the fold and available to play in the last warm-up game against Finland in Helsinki, and both scored in the 2–1 win. Amazingly, this proved to be the only time that Bobby played an international fixture outside of the Home Countries.

The selectors now announced that they would take just 13 players to the Finals, two of which were goalkeepers. The obvious captain for the event, a fit George Young of Rangers, was excluded because he had been injured when the initial pool was selected, though he was probably more accurately a victim of a club versus country dispute, with Rangers having decided to play him in a League game a few days prior to the England international. Then came the announcement that Bobby Johnstone too was injured and unable to participate. Bobby simply had to be replaced, and Aberdeen's George Hamilton was the lucky man, although he made no bones about his preference to stay at home and play golf. In the event, he wasn't called upon. One might readily conclude that Bobby, guessing that the trip was likely to be shambolic, had decided that a summer on the greens, cricket fields and baize of Selkirk held greater appeal. The travelling party was shorn of teammates Gordon Smith and Lawrie Reilly, of course, and Eddie Turnbull was amid his eight-year spell in the international wilderness. Further, the 'error' by Harry Swan over the tour dates for Germany might be interpreted as indicating Hibs' position on the club versus country debate at that time – ambivalence at best. Thus Willie Ormond was the only Hibs man with the fortune to represent his country at the 1954 World Cup. The tournament did indeed turn out to be a disaster, a complete embarrassment to one of the world's oldest footballing nations. In the first game against Austria, Scotland suffered a 0–1 defeat. Two days later, on the eve of the Uruguay fixture, the manager, Andy Beattie, quit, although it later emerged that he had done so before flying out to Switzerland! The following day Scotland lost 7–0. There were no training bibs, no pennants to exchange with opponents and no goals, though perhaps Scotland could consider themselves unlucky: firstly with injuries but subsequently the 'luck of the draw', which had them facing the sides that would go on to finish third and fourth in the tournament. It would be many years yet before Scotland properly sorted out their managerial and organisational approach to international football. The prevailing air of insularity and disinterested superiority was to cost them dear, and Eddie Turnbull's retrospective view was crystal clear: 'A lot of blame lies with the SFA. They were just a bunch of tattie merchants running a game they knew nothing about.'

The Selkirk Common Riding is an annual pageant that commemorates the time when the King repaid the gallant Selkirk folk for their support at Flodden by granting them land, and to this day the boundaries of the Royal Burgh are ridden on horseback in a symbolic spectacle. The Riding, one of the largest equestrian events in Europe, is held in June each year and forms the centrepiece to a weekend of celebration. The greatest honour that can be bestowed on a Selkirk man is to be the standard bearer at the Riding, and, as a true Souter Bobby was no different. The honour can only be bestowed upon a competent horseman, a bachelor and resident within the burgh boundaries. Further, convention holds that prior to the supreme honour aspirants perform the role of attendant to the standard bearer and ride as part of the mounted cavalcade supporting him on at least two or three occasions. As a child, Bobby had not learned how to ride, and initially there may have been some question too over his address – Linglie Road lies on the northern side of Ettrick Water and technically outside of the town boundary.

After the war, Bobby did begin horse riding. In 1951, dressed in full, formal riding gear (riding hat, jodhpurs, knee-length boots with riding crop), Bobby had proudly taken his place as an attendant during that year's Common Riding. Sadly for Bobby though, that was the height of his achievement in this regard. One or two of Hibs' subsequent summer tours clashed with the Riding, but in any event Hugh Shaw put a stop to Bobby's riding activities in case he fell off and broke a bone! Bobby would never achieve the ambition of all Selkirk men, but he did not like to miss the Common Riding. Unfortunately the 1954 event, social high point of this and all other years, coincided with football's World Cup. On the day that Andy Beattie quit, the minds of Bobby and the folk of Selkirk were engaged elsewhere, as their festival began, as usual, in the very early hours. By the following day, over 24 hours after celebrations had begun in earnest, many burghers might have struggled to accurately compute the seven goals that Uruguay managed against their countrymen.

Coincidentally, Bobby's interest in the Common Riding this year was keener than usual, because his close friend Davie Grieve had entered the Common Riding Games sprint. Bobby had helped train his mate, taking him on runs and coaching him on Selkirk Hill. They were both delighted when Davie won, an achievement that realised at least one Selkirk schoolboy's dream. Davie and Bobby had been great friends since those days, and strangely it was Davie who first seemed to be on the way to a professional football career. Unlike Bobby, he got to represent Scotland in both Boy and Junior level internationals, and after leaving Selkirk FC he went on to enjoy a modest career as a professional footballer in the Football League, playing for Reading, Crystal Palace (where he was signed by the great Ted Drake) and non-League Worcester City. Both lads also excelled at cricket, enjoying their time together playing for Selkirk Cricket Club. Graham Bateman recalled Bobby's ability with a cricket bat: 'he was an exceptionally fine cricketer, and the old-stagers at Philiphaugh still talk about the running between the wickets of those two'. Bobby was almost as fond of cricket as he was of football, and his exploits in the summer of 1954 demonstrate that passion. 'Oh, I loved cricket, aye. Cricket was one of the best games we ever played I think; once you're out in the middle, at cricket you're on your own, it's up to yourself. We'd all played as boys too, and most of the lads that went to the cricket club at that time were very keen. Then, there was no television, so you used to have to get up to the club by about six o'clock, or it was impossible to even get a go in the nets.'

The 1954–55 season began with Eddie Turnbull taking over from wing-half Bobby Combe as captain of the side and Gordon Smith back fit. But Lawrie Reilly was still recovering from the illness that had kept him out since January, and there was a disappointing failure to qualify from the League Cup section. Bobby also missed two of those games through injury, though he did manage to score twice in the final group match, a 5–3 victory at Queen of the South. The League programme got off to a tough start once again, and a promising point at Ibrox was followed by a home defeat to Hearts and a 1–3 defeat at Aberdeen, who would be crowned Scottish League Champions for the first time later in the season. Bobby scored in the latter two games, and he did so again the following Wednesday, when Hibs inflicted a first-ever floodlit defeat on Leeds United at Elland Road. Gordon Smith and Bobby played really well on the right, treating the crowd to their array of tricks, and Bobby scored a goal from an oblique angle, which completely bamboozled Leeds 'keeper Scott and indeed most of the crowd. Gordon Smith also scored twice in that 3–1 win, but the best news of the night was probably back in Edinburgh, where Lawrie Reilly, clearly not yet ready for first-team duty, returned in a reserve-team game against Hearts at Tynecastle. The following Saturday, as the season entered October, Raith Rovers won at Easter Road for the second year running, and so it was not until the fifth game that a League victory was secured, a second win in Dumfries.

Bobby now had his own car, but as he wasn't allowed to drive on the day of a match, he would either get the bus or the train, or take a lift into Edinburgh. Lex Millar remembers one trip, probably not quite the mode of transport the club had in mind: 'Someone had to drive him in, but one day Selkirk were at home in the morning, and Bobby wanted to watch the game. He had arranged for a baker's driver to pick us all up in Selkirk, and take us into Edinburgh, to a place near the top of Leith Walk, Littlejohn's, where we all had lunch. All the players met there for lunch, it was good for fish and such, Harry Swan's place I think it was. Anyway, we had a lovely meal with Bobby and his teammates, and then we all went off to Murrayfield for the rugby! And Bobby would have come with us too, if he could have.' Whenever his playing commitments allowed, Bobby would arrange to go with whoever fancied a trip to Murrayfield for rugby, or Musselburgh for the horse racing. In October the Hibs boys took part in an annual golf pro/am tournament that was sponsored by the *Daily Record* and played at Cawder. Hibs' team was Bobby, Eddie Turnbull, Lawrie Reilly, John Paterson and Willie MacFarlane, with the best three rounds counting. Bobby was playing well at the time, and at one stage had got his handicap down to eight, but some of his teammates, especially Lawrie, were even better than that. Golf was one of the few ball sports where they stood a reasonable chance of extracting a couple of shillings from Bobby's pocket.

Back with the football, in mid-October Hibs unveiled their own floodlighting, mounted on 100-foot pylons. The system was reckoned to be the best in Britain, yet while Hibs claimed to be 'leading lights' just off the pitch, on it their city rivals Hearts won the inaugural friendly, Hibs suffering a 0–2 defeat that saw gloom descend on to Easter Road. Bobby scored twice in the next League match, a 3–6 defeat to Clyde, and then in early November he went off to Largs to prepare for the international against Northern Ireland at Hampden Park. There he was capped for the 12th time, and he scored his seventh goal at international level when equalising to force a 2–2 draw. At this point Hibs routinely embarked on a run of top form up until the end of the year, and this year was no different. A consecutive winning run of nine games was punctuated only by a 0–5 defeat at home to Celtic.

During that spell, in December 1954 Bobby experienced the thrill of playing against the famous Hungarian side, something that he always recalled as one of the highlights of his career. The Hungary team featured seven of the team that earlier in the year had unexpectedly lost the World Cup Final, including Puskas, Hidegkuti and Kocsis, who had finished top scorer in that tournament with 11 goals. That surprise defeat against West Germany, whom they had defeated 8–3 in a group game, was in fact their only defeat in five years, and there were not too many who fancied Scotland's chances before the game. A crowd of 113,000 assembled at Hampden Park, and in the early stages it seemed that Scotland would be overrun, and Hungary raced into a 2–0 lead after just 25 minutes. But Scotland began to settle to some good football, and five minutes before half-time came the moment the massive crowd had been waiting for: Bobby Johnstone weaved his way brilliantly past two defenders and played in Tommy Ring, who smashed in a goal that gave Scotland great hope. Sadly, that hope didn't last too long, and just before the break Sandor restored Hungary's two-goal lead.

The second half was only seconds old when McKenzie took a free-kick, and centred for Bobby to restore Scottish hopes with an excellent headed goal. Newspaper reports describe how Bobby 'rose like a gull', to score the best goal of the match, 'Johnstone's header rocketed the ball past Farago, who didn't have a chance – and the match was wide open' another opined. Later, Scotland's captain Willie Cunningham was carried off on a stretcher, seemingly with a serious injury, and this disrupted the pattern of the game, with Tommy Docherty in particular 'guilty of some extremely robust play'. The young full-back, Harry Haddock of Clyde, one of four debutants, played superbly, and the no-nonsense defending served to knock the rhythm out of the Hungarian game. The Hungarians were knocked out of their stride and began to retaliate, and 'make the most elementary mistakes and childish fouls'. Then Willie Cunningham unexpectedly reappeared, and the Scottish assault continued, although later several Hungarians complained about rough tactics. Puskas himself declared 'the Scots tackled too hard – that is not football'. In the latter stages, Hungary resorted to wasting time with long back-passes and hefty clearances into the stands, before Lawrie Reilly almost scored an equaliser that Farago saved with a diving punch. In the last minute, Kocsis finished off a good move with a great piece of skill, to score the final goal in a game that the famous Charles Buchan described as 'a fighting exhibition that at times left me gasping. At one point of the game I thought Scotland were going to end with honours even.' So Scotland lost the match, 'but only 2–4', according to Bobby, who always enjoyed reminding everybody that England had conceded six at Wembley. It was widely felt to be the best Scotland international performance for some years, and Bobby was proud to have scored his eighth international goal against the

Magyars. He won a set of golf clubs for being nominated as Scotland's Man of the Match, but his overriding memory was one of privilege; he had played against the man he believes to have been the greatest player he ever saw, Ferenc Puskas. Bobby drew some useful lessons from seeing the master at work, and some of the tactically innovative play would have a bearing on his future career.

* * * *

Hibs had enjoyed a great run during the autumn of 1955, surged up the table, and given the fans a treat by beating Rangers 2–1 on Christmas Day. When Bobby scored at Tynecastle in the customary defeat at Hearts on New Year's Day, this time 1–5, he was ending a run in which he had scored nine times in 11 games, yet Hibs would gain no points at all from their four January League games. Down in England, Manchester City began their New Year by negotiating a safe passage past a struggling Derby County side in the third round of the FA Cup, winning by 3–1 at the Baseball Ground. Derby were in decline, and about to fall to the Third Division, a second relegation in three seasons, and a sudden fall for a club that had enjoyed two top-four finishes in the late 1940s. On the same day, Hibs lost against Falkirk at Brockville by 1–3, with Bobby Johnstone scoring Hibs' consolation. It was to be his last goal for Hibs.

The following week, Hibs' game against Queen of the South at Easter Road was the only senior game in Scotland to escape postponement due to the heavy falls of snow sweeping the country. Due to the difficulties of travelling and the obvious risk that the game may not conclude, not to mention the freezing cold, most sensible people stayed at home, leaving only 6,000 hardy souls in attendance. After 69 minutes, with Hibs leading 3–0 from a Bobby Johnstone hat-trick[2], the referee found himself with no option but to call a halt to the proceedings because the snow was obliterating the line markings. It was the first game to be called off at Easter Road for seven seasons due to ground conditions, a notable feat and tribute to the Hibs groundstaff. Bobby Johnstone never scored a hat-trick again for Hibernian. His next hat-trick, less than a year away, would come in a blue shirt.

Saturday 29 January was FA Cup fourth-round day in England, and it proved pivotal. Manchester was buzzing with excitement – City faced their derby rivals United at Maine Road in their only home draw of their Cup campaign. On the same day, around 200 miles to the north, Hibernian faced Clyde in a Scottish A League match at Easter Road. That day Bobby Johnstone came up against his Scottish international teammate Harry Haddock, who had a 14-year long career at Clyde, gaining six international caps and twice playing alongside Bobby for the international team.[3] The programme records that the players had had difficulties training because of the weather – Bobby had lost his footing twice on a run around Arthur's Seat, but the players had managed some links golf, with Bobby regaining his hurt pride by partnering Gordon Smith in a victory over John Paterson and Lawrie Reilly, the losing partnership being a strong one.

With headed goals from Ormond and Reilly, the latter after a great run and cross from Bobby, the Hibees were coasting to two points with 20 minutes to go, but a mistake by Jackie Plenderleith presaged a three-goal burst in just seven minutes, and

Hibs unexpectedly lost 2–3. Bobby had at least three or four good chances to score, and indeed all of the forward line were in good form, bar Eddie Turnbull, who had been a late inclusion in the side following a long absence. The events of that late January day were firm evidence of the contrasting fortunes of the two clubs involved in Bobby Johnstone's first major transfer. Manchester City left their local rivals to concentrate on the League – which was won by Chelsea, incidentally – and as Hibernian stumbled in this relatively straightforward League match, nobody could have guessed that the Famous Five were appearing together for the last time.

Perhaps the minds of the players were not fully focused? Even the manager's column that day states that his players might have half an eye on their subsequent fixture: Hibs had a Cup derby of their own to contend with, as the following week they faced Heart of Midlothian in a Scottish Cup fifth-round tie. Fittingly, Hibs were demolished 5–0, and Bobby would never achieve Cup success with Hibs. It was a strange state of affairs, but there seemed to be some peculiar force at work that seemed to conspire against Hibs, preventing them earning Cup glory. The reason most often proffered is bad luck, but Eddie Turnbull, as usual, has a less romantic view. 'We could do it in the League, but when the chips were down we often didn't have enough players full of blood and guts. That's what you need in Cup ties and perhaps that was the only weakness in our team throughout the '50s.' Another piece of the jigsaw that would see Bobby Johnstone moving south had dropped into place.

It is clear in retrospect that Hibernian had peaked and that there was a shift in the Edinburgh soccer power base across the city to Tynecastle. Out of the Cup, Hibernian now faced playing out the season with a series of relatively meaningless fixtures. Perhaps Hibernian were vulnerable. Was it possible that some of their prized possessions might be prised away? Immediately after the Cup defeat, Harry Swan emphatically denied the rumours that swept through the club. These concerned Eddie Turnbull, and the fact that representatives of Manchester City had been seen in the stands. The following week Lawrie Reilly scored a hat-trick in a 3–0 win at Rugby Park, home of Kilmarnock, and it turned out to be Bobby Johnstone who was making a final appearance for Hibernian. That same day, Manchester City won 5–0 at Old Trafford in a League match, and then made further progress in the FA Cup with a win at Luton Town in the fifth round with both goals from Roy Clarke.

In late February Harry Swan, the chairman, declared 'There is no financial necessity to transfer any player, and the club wishes to keep the squad intact. If any player were to be transferred it would not be for money, but in pursuance of club policy...' A few days later, on 2 March 1955, Bobby Johnstone signed for Manchester City.

* * * *

Many years later Bobby revealed that he 'would never have signed for Manchester City if they'd guaranteed me a benefit, but there was no guarantee coming. Lawrie Reilly agrees that ultimately Bobby left for City because he didn't get his benefit match. 'Aye, but if Bobby, Eddie and Willie had stuck by me, I'd have got a promise for them that they would have played a testimonial for each of us individually. I'm sure we would have won the case, but the others changed their minds and signed. If the four of us had stuck together they would have got their testimonials as well, because the Hibs could nae have manage without the four of us.' In spite of Harry Swan's entreaties, it later turned out that the clubs had been talking for some while, certainly a few weeks, and that, unofficially, Bobby had been on the transfer list.

The Hibs supporters were devastated at the news that Bobby had been sold, and none of the newspaper articles, or indeed letters to the club, were supportive of the club's decision to sell. Some talked about staying away from the ground, and others were critical of the succession policy, seeming, as it did, that there was no suitable replacement available. One published letter lamented the 'ridiculous state of affairs... even contemplating selling a star player when there is not even the semblance of an adequate substitute.' Bobby was known as a private man, not readily given to discussing his business abroad, but the publicity created by the news of his move was a surprise even to his close family. Betty Johnstone still lived at home, and she recalls that Bobby simply came home one night and said he was signing for Manchester City. Margaret, who was nursing in Edinburgh at the time, found out from the newspapers! While it was undoubtedly a massive step for a wee lad from the Scottish Borders, maybe Bobby drew comfort from the knowledge that, faced with a similar path, his boyhood heroes Andy Black and Alex Massie had both left Edinburgh to play football in the north west of England and both had flourished.

By this time preparations for City's FA Cup quarter-final tie against Birmingham at St Andrews were well in hand. The same month, a crowd of less than 1,000 turned out to see Hibernian's home game against Stirling Albion. Bobby had seemingly moved on to bigger and better things.

Hibs were to finish empty-handed, in fifth place in the League for the second successive season. Having been either Champions or runners-up in the five previous seasons, this was difficult to come to terms with. Hearts had already won the Scottish League Cup, and with that trophy would go on to a purple patch of their own, ironically under the astute management of Tommy Walker, one of Bobby's boyhood heroes from the 1930s. By the end of the decade Hearts would be able to look back on six pieces of silverware in six seasons, including two Scottish League Championships.

A Hibs fan wrote the following poem in 1955. Evidently devastated at the loss of Johnstone, he also mourns the passing of the Famous Five era...

Auld Reekie's Lament.

What gars the toon in mournin' lie,
An' darknin' clouds o'ercast the sky?
Has weary winter drawn their tears?
Or Castle fa'en aboot their ears?
Have a' the dugs at Pooderha'
Cam oot on strike for better straw?
Has floral clock run doon at last,

Or Gun been fired at twenty-past?
Alas, tho' dire these things appear,
They'd scarcely bring the tricklin' tear.
A sadder blow has stunned the toon.
And plunged them a' in deepest gloom.
A blow that's shaken Arthur's Seat,
And shut the shops in Princes Street.
Calamity has struck us a'
Oor Souter Lad's been ta'en awa'!
Ah, Bobby lad! it gars me greet.
Nae mair your magic twinklin' feet,
Will charm us a' at Easter Road.
And banish cares o' weary load.
Tae watch ye play was sheer delight,
The very ba' seemed green and white.
Noo English gold's been dearly bocht,
An' left us a' the poorer o't.
But courage, lads! tho' stricken dumb,
Perhaps the best has yet tae come.
Tho' days o' Famous Five are gone,
To-morrow's day has yet tae dawn.
Wi' Gordon gay and Reilly fit,
The magic spell's no' finished yet.
So lift the heid, stick oot the chest,
And wish oor Bobby 'A' the Best'!

(J.S)

The Johnstone Years

Before we close finally on Bobby Johnstone's nine years at Hibs, the club's overall record during his years there is worth closer scrutiny. Looking back from the end of the 1954–55 season, by which time Hibs' star was clearly waning, analysis of the statistics show why the Famous Five will forever be revered by Hibernian fans who have since waited half a century to see the Scottish League Championship return to their part of Edinburgh. In the nine years since the end of the war, Hibs had been battling constantly for the Scottish game's major honours with a Rangers side that had won the title four times to Hibs' three. Thus, Hibs were the only side capable of halting what otherwise would have been a period of total domination for the Glasgow giants, and whenever Hibs finished above Rangers they won the flag. Rangers scored 589 goals during that nine-year period, over two goals per game, and they finished outside of the top two only in 1953–54 and the following year. Over that same period, Hibs scored 715 League goals.

In addition to scoring a good number of goals, Bobby established himself primarily as a brilliant provider of the perfectly weighted 'killer' pass. It was a supply in which the predatory forwards alongside him could, and frequently did, gorge themselves. From the time Bobby came into the first team in 1949–50, until the end of 1954–55, his last season, Hibs scored 485 goals, with the emerging Hearts side clocking up 430. Rangers were almost a century of League goals behind with 386 in those six seasons. Hibs were top scorers in Division A of the Scottish League every season between 1948 and 1953, though their flamboyance had never carried them all the way in the Cup, something of a sore point with the players. Perhaps Bobby reflected on these issues as his train made its way south, where the newspaper photographers were waiting to greet him at Manchester's Victoria station – though even he cannot have dreamt that within 14 months he would make footballing history.

Lawrie Reilly believes that the ability displayed by that side was never recaptured after Bobby left. 'The football ability on the right wing with Gordon and Bobby was unsurpassable. On the left wing, football ability and skill-wise, you would nae compare them, what a contrast they were. Eddie was strong, had a good shot, Willie Ormond had pace and a great left foot, but no right foot. It wouldn't have gelled if we'd had the same football skills on both the right wing and the left. But when we interchanged – and we used to interchange a lot – it fitted in superbly. It was just one of God's gifts, I think. Just a big coincidence.'

One interesting aspect of Bobby's departure was that he missed the opportunity to play as part of the Hibernian side that became the first British side to play in the European Cup later in 1955. That inaugural event was an invitational affair, organised by *L'Equipe*, the French sports publication. The sides selected were generally the most outward looking and appealing clubs within the major European soccer powers, and one decidedly futuristic aspect was the absence of any requirement to have actually won one's domestic Championship. Hibernians faced Rot Weiss (Red White) Essen, then a top side, who were incidentally the German national Champions. Bobby Combe reclaimed a place in the forward line alongside the now Famous Four in Hibs' historic, and victorious, first-ever European Cup tie.

Notes

1. Lawrie's testimonial was eventually played in 1958, after his retirement from football. By that time Lawrie was unable to play himself. Hibernians played against an International Select XI and won 9–3. The attendance, on a night affected both by the dreadful weather and non-appearance of Stanley Matthews, was less than 7,000. Joe Baker, Gordon Smith and Willie Ormond each scored two, while Eddie Turnbull also scored. Bobby played against Hibs and also got two goals.

2. According to the author's calculations, the elimination of this hat-trick from the records ultimately left the Famous Five one short of having collectively scored 50 hat-tricks for Hibs. The total of 49 includes eight scored by Gordon Smith during the war years, when Scottish Southern League fixtures were played. Lawrie Reilly scored the last hat-trick in 1956. Bobby Johnstone achieved the feat four times for Hibs, but only once at Easter Road.

3. Interestingly, the records also reveal that Harry also played one Football League game for Exeter City in the 1946–47 season, this presumably being connected to his national service.

Cannon Street in Selkirk, seen from the south side of Ettrick Water during the 1920s. The Johnstone family lived at number 11 until the early 1940s.

Selkirk's Border Cup-winning side of 1930–31. Bobby's father Hopey is the tallest man on the back row, and the picture also features two of Bobby's uncles. Back row, left to right: W. Douglas (trainer), T. Johnstone, J. Buckham, A. Greig, W. Henderson, G. Johnstone, J. Pringle, T. Nichol, A. Johnstone (president). Front row: W. Monks (treasurer), A. Higgins, J. Douglas, P. Sheridan (captain), G. Robertson, J. Nixon, A. Welsh (secretary).

A Century of Soccer in Selkirk, G. Bateman

Bobby, aged three, with
his youngest sister Betty,
in spring 1933.

Courtesy of B. and M. Johnstone

The small schoolyard at Philiphaugh School. Bobby and all of his sisters attended the school until aged 11.

Bridgend Fives in approx 1943. Back row, left to right: Graham Bateman, Jimmy Douglas, Ted Price, Andrew Mair, Tom Douglas. Front row: Bobby Johnstone, Davie Grieve, Tom Hope, Will Lindsay, Tom Simpson.

Courtesy of G. Bateman

Selkirk FC, East of Scotland Qualifying Cup Finalists, 1946. This picture features the rare sight of Bobby Johnstone in a Selkirk shirt. Back row, left to right: G. Inglis (trainer), G. Turner, B. Turnbull, T. Hope, T. Wilson (secretary), A. Smail, J. McGirvan, J. Lawrie, R. Lindsay (president). Front row: D. Grieve, R. Johnstone, T. Simpson, D. Smail, H. Mullins.   *A Century of Soccer in Selkirk,* G. Bateman

The other famous five. Bobby pictured with his sisters, in 1950, (left to right) Betty, Jenny, Margaret and Sheila.   Courtesy of M. Johnstone

HIBERNIAN F.C. PROGRAMME

No. 17.   SATURDAY, 19th NOVEMBER 1949.   Kick-off 2.25 p.m.

SCOTTISH LEAGUE

Photo by *Roy Cameron*

HIBERNIAN
VERSUS **EAST FIFE**

3d...

Programme for the Scottish Division A game between Hibs and East Fife in November 1949. Bobby scored twice, his first League goals at Easter Road.

OFFICIAL PROGRAMME

The RANGERS FOOTBALL CLUB LTD

IBROX STADIUM GLASGOW

Directors:—Councillor J. F. Wilson, D.L., J.P., (chairman), William Struth, J.P., (vice-chairman), Alan L. Morton, G. C. P. Brown, M.A., William G. Bennett, M.P.
Secretary:—J. Rogers Simpson, C.A.   *Manager :*—William Struth, J.P.

No. 85	10th February, 1951.	Price Threepence

RANGERS 2

1
BROWN

Right | | | | Left

YOUNG
2

WOODBURN
5

SHAW
3

McCOLL
4

SIMPSON or
WILLIAMSON   *Thornton*

RAE or COX
6

WADDELL
7

FINDLAY
8   *Thornton*

WILLIAMSON
9   *2*

THORNTON
10   *Rae*

PATON
11

1873   **1951**

ORMOND
11

TURNBULL
10

REILLY
9

JOHNSTONE
8

SMITH
7

GALLACHER or COMBE
6

PATERSON
5

BUCHANAN
4

OGILVIE
3

GOVAN
2

Left

YOUNGER
1

Right

HIBERNIAN 3

Referee—
      J. A. MOWAT, Rutherglen.

Linesmen—J. BLACK, Bonnybridge.
          J. CADDEN, Gourock.

Our Sporting Rivals

HERE we are again at The Stadium thanks to the luck of the draw in the Cup.   It is a coincidence that we were due to meet this afternoon at Easter Road in the League. When Hibernian were here in search of points in November, we were regaled by a ninety minutes straining contest which ended in a 1-1 draw.   Since the League was resumed after the War, Hibs have won twice in the League at The Stadium compared with one success by ourselves, while two games have been drawn.   No matter the outcome of today's tie, we know it will be fought out in the best sporting spirit.   We do not forget that when we pipped Hibs on the post for the League Championship last season, they were gracious enough to send a telegram of compliment on our hard won success.

Bobby on his Scotland international debut at Wembley in April 1951. He is being closely monitored by full-back Alf Ramsey, as 'keeper Bert Williams saves a certain goal.   Courtesy of G. Bateman

Hibernian 1951–52. Back row, left to right: Combe, Howie, Paterson, Younger, Mr Hugh Shaw, Govan, Gallagher, Buchanan. Front row (players only): Johnstone, Smith, Reilly, Turnbull, Ormond – it seems that Bobby and Gordon Smith are in each other's seats.

New Hotspur *Famous Teams in Football History* 2nd series

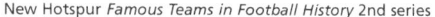

Opposite: Programme for the thrilling 1951 Scottish Cup second-round tie at Ibrox Stadium. Bobby scored a very late winner to stun most of the 106,000 crowd. Pencil-marks record the fact that three of the Famous Five scored.

Obverse of Bobby's first Scottish League Division A Championship medal. Note the inscription, Edinburgh Hibernian FC.

Reverse of Bobby's second Scottish League Division A Championship medal for the 1951–52 season.
Courtesy of Hibernian FC

Bobby on horseback (centre) riding as an attendant within the mounted cavalcade at the 1951 Selkirk Common Riding.

Below: Bobby with his great friend Davie Grieve on the cricket ground at Philiphaugh. Bobby trained Davie to win the sprint race at the 1954 Selkirk Common Riding.
Courtesy of G. Bateman

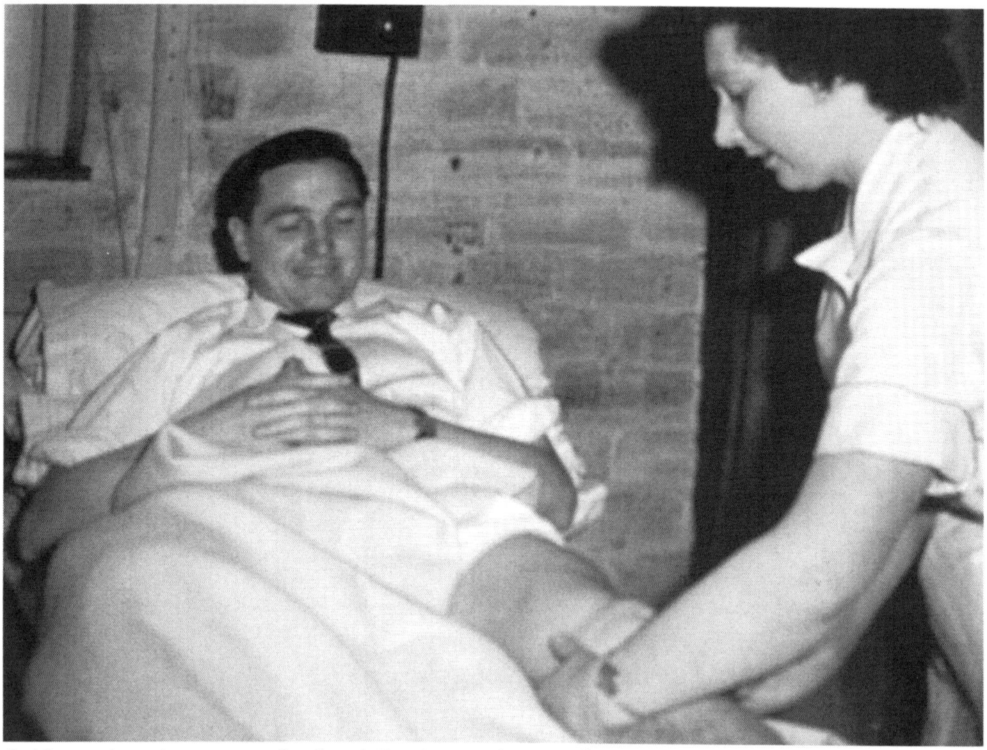

Bobby undergoing an examination following a minor cartilage operation at the Western General hospital in Edinburgh in the summer of 1952.

Courtesy of M. Johnstone

The badge on Bobby's shirt from the Scotland versus Sweden international in 1953. Bobby scored in a 1–2 defeat at Hampden Park, Glasgow. Note the beautifully embroidered detail.

Courtesy of Mr R. Russell

Cigarette cards from 1955–57.

Bobby gives his first autograph at Victoria railway station in Manchester, having just signed for City.

Courtesy of *Manchester Evening Chronicle*

Bobby Johnstone shortly after his arrival at Manchester City in 1955.
Courtesy of C. Buchan's Publications Ltd

This picture appeared in the 1955 FA Cup Final souvenir brochure, produced on behalf of the Manchester City players. Bobby, who had been at City less than two months, was shown in a Scotland shirt.

Courtesy of Manchester Evening Chronicle

HRH The Duke of Edinburgh shakes hands with the former prince of Edinburgh, prior to the 1955 FA Cup Final.

Courtesy of R. Conner and Kemsley Newspapers Ltd

Bobby Johnstone's shirt from the United Kingdom versus Rest of Europe fixture played at Windsor Park, Belfast, in August 1955. The hosts played in emerald green shirts, and note the beautiful detail showing the badges of the four home Football Associations.

Courtesy of Mr R. Russell

Bobby Johnstone lines up with the United Kingdom squad before the fixture against The Rest of Europe in 1955. Teammate Don Revie is immediately behind Bobby, on the back row.

Courtesy of I. Whittell and *Manchester Evening Chronicle*

Team line-ups for the United Kingdom versus Rest of Europe fixture, with Stanley Matthews lining up on the wing alongside Bobby.
Courtesy of T. Wright, Scotland in Pictures, Edinburgh

HOW THEY WILL TAKE THE FIELD

Referee—MR. JUST BRONKHORST (Holland)   Linesmen—Mr. J. HELGS (Denmark), Mr. A. ALSTEEN (Belgium)

UNITED KINGDOM
(Green Shirts, White Shorts)

EUROPE
(Red Shirts, White Shorts)

11 LIDDELL (Scotland)
6 PEACOCK (Ireland)
7 SOERENSEN (Italy)
4 OCWIRK (Austria)

3 McDONALD (Scotland)
10 McILROY (Ireland)
8 TRAVASSOS (Portugal)
2 HANAPPI (Austria)

1 KELSEY (Wales)
5 CHARLES (Wales)
9 BENTLEY (England)
9 KOPA (France)
5 GUSTAVSSON (Sweden)
1 BUFFON (Italy)

2 SILLETT (England)
8 JOHNSTONE (Scotland)
10 VUKAS (Yugoslavia)
3 VAN BRANDT (Belgium)

4 BLANCHFLOWER (Ireland, capt.)
6 BOSKOV (Yugoslavia)

7 MATTHEWS (England)
11 VINCENT (France)

PRE-MATCH ENTERTAINMENT

Organised by Central Council of Physical Recreation   Commere—MISS J. ROBINSON (C.C.P.R.).
Music provided by THE ROYAL INNISKILLING FUSILIERS BAND (Conductor, Mr. G. H. Churchill) and
AGNES STREET TEMPERANCE SILVER BAND (Conductor, Mr. E. Ruddock).

1.00—1.30—Musical Selections.
1.30—1.45—Exhibition Netball Match.
1.45—1.55—Musical Selections.

2.15—2.25—National Dances of Europe by selected members of the Women's Keep Fit Association, N.I.

2.50—The Teams will take the field.
2.53—National Anthem.

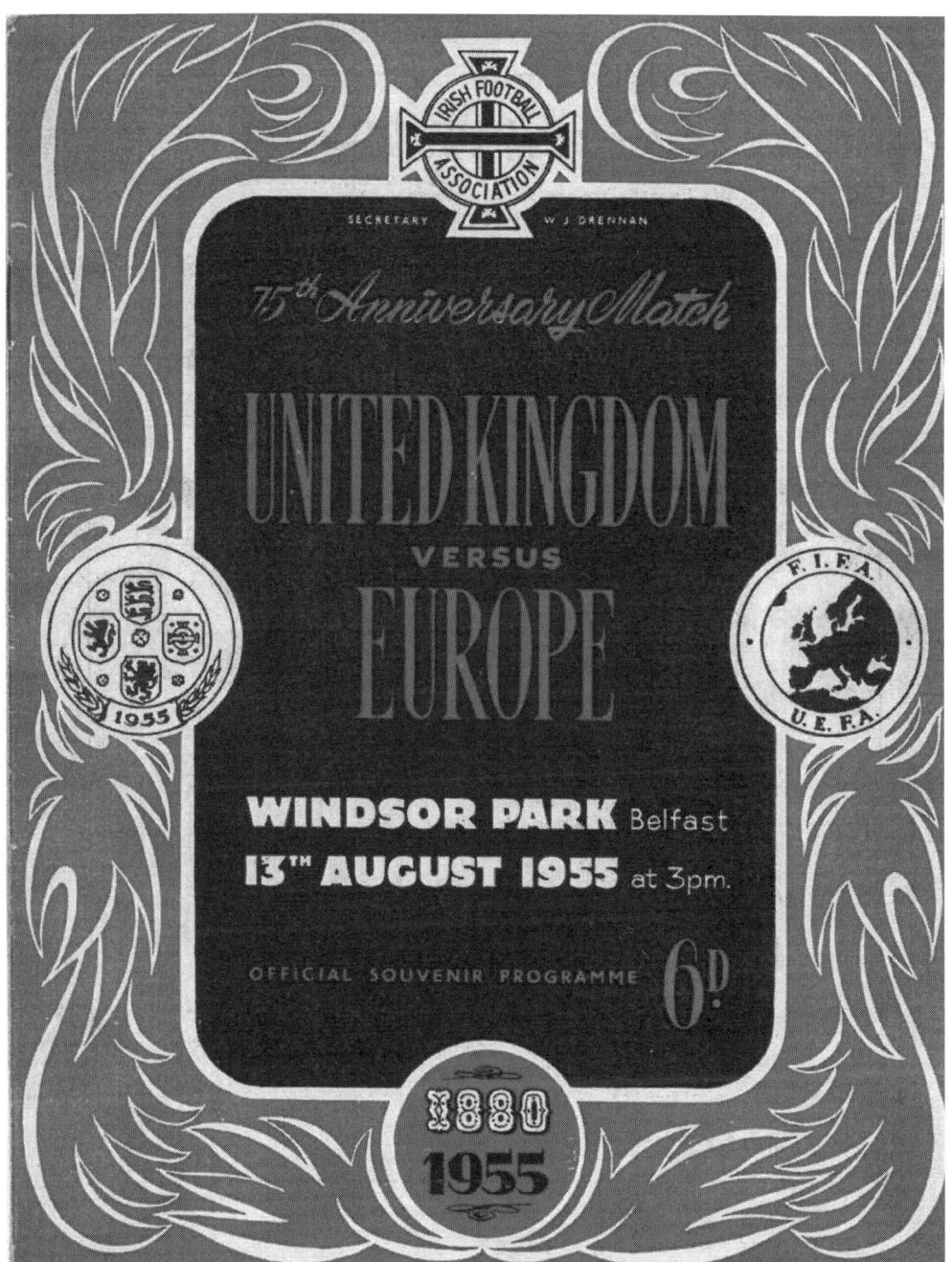

United Kingdom versus Europe match programme from August 1955. Bobby scored Britain's goal in a 1–4 defeat.

Courtesy of T. Wright, Scotland in Pictures, Edinburgh

HIBERNIAN F.C. PROGRAMME

VOL. 7   No. 16   TUESDAY, 1st NOVEMBER 1955   Kick off 7.15 p.m.

Floodlit Challenge Match

Photo by "Scottish Daily Mail"

HIBERNIAN   *VERSUS*   6D

MANCHESTER CITY

Bobby returned to Easter Road as a Manchester City player in November 1955. Part of the second half of this floodlit Challenge Match was shown live on BBC television.   Courtesy of Phil Noble

CHAPTER 5

Breaking up and Breaking Out – 1955 and Manchester City

Bobby had taken the momentous decision to leave Hibernian, his native Scotland, and a diminishing army of loyal supporters behind him... but what sort of club had he joined?

Manchester City were one of the leading clubs in England, although they had never enjoyed a spell of dominance comparable to that enjoyed by the Huddersfield Town or Arsenal teams of the 1920s and 30s. They'd won the FA Cup in 1934 and been crowned League Champions in 1936–37, but there was always something enigmatic lurking. This was demonstrated perfectly when they were relegated the year after winning the League Championship. During the 1930s, enormous crowds often watched City, whereas, by comparison, near rivals Manchester United struggled to survive. At this time the red half of Manchester had the reputation for inconsistency, with United managing to retain a First Division place just once during the 1930s, prior to the intervention of World War Two[1]. Jimmy Armfield, the legendary Blackpool and England full-back of the 1950s and 60s, referring later to the Manchester United of the immediate post-war period, said 'City were as big and often bigger, as they paraded stars like the great Frank Swift and Peter Doherty'.

The man who became Manchester United's saviour was a wing-half from Lanarkshire: Matt Busby, the former Manchester City and Liverpool player. He had appeared in two FA Cup Finals for the Sky Blues, collecting a winners' medal in 1934, and coincidentally had also been a wartime guest player for Hibs too. He engineered the post-war renaissance of Manchester United to the extent that, by the mid-1950s, United were long-established as a force to be reckoned with.

City's manager was also a Scot, Les McDowall, now five years into the job having replaced Jock Thomson in 1950. He was a former stalwart City wing-cum-centre-half, described by the legendary Peter Doherty as 'A great player, a fighter, a good footballer; he never gave in.' This was praise indeed, and McDowall was shrewd to boot. He was given huge credit for introducing the first significant tactical change of the post-war period, which ultimately became known as the Revie Plan. In essence, the centre-forward (usually Don Revie) wore the number-nine shirt but operated behind the forward line, in a deep-lying, 'scheming' role. City were moving in the right direction under McDowall – they were in the FA Cup quarter-finals and were placed handily for an assault on the League Championship. For the first time since the war their crowds would exceed those of their near rivals. This was the Manchester soccer scene as Bobby

Johnstone came south for a transfer fee variously reported as being between £20,000 and £22,000.

Back up in Edinburgh in March 1955, with Hibs on the wane and out of the Scottish Cup, they had seen fit to talk business, and Manchester City were front-runners. It is thought that City were mainly interested in Eddie Turnbull, and one audacious rumour suggested that Newcastle United were prepared to offer £120,000 for the entire Famous Five. Eric Thornton, the well-known Fleet Street journalist, and then Manchester City correspondent for the *Manchester Evening News*, recorded the fee for Johnstone as £25,000 – probably an exaggeration – but the fee was certainly among the dozen or so highest-ever paid for a footballer. Walter Smith, the City chairman, was desperate to sign the Scot, and he agreed to pay a high price. Thornton records the transfer as taking place on 9 March, although the previous weekend's programme for the Tottenham Hotspur game congratulates City on their brand new capture, so the transfer was common knowledge before the contract was finalised.

The signing of Bobby Johnstone had controversial aspects. There had been rumours and probably even bids for Johnstone over the previous couple of years, but Hibs simply would not sell part of their crown jewels. Matt Busby was a known admirer of Bobby's abilities, and it is thought that Manchester United may even have been promised first refusal should he become available; they were certainly in the running for his signature. Hibs had established close links with many of the big clubs in England, playing several floodlit friendlies against English opposition both north and south of the border. In fact, both Manchester clubs had played the senior Edinburgh clubs several times as floodlit soccer was becoming possible. 'I know Matt Busby wasn't very pleased when I moved to City,' Bobby said later. 'He'd played for Hibs during the war, and the club may have promised him first refusal if any of the forward line came up for sale. I don't know if it was coincidence, but Hibs used to play Manchester United regularly in friendlies, but when I signed for City, they stopped.'

There was a split among City fans. One quarter assumed, quite reasonably, that the new man must play his way into a side that were doing well before his arrival. Some questioned McDowall's rationale... City certainly did not appear to need Johnstone, as there were several well-established forwards at the club. Had McDowall purchased an expensive luxury? Others supposed that someone had to make way for the new signing, and the debate centred around who that might be. Unfortunately, Bobby went into print in a *Manchester Evening News* article and rather ill-advisedly wrote about 'his Wembley dream' and his own prospects of a Cup medal. The club now found themselves having to placate some of their own fans, although the chairman's private view was that he hadn't negotiated a major transfer just to see his man warming the trainer's bench. Perhaps mindful of the furore, McDowall chose not to select Bobby for the quarter-final tie against Birmingham City at St Andrews, which City won with a goal from Johnny Hart. On the evening after the match, Johnny wished that Bobby had played: 'Against Birmingham I remember getting kicked all over the park by a lad called [Len] Boyd. I was already sore because I'd fallen downstairs at home, from top to bottom, on the Thursday morning before the game. We lived at Golborne then, and I'll never forget the fall because, unusually, I wasn't carrying my son Paul down in my arms. Anyway, I was already black and blue, all down my back, but I didn't tell the club about it because I wouldn't have played.'

The club were now eagerly looking forward to the semi-final, but Bobby Johnstone's priority was his debut for City, which came the following Wednesday afternoon against Bolton Wanderers. He took the number-10 shirt in a 4–2 win at Maine Road, and while Joe Hayes scored a hat-trick Bobby played a blinder, winning over many of those who felt that he had not yet earned his selection. In those days, the gates used to be thrown open to early-leavers at around 'three-quarter time', and it was common for locals, especially young boys, to sneak in and pinch a few minutes watching the closing stages. One local lad, Roy Conner, recalls running up to the back of the Platt Lane stand with two of his mates, Dave Goodwin and Neil Young,[2] who years later would become a Cup Final hero for City. Roy recalled 'City were 3–0 up when we got in, but Bolton pulled it back to 3–2 before Hayes scored again… but the main thing was that it was our first sight of Bobby Johnstone.'

Initially, Bobby was provided with club lodgings at the eastern end of Claremont Road in Rusholme, very near to the ground, in a terraced house the club used to board players. He was looked after by an elderly landlady, who took footballers in to supplement her income, but it is clear from Bobby's earliest days at the club that, as in Edinburgh, he was a young man who liked the social life that a large city had to offer. It wasn't too long before Bobby gravitated towards the city centre, and for a short while he resided in a public house, The Crown, on the corner of Fountain Street and Booth Street in Manchester, an arrangement that the club were not officially aware of. Both on and off the pitch, Bobby's life was far from settled. Team selections at this time make clear that there were too many players for too few shirts, and it seems that Johnny Williamson, Don Revie, Paddy Fagan, Johnny Hart and now Bobby Johnstone were competing for three places in the team. With such a large transfer fee having been paid, Bobby's arrival was unsettling for many of the recognised first team, and Johnny Hart thought that Bobby had been brought to replace him: 'I wasn't too pleased – but the club didn't give me any inkling of that though. And I'll bet I wasn't the only one who thought it either… Billy McAdams, Don Revie, Johnny Williamson, they probably all thought the same. I didn't particularly get on with McDowall, but in the first game Johnstone played, against Bolton, McDowall said he wanted me to play at centre-forward. I'd always said that even my son, then aged 18 months, could play Revie's game (the deep-lying centre-forward). To be fair, McDowall had the decency to have me in the office; he didn't just put it on the notice board as he had done sometimes with the instructions and things. He told me "You've always said you can play centre-forward, and I want you to play it against Bolton". So I said "Oh, so you've bought Johnstone to replace me!" Revie didn't play, and Bobby took my place. I'll never forget it because their marking was all over the place. I'd agreed to play centre-forward against Bolton, provided I was back at inside-left or inside-right for the Huddersfield game on the Saturday. McDowall said "I'll grant you that", and Revie came back in at centre-forward at Huddersfield.' Over in Yorkshire, Paddy Fagan lost out in this re-shuffle. It seemed that McDowall had no fixed idea of how to best solve the puzzle. Eric Thornton commented 'It was a problem they were postponing but never had to face up to because fate took a hand.' In that game at Huddersfield Town Johnny Hart suffered a broken leg in a 0–0 draw. Over the weekend, Huddersfield Post Office was inundated with thousands of cards, telegrams and get-well messages for the hard working but modest Hart, who had always gone about his job quietly.

Johnny was in so much pain that he didn't know where he was for a while, but then later, as the painkillers started to wear off, he began to come around: 'I knew I wasn't in Huddersfield Royal Infirmary, because there were no other beds in my ward. They'd set my leg, and I had a cage over it, and about 1am on the Sunday, I couldn't sleep. I kept thinking about my leg, it's clicked, it's moved, but of course it couldn't – it was set. Then I heard a woman scream, and at about 6am I heard a baby crying, and I realised I was in a maternity home. I was there a while, I can't remember how long, but it was quite a few weeks, and on my first night back at home we had a burglar, and I put my recovery back by standing up on the leg, trying to get up.' Clearly Johnny Hart was out of the frame for the foreseeable future, but what about the other players affected by Bobby's arrival?

Johnny Williamson, who certainly played the deep-lying centre-forward system in the reserves before Revie, also harboured concerns about his future – and with good reason. He played in the same team as Bobby Johnstone just once, when he scored in a 3–0 win against Wolves. This proved to be Johnny's last match in a City shirt, though he stayed around for almost a year before being transferred to Blackburn Rovers. Revie's position also bears further examination. He was a complex character, and he is the man after whom the Revie Plan was christened, although many feel this was rather too simplistic a title for a system that had involved the thoughts and deeds of many players at Manchester City.

In truth, it was generally reckoned that Revie was going to leave the club, and most observers felt that McDowall had bought Bobby as a direct replacement for the deep-lying role. In fact, McDowall's view was that Bobby would improve an already effective system, quite a judgement considering that Revie had recently broken into the England team. According to Ken Barnes, who didn't share his manager's view at that time, 'McDowall thought that Don was on his way, and so he wanted Bobby. When he first arrived he was such a quiet lad, but when he got on the pitch he was in a another world.'

Les McDowall had a legendary appetite for tinkering with the side, but Bobby, unusually, found him to be quite fair in his approach. In contrast with the recollections of many of City's players of the time, who felt McDowall to be aloof, if not arrogant, in his dealings with players, Bobby said later 'Usually he was pretty fair... McDowall did have some funny ideas – he tried to sign as many inside-forwards as he could. He wanted a whole forward line of inside-players. I couldn't understand it...' Johnny Hart's view was less positive 'I didn't particularly like McDowall, but when I think back, I remember arguing with him, talking tactics. I can remember him saying "we'll not make a tackle in their half, we'll all retreat to our half," and I felt we were giving way territorially. He wanted us to drop back. Looking back I was perhaps a bit unfair, I didn't know it all. I didn't get on with him at times, and I was put on the transfer list. Earlier, when they'd brought Revie and Ivor Broadis, and put them at inside-forward, they put me out on the wing... I must have asked him 12 weeks running to go and see the chairman and put my transfer request before the board, but he didn't.'

Bobby's high-profile transfer was always going to have repercussions, but the injury to Hart meant that whatever plans there may have been, these were now in disarray. It was a shattering blow for the loyal Hart, but it cleared the way for Bobby Johnstone to appear in the FA Cup semi-final against Sunderland the following week. Hart's career barely recovered; he struggled to regain full match fitness, enduring six operations and making only 11 more League appearances in the six years before his retirement, by which time all other factors in this puzzle had moved on.[3]

Just 10 days after that first-team debut against Bolton, Bobby travelled to Villa Park for his FA Cup debut – a semi-final. The team had arrived in Birmingham the previous evening, and it had rained throughout the night. The pitch had been turned into a quagmire, and there were large pools of standing water on the surface. Conditions were so bad that at around 2.15 the players were led to believe that the match was going to be called off, but soon came the news, supposedly after an inspection, that it wasn't. Some sources say that the senior linesman made the decision, with the referee stuck outside the ground in traffic, but others attribute it to the Chief Constable. He had earlier decided to allow the crowd into the ground and out of the rain, and he could reasonably anticipate a major logistical problem had the match been postponed with a crowd of almost 60,000 largely in place, and severe traffic problems outside – not to mention the difficulty of re-scheduling the whole event within a few days. The match would go ahead!

Bobby ran out on to that pitch knowing that he had been fortunate to get the opportunity to help City into the FA Cup Final, but the conditions militated against good football. Len Shackleton, Sunderland's best ball player, was unable to flourish in such circumstances, and the teams mustered just one goal. In Bobby's own words, 'It must have been one of the poorest semis in history. Roy Clarke scored the only goal early in the second half and then went off with a cartilage injury.' In the 56th minute Joe Hayes sent in a cross that was too high for Bobby, but Royston Clarke, who anticipated that Bobby wouldn't be able to reach it, dived to connect with an astonishing header. The ball took an age to reach the net, and it seemed that City fans were holding their breath before they exploded with elation. Clarke was carried off later, injured and exhausted, only realising that City had won when his jubilant colleagues joined him in the dressing room at the end of the game. His own feelings were mixed, as he felt he would be out of the Final, and he was right – though he did return to the side some weeks later. A re-occurrence of the knee injury meant that he missed the showpiece, against the other North-East giants, Newcastle United – and things would not improve for City in the days leading up to the Final.

But these worries could be attended to later. For now the City fans could enjoy the prospect of a first post-war trip to Wembley, and they were in great spirits. Ian Niven, then a young City fan, but a man who would later sit on City's board of directors, recalled travelling back from Birmingham with the rest of the Rusholme branch of the supporter's club: 'There were about 12 of us on a small bus we'd hired from Hackett's Coaches; there were no motorways then of course. We stopped in a pub, somewhere in Staffordshire, and I remember nipping into the toilet to wring my clothes out after the game. We were a boisterous bunch, but not unruly. We had a few pints, and the landlord was happy to let us enjoy ourselves. They had a piano, and he let us play it, and I can still recall us singing, the song went on and on, and we kept making up new verses:-

> For me a Johnstone, for me
> You're nae a Johnstone,
> You're nae use to me,
> Stanley Matthews is braw,
> Willie Waddell and a',
> But our wee Bobby,
> Is the pride of them a'.
> Who said City couldn't play,
> City couldn't play, City couldn't play,
> Who said City couldn't play,
> City couldn't play football,
> After the ball was centred,
> After the whistle blew,
> Clarkey got his temper up,
> And down the wing he flew,
> He passed the ball to Johnstone,
> Johnstone passed it back,
> Clarkey took a flying head,
> And in the net it went.
> Who said City couldn't play,
> City couldn't play, City couldn't play,
> Who said City couldn't play,
> City couldn't play football...

Having qualified for the Cup Final, City could turn their attentions to League matters, where they were still technically involved in the Championship race, although it was looking increasingly likely that Chelsea would triumph for the first time in their history. The draw at struggling Huddersfield had been something of a blow, and Bobby missed the next two games due to his international commitments. While he was away, City drew 2–2 with Sheffield Wednesday at Maine Road, and any lingering hopes were finally extinguished in a 0–1 defeat at Portsmouth. City were seriously weakened in that match because, in addition to the loss of Bobby, both Don Revie and debutant Jimmy Meadows were in the England side preparing to face Scotland at Wembley. Portsmouth took advantage, leap-frogging City into third place, a spot they retained until the end of the season. Of all City players on international duty that day, Bobby's was the blackest – his side were crushed 2–7 in a match that was perhaps more notably the start of Duncan Edwards's international career. Charles Buchan's *Football Monthly*, in a report titled 'It was too easy for England', told his young readership that 'Strangely, the [Scottish] forwards had quite a good game… inside-forwards McMillan and Johnstone worked the ball cleverly and passed neatly, but Reilly was too slow to get the better of Billy Wright.' Scotland's defence was poor, allowing England to rack up their (then) record score in this series, and a first home win against Scotland since 1934. After the heavy defeat, Liddell, another English-based Scot, plus George Young and Gordon Smith, were recalled for the next game, but Bobby wasn't available as he was now preparing for the Final. Incidentally, viewed solely from the financial viewpoint, the £50 each player received for each international appearance exceeded the amount that Bobby would earn in wages, appearance money and bonuses during Cup Final week – even should he earn a winners' medal!

Bobby returned to Manchester for a hectic spell of five games in 13 days, and the first of these, the Good Friday fixture against West Bromwich Albion, brought a 4–0 win and Bobby's first goal for City – in just his third game. The Maine Road crowd, almost 58,000, was the highest of the season, but it was surpassed the very next day when Don Revie scored City's only goal in a 1–0 victory against Sunderland. Remarkably that turnout, over 60,000, was higher than the attendance at the Villa Park semi-final. Bobby scored at Charlton the following week, but in truth the League season was running down and all thoughts were now on the Cup Final. There was a notable 3–0 victory over Wolves though, in which Bobby was the star, producing 'brilliant footwork and shrewd passing. He has proved himself worth every penny City spent on him.' He picked up a slight injury in that match and would miss the next one, another surprise result.

* * *

Besides his family, Bobby had left many friends behind in Selkirk. Lex Millar, one of Bobby's ex-school pals, had been sorry to see Bobby go, 'but we all knew he was bettering himself. City were a big club, it was a big opportunity, and he took it. When he came back in the summer, he told me that the first thing they'd done was send him to be measured for two new suits! No doubt this was related to City's success in the FA Cup, of course, but it was a good yarn for the folks back home.' Having started to establish himself at the club, Bobby quickly began to make new friends – more accurately acquaintances at this early stage, when one has to be wary about who may merely be star-struck. One new acquaintance was Vic Gledhill, who would later be influential in Bobby's career, though for the moment he was not actively connected with football, but he was a City supporter! He lived in Dargai Street in the Clayton area of east Manchester, and just down the road there was a licensed social club with its own bowling green. There Vic introduced Bobby to another resident, Roy Allison, who was also a City fan. 'I was a City supporter, and first went to Maine Road in 1936, aged 10. I stood in the boys corner. I don't recall Busby playing, though I may have seen him, but I did see Peter Doherty.' Roy had been a footballer himself, playing as an amateur in Scotland, and had also spent some time on Blackpool's books without ever threatening the first team. But it was a useful introduction to the conversation with Bobby, and the two hit it off straightaway. 'I had married Margaret in July 1954, and we were living at my grandfather's, directly opposite Vic's house. Being the sort of man he was, and a good City supporter, Vic went out of his way to be friendly with players if he could, and he introduced me to Bobby. It was a nice day, in the April, I think, of 1955. Vic shouted me across; he thought I'd want to meet Bobby, and we had a few things in common. I was a decent amateur footballer myself, and had been stationed in Scotland, just outside Paisley at Linwood, an army base, while I was in the REME. In the 1940s they had a works team, Linwood Thistle, which was a reasonable standard, and Bobby knew a couple of blokes I'd played with, ex-pros. We just got on extremely well.' Roy recalls Bobby being invited around to Sunday lunch at the Gledhills, not long after he had arrived in Manchester. When Roy asked him if he'd enjoyed the meal, Bobby was matter-of-fact and said that 'No, he hadn't actually... the food was awful.' He'd been given salmon, a luxury in post-war Manchester, but something that Bobby was heartily fed up of!

Bobby was known as quite a reserved character, but Roy and Margaret struck up a long-lasting friendship with Bobby. 'He was a lovely man, very ordinary. Some people are very pushy to make contact with footballers, famous people, but he didn't care for the publicity. He was easy to get on with – if he liked you. Many a time, on a Saturday, we'd come straight back up here from the match instead of going to the Lord Lyon near the ground. I remember us going down to queue for fish and chips at Clayton Supper Bar, and Bobby would put a cap on so that he wouldn't be recognised. We'd be queuing, and one or two of my pals might say "Hey, Roy, what was your mate playing at today, he should have scored that one," something like that, and he'd be stood there in the queue with me, collar turned up, cap down. I just found him very ordinary, he used to get a bit embarrassed if he was recognised.'

Bobby had been at the club just two months, and he had barely settled in, but already he had the chance to earn a Cup-winners' medal. In spite of all Hibernian's success, Bobby had never played in the Scottish Cup Final, although the size of the English equivalent held no fears. He had plenty of experience of playing in front of massive crowds, and in fact the 1950 Rangers versus Hibernian League match had been witnessed by a crowd of 101,000, an attendance greater than the capacity of Wembley Stadium. He was fast becoming a cult figure in England too, and Ian Niven still couldn't believe that City's board of directors, whom he felt were 'fuddy-duddies', had actually signed him. A Scot and a City fan all his life, Ian first recalls seeing City in the late 1920s. He believed that, while City had often gone out and spent big money on players with great potential, only occasionally had they purchased the finished article. As far as Ian was concerned, Bobby's signing was very much in the latter category. 'Clarke, Paul, Revie and Broadis – they were superb, top-class signings. Bobby too was an established star. I couldn't believe it.' He also recalls the clamour for tickets for the Cup Final. He had been for a night out with four of his mates to the Lord Lyon on Claremont Road, one of the main approaches to the ground. 'As we left to go home, the queue for Cup Final tickets was already back past the pub door, a good half mile. Anyway, three of us stayed in the queue, while the other two went home for blankets and money. We camped out all night. I always remember then, thinking, if I ever got into a position to do anything to avoid this, I would. It wasn't just us, the inconvenience of queuing, we had a choice, but the neighbours, the noise... for people living nearby, their nights were so disrupted...' Later, as a director, and now life president of the club, Ian would indeed be in a position to have some influence.

City's opponents, Newcastle United, had a tremendous recent Cup pedigree, but their respective runs to the Final contrasted greatly. Newcastle were in the Final for a record tenth time, and having won the Cup in 1951 and 1952, they were hoping to win the trophy for a third time in five seasons. City hadn't played in a Cup Final since overcoming Portsmouth in 1934. Current form simply served to confuse potential punters though, as City had endured a series of tough challenges in their run to Wembley, with only Derby County a seemingly 'easy' tie. Having overcome two First Division sides in Manchester United and Sunderland, City's fifth and sixth round opponents had been Luton Town and Birmingham City, both in good form, and both on the point of promotion to the top Division. Yet City had progressed smoothly, without recourse to replays, in spite of being drawn at home just once. Indeed, in making their way through to Wembley, only Derby County had managed so much as a goal against City. Since the semi-final though, City's game had faltered, and fans must have worried when, in their last home League match, Blackpool promenaded to a 6–1 win. Bobby was absent with a slight injury, and Jimmy Meadows, who would have probably been better engaged in his usual full-back position, replaced him in the forward line.

Newcastle, meanwhile, had faced just one First Division side, and even that was a declining Huddersfield Town, who were to lose their status in 1956. The Geordies had almost come unstuck against sides from the lower Divisions, and at least four late Newcastle goals had been features of their run. In the semi-final they met York City of the Third Division North and had needed a late equaliser to force a replay before 'triumphing' 2–0. Hard work had been made of fortuitous Cup draws, and they'd taken nine matches to see off their five opponents. The Newcastle side seemed to lack the quality of the early '50s teams, with Jackie Milburn evidently past his best. City had the incomparable Trautmann, Ken Barnes, and Footballer of the Year Don Revie, plus, of course, the new signing from Scotland, wee Bobby Johnstone. City were clear favourites.

After the final League game, a 0–2 defeat at Aston Villa, Bobby and his teammates travelled down to Eastbourne, staying at the Grange Hotel and maintaining their fitness in the run-up to the Final. Back in Manchester, the *Evening Chronicle* produced a souvenir brochure entitled *The Road to Wembley – Official Souvenir Brochure*. Ostensibly a service to City supporters, the publication provided up-to-date information, including pictures of the players and a double-page picture of the team. There was a distinct lack of written material, yet sufficient space for six pages of advertising was found, though the product did at least benefit from an analysis of City's Cup run. In fact, the brochure's primary function was to earn revenue for the players 'pool', and such publications were accepted at the time as one of the legitimate perks allowing players to earn a few pounds from their success. It was expensive at two shillings – comparing poorly with the FA Cup Final souvenir programme, which cost just half that, while a standing ticket for the match itself was only 3s 6d (three and a half shillings). Bobby was the man whom supporters, even the keenest City followers, were least familiar with, and he is described as 'the centre of much discussion when he signed a few weeks ago. Got his chance when Hart broke his leg. Quick off the mark, he possesses the genuine footballer's brain, and some of his passes have to be seen to be believed.'

With the squad now at their London team hotel, the night before the Final brought problems. A nurse had to be called to Jimmy Meadows during the early hours, and she advised him not to play as he had a high temperature. How different things might have been had that advice been heeded. The players' wives all stayed at a hotel in Gloucester Road, and this year there were a couple of injured players with that party, Roy Clarke and Johnny Hart. Johnny was still only mobile with the use of a walking stick. On the morning of the match, he asked Roy how the two of them might get to the stadium. 'We'll go about 11o'clock, we'd better get a taxi, get down there. I said "I'm not going that early, we'll wait 'til about half 12, the coach won't be there until half one." Anyway, we got down there. I was still on crutches, and as we got out of the cab I thought they'll never let us in. Clarkey said "come on, they'll know me." The bloke on the gate says "I don't care who the bloody 'ell you are, wait over by that wall until your coach comes." We stood by this wall for ages, about an hour. After a bit, the bloke comes across to me and says "Are you Johnny Hart? Oh, right, you come in." But he left Clarkey there! He must have took pity on me with the crutches and that, and then realised who I was.' Roy Allison had no worries about getting into the ground, as Bobby had given him two tickets, so he could take Margaret, and he travelled down with the ladies.

Out on the pitch later in the day, City cut a dash in their bright blue tracksuits. They were the first to wear them before a Cup Final, though the Hungarians had worn them at Wembley in 1953. The teams were introduced to Prince Philip, the Duke of Edinburgh, and the Prince was gracious enough to find a few words in Bert Trautmann's home tongue as he was about to become the first German to appear in an FA Cup Final. Seventh in line, Bobby Johnstone was probably just too far away to have heard that conversation, had he cared to listen. More likely he was concentrating on trying to relax himself before the match began and reflecting upon his good fortune in appearing at Wembley only 52 days after his Football League debut. It is difficult to substantiate, but at least one article written at the time claims that this was a record.

Shortly after those handshakes, and just 45 seconds of the match, Len White crossed from a corner and an unmarked Jackie Milburn headed Newcastle into the lead. After more good play by Newcastle, Manchester City's serious injury jinx now struck for a third time, and after 20 minutes full-back Jimmy Meadows had to leave the fray with a cruel knee injury. This was later diagnosed as a torn cruciate ligament, and in those days that was an injury that meant the end for many professional footballers. Six weeks previously, on Meadows's international debut, the Wembley turf had been much more giving. Then he had faced Bobby Johnstone in a Home International match, with Scotland being defeated heavily. It seemed that Meadows would go on and carve a successful international career, but now that dream was over, and he never recovered sufficiently to play first-team football[4]. Ironically, Meadows had only got the chance to establish himself when Ken Branagan became ill with appendicitis, and Ken, who was 12th man and a tailor-made replacement for Meadows, had to sit and watch these whole proceedings from the bench.

With Meadows in the treatment room, 10-man City managed to produce a good spell of possession towards the end of the first-half. For the first time in his career, Bill Spurdle had to drop deep and provide cover at full-back, and up in the stands his wife quietly cursed her husband's luck – she had brought their four-week-old child along to witness this momentous day, and things seemed to be turning sour. Then, suddenly, just before the half-time interval, Bobby Johnstone equalised with a classy diving header, after good work by Joe Hayes. BBC radio commentary describes the build-up to Bobby's goal in the inimitable fashion of the day. 'It comes out now to Johnstone, just outside the Newcastle area in, past one man, out to Fagan, he shoots across the goal, it's flicked forward there by Stokoe and away, and cleared in desperation, back by Roy Paul, now out through, now to Hayes, he turns on the ball, terrifically in there... header there, by Paul, oh it's a goal! Johnstone! It's a goal, and Johnstone has scored. Well, that was a typical Manchester City goal. He flung himself across the goal and from 10 yards out nodded it into the far corner of the net. I thought for a moment it was Paul, but it was Johnstone, and Manchester City have equalised, almost on the stroke of half-time.' It was not a typical Manchester City goal at all. Firstly, Bobby had not long been at the club, of course, and further it was unusual for any player to score with such an accurate header, which was actually from a spot not far inside the penalty area.[5] Shortly afterwards, Bobby wriggled through to create a chance for himself, which he struck against the onrushing Simpson's legs – he might easily have put City into the lead, but it wasn't to be.

Ian Niven was in the crowd and remembers the devastation felt when City were stricken by the injury to Meadows: 'In your heart, you gave up when you went down to 10 men. The City fans were grouped in pens behind one goal, and Bobby scored right on half-time, but it was at the other end. His diving header was fantastic, believe me. For me to remember that goal, it was something special.' He has another warm memory of the day, too, with the City fans packed into the terrace behind the goal. After his soaking at Villa Park in the semi-final, he wasn't going to be caught out again; this time he wore his thick crombie overcoat, and it turned out to be a boiling hot day!

In the first quarter-hour of the second half, Newcastle effectively killed off the match. Their second goal went in at the near post, having been driven in from a wide position by Bobby's fellow international Bobby Mitchell, who, along with Milburn and Bobby Cowell, was set to gain his third FA Cup-winners' medal. Mitchell, more than anyone, deserved it. He had played well, while some teammates had struggled for form, and this was his 23rd goal of the season. City goalkeeper Bert Trautmann blamed himself though, maintaining that the goal had been due to his error; he had moved forward anticipating a cross, and the ball went in at his near post. Later, on the hour, Mitchell's shot was parried by Trautmann, but only out to George Hannah. Hannah, who would later spend six years at Maine Road, thumped the ball through a crowded box and high into the net. Newcastle spent the rest of the match almost 'shadowboxing' against a City side that was incapable of raising a response in the face of inevitable defeat. Perhaps charitably, Newcastle did not push too hard for more goals. For the second time in four years the Geordies claimed the Cup against a side that had been depleted numerically because of injury, and one of the features of press coverage over succeeding days was the debate and, in some quarters, clamour for the introduction of substitutes.

Might City have made a better fist of it with a full side? Probably not – the Newcastle players were more experienced on the big occasion, were playing well and had wisely saved one of their better Cup performances for the Final itself. Although City had not called upon Lady Luck too often during their Cup run, she seemed to turn away from City once the semi-finals were resolved. Trautmann had kept City in the Final at 0–1, and Bobby seemed to have provided a brief foothold, but the half-time score of 1–1 certainly wasn't kind to Newcastle. In summary, Manchester City had survived a tough FA Cup run, fought hard to reach Wembley, but luck had deserted them after the semi-final. It wasn't their year. They would have to wait.

At the rather downbeat City banquet, Roy Paul was persuaded, against his will, to say a few words. He echoed the words of Sam Cowan, City's captain in the 1933 FA Cup Final. After defeat by Everton, Cowan had promised to return and collect the Cup in 1934, and he delivered on his promise. 1956 would see Roy Paul and Manchester City attempting to follow suit. For Bobby Johnstone, it was the bitter taste of disappointment in a major Cup Final once again, a blow barely softened by the fact that City had suffered appalling luck with injuries. The Revie Plan had failed to prosper, although its chief exponent was named Footballer of the Year. Never one to bear a grudge, Bobby collected his mate Ken Barnes, and they went over to the Newcastle post-match function, where things were a bit more upbeat, and they had a good night with Jimmy Scoular, the Newcastle captain.

In the days following the Final, there was some suggestion among supporters, and this was reflected in the press, that City, and Roy Paul in particular, had erred at the point where Jimmy Meadows was injured. The critics suggested that Paul should have gone to replace Meadows himself and let Bill Spurdle take the wing-half slot. Paul himself claimed to have considered this but always maintained that, though City should have won the Cup, on the day the Final was played Newcastle were simply the better side, and they would have won with both sides at full strength. Paul felt that City had peaked too soon – several weeks earlier in fact.

Later, Bobby was asked about his recollections of the match, given that he was so new to English football: 'I scored one of the best goals I think I ever scored in my life in that Final, with a header, and it was from about 17 or 18 yards out, and how I got a header that far I don't know, it was just one of them things. Anyway it went in, and Ron Simpson, who later on played for Celtic in the European Cup, was in goals for Newcastle, and I'd been in the army with Ronnie, so that was one up for me.' Ronnie Simpson enjoyed an amazing football career, having first played for Queen's Park against Clyde during the war when he was aged only 14. On the resumption of League football, he became the Scottish League's youngest-ever player when he played against Hibernian at Hampden Park. He and Bobby first met when they completed part of their national service together at Edinburgh castle, and they later faced each other in the Scottish League during the early 1950s, when Ronnie was at Third Lanark. This current season had been a difficult one for Ronnie, as it began with him at loggerheads with the club over wages. Under the retain and transfer system, Newcastle United's offer to him was a weekly wage to be reduced by

£2 per week, to £13. He was upset and even considered quitting the game, but in the end he decided to accept and soldier on. Even now, 10 years after his first-team debut, his first international cap was still a distant 12 years away. He would be 36, and the oldest-ever Scottish international debutant, when that recognition came in 1967. That same year he gained fame as part of the Celtic 'Lisbon Lions' team that became the first British club to win the European Cup.

The following week, Bobby and his teammates set out for a five-match programme of games in the border area of France and Eastern Germany, a tour that generated considerable interest because of the involvement of Bert Trautmann. Bert was less than impressed at the approach of some of his colleagues, and said so, as City rather stumbled through the fixtures. There was a defeat to an amateur side, and only one win, against Eintracht Trier, when Bobby's solitary goal of the tour was overshadowed by four from winger Bill Spurdle. Bobby also made a few trips back to Scotland during the summer, where he played a lot of cricket and enjoyed the Common Riding. Bobby bumped into Bill Stark as they queued to get into one of the events, and knowing Bill liked a bit of poetry, he showed him the verses that had been written by the Hibs fan when Bobby had left there. On another trip north, Bobby invited Ken Barnes to travel up with him, something Ken particularly remembers because Bobby was one of the few players with his own transport. 'Bobby had a car even in 1955. I remember him being late to pick me up once, he was nipping back up home to see the family and whatever, and I went with him. There were nightclubs and things open down here in Manchester, but it was so much quieter up there, there was nothing like that. One time when we were up there, we came back early – it must have been a Sunday. Bobby was saying the pubs don't open until such and such a time here, let's go back to Manchester. He wasn't one of them fellows that looked around for birds and all that kind of thing, but I think it was such a difference from where he'd come from, down here he thought the whole city was a nightclub!'

On 13 August 1955, just a week before Bobby was due to start his first full season in England, he received a great honour when he was selected to play for the Great Britain side chosen by the England manager, Walter Winterbottom, who rated Bobby very highly. The game, against 'The Rest of Europe', was played at Windsor Park, Belfast, and commemorated the 75th anniversary of the formation of the Irish Football Association. In the past, Windsor Park had proved a happy hunting ground for Bobby – he scored twice there for Scotland in October 1951, and after 25 minutes here he scored the game's opening goal in front of the 58,000 crowd. Despite the presence of other luminaries such as Stanley Matthews, Danny Blanchflower, goalkeeper Jack Kelsey, and John Charles, the host team went down 1–4, with Vukas of Yugoslavia scoring a pure hat-trick in the last quarter of an hour. Each player was presented with a small commemorative plaque containing two crests in silver, one incorporating the flags of the four home nations, the other showing a relief map of the rest of Europe.

The following week, Manchester City kicked-off the new season against Aston Villa at Maine Road. Following the Cup Final ticket debacle of the previous season, when the whole of the Rusholme and Moss Side areas had been seriously inconvenienced by supporters queuing for Cup Final tickets, the directors, with an amazing display of foresight, introduced a new feature into the Maine Road match programme: the token. Four games in, in early September, Bobby had his first experience of the Manchester version of the football derby, and he grabbed the headlines following an excellent performance. City won 1–0 and so gained their first win of the season, with Bobby, who had a goal disallowed, also setting up Joe Hayes's goal in what would prove to be his only victory in the Manchester 'derby'. After a 0–0 draw at Highbury, Bobby then ran into a timely spot of goalscoring form, with three goals in successive games before his next international call-up caused him to miss a League game against Sheffield United early in October. Bobby gained his 15th cap at Windsor Park, Belfast, but Scotland's Home International campaign got off to a poor start as Jackie Blanchflower and Billy Bingham scored for Northern Ireland. Though Scotland then applied great pressure, all they had to show for it was a Lawrie Reilly goal in the 62nd minute.

Having missed two games due to injury, it must have been strange for Bobby when, at the start of November, his return to first-team football came in a floodlit Challenge Match against Hibernian at Easter Road. The second half of this game, a 2–1 home win, saw live BBC television coverage, the first such from Edinburgh, though again Gordon Smith missed the occasion. The following week Bobby again met up with former teammates when Tommy Younger and Lawrie Reilly joined him in the Scotland team for the second Home International match at home to Wales. Not surprisingly, Smith was now fit, and Bobby played alongside all three against a strong Wales side that included Jack Kelsey, the Charles brothers, Mel and John, Roy Paul, and Ivor Allchurch. One of the strongest-ever Welsh sides was no match for Scotland on this night, as Bobby scored early goals (in the 14th and 25th minutes) in a 2–0 victory. These goals, his ninth and tenth at international level, would prove to be his last.

While Bobby was now enjoying peak form, and on the international stage at that, Don Revie's star had seemed to wane further after the Cup Final, and later in November he was dropped for a League game at Everton. It seemed that Bobby had finally supplanted him, with the Scot now assuming the deep-lying centre-forward role and the number-nine shirt that went with it. The *Daily Mail* told its readership that the Revie Plan would now go ahead without Revie, while the suggestion in the *Manchester Evening News* was that Revie, who had been suspended for two weeks in the August and had enjoyed, at best, a delicate relationship with management in recent months, had now decided that he wanted to move. Further, it was stated that his relationship with Bobby Johnstone had run to ill-feeling. While the club would not officially discuss the problem, it was clear that the rift between Revie and McDowall would not heal, and with Johnstone now becoming the star player, it seemed a matter of time before Revie went. The Everton game finished 1–1, perhaps justifying McDowall's decision following a couple of defeats, and the team then went on an unbeaten run, ending the year with a narrow derby defeat at Old Trafford on New Year's Eve. Manchester United were no mean side, though, and would later be crowned League Champions for the second time under the management of Matt Busby. Don Revie would play just nine more games this season, eight of those as a replacement for Bobby Johnstone. And this the Footballer of the Year.

So, all in all, the year ended on a most satisfactory note for Bobby. Heather came down for Christmas and New Year, and stayed with the Allisons, who had just bought a new house in Droylsden. Margaret remembers that time well… 'The first time Heather came down to stay, she came down by train. We all went to the cinema on Deansgate, then Bobby picked her up from Victoria station.'

Notes

1. After relegation to Division Two in 1930–31 Manchester United avoided a drop into the Third Division North in 1933–34 only by virtue of a last-day victory at Millwall, who were relegated instead.

2 Neil Young scored the winner for Manchester City in the 1969 FA Cup Final and also scored in the European Cup-winners' Cup Final victory in April 1970. In addition, he top scored in City's Second and First Division Championship-winning seasons (1965–66 and 1967–68).

3. Johnny Hart's last League appearance for City came in April 1961, when he replaced the injured Denis Law against Preston North End at Deepdale. In 1973, then as City's manager, Hart signed Law for a second spell at City. For many City fans, this act was one of the most important of all his contributions.

4. In 1958 Manchester City granted a benefit match to Jimmy Meadows, and there was even an attempted comeback in 1961, when he was given a short-term contract at Maine Road. But it was not to be, and so Meadows retired for the second time that summer and turned his attention to coaching and management.

5. Bobby Johnstone now joined a select band of Scots that had scored FA Cup Final goals at Wembley. In 1924 Neil Harris became the first Scot to score there in only the second Wembley Final. Three years later Hugh Ferguson scored the Cardiff goal that beat Arsenal and took the FA Cup out of England for the only time, and in 1928 Alex Jackson scored for Huddersfield. (Jackson, part of the famous 'Wembley Wizards' side, scored a hat-trick in the 5–1 defeat of England that same year). Alec James (1930) scored for Arsenal, while Jimmy Stein and Jimmy Dunn both scored for Everton against Manchester City in 1933. In 1938 George Mutch scored the first Wembley FA Cup Final penalty, which won the Cup for Preston against Huddersfield. In both the 1953 and 1954 Cup Finals Scots had scored – Willie Moir for Bolton in the 'Matthews Final' and Angus Morrison for Preston in a 3–2 defeat by West Bromwich Albion. Two Scots scored in the 1955 Final.

CHAPTER 6

1956 – History is made

Having left Hibs in March 1955, Bobby had played in almost all of City's games since establishing himself in the side. His first Hogmanay away from Scotland saw less than perfect preparations for what would be his historic year.

As 1956 dawned, Bobby Johnstone was enjoying a decent spell of form. Two days in, on Monday 2 January, City faced a home game against Portsmouth, and one of the largest crowds of the season, over 43,000, had turned up at Maine Road. One former colleague recalls that when Bobby arrived at the ground, it was obvious that he had been enjoying himself during the New Year festivities. This was his first in England of course. 'Even as juniors, and on the ground staff, we all knew Bobby liked a pint, but we could smell alcohol on him that day, and we feared the worst. The club had let him lodge in a pub literally around the corner from the ground, on Claremont Road, in Rusholme – not the brightest thing to do!' Bobby's mate Ken Barnes was less than impressed with Bobby's preparations and told him so, 'he looked over at me in the dressing room, and asked me to get him some aspirin, so I nicked a couple for him out of the trainer's bag. I gave him a right rollicking actually, but I did keep him out of the trainer's way – then he went out and scored three bloody goals with 'is 'ead.' It was Bobby's first hat-trick for City. 'It was laughable really,' recalls Barnes, 'afterwards I told him "Get drunk before every game if that's what you do!"'

As with the start of every new year, footballing thoughts quickly turn to the FA Cup, yet City fans were not overly confident about the team's chances of converting Roy Paul's brave words into deeds. On the Saturday following that remarkable Portsmouth game, the FA Cup campaign began – badly – with a third-round tie against Blackpool at Maine Road. Blackpool scored within the first 10 seconds, with Bert Trautmann conceding the quickest goal of his long career. Jack Dyson scored an equaliser from the penalty spot for City, but newspaper reports suggest that many spectators were unaware of this, due to the dense cloud of fog that had enveloped the ground. Ten minutes later it was announced that the referee had abandoned the match. Thankfully for Trautmann, the record, if not the memory, of that goal was wiped clean.

The replay was arranged for the following Wednesday afternoon at 2.15pm – a 'normal' working day. In spite of this, an additional 10,000 supporters turned up, forming a crowd of over 42,000. One might assume that Manchester had fallen under the spell of some mystery virus, a strain serious enough to prevent people from attending work, but not so debilitating as to affect recreational activities. Yet it was the attendance for the replayed game that was usual here; the previous Saturday's turnout had been remarkably low. That 'gate' had been badly affected by Friday evening press reports of a cloud of smog drifting up from the Midlands, and most supporters were aware of this serious threat to the game. Quite simply, many assumed the match would not start, and so were not prepared to risk travelling to a match that might well be postponed, or worse, of course, started and then abandoned.

Bobby Johnstone scored just before half-time, only for Blackpool to equalise even later in the half. Jack Dyson scored for City 10 minutes into the second half, and City held out to scrape through 2–1. There was relief at this outcome as some of the players had been fearful prior to the replay because of the quality of the football that Blackpool had produced in the abandoned game, but they were through and on their way. The week after Bobby scored City's goal in a 1–4 League defeat at Cardiff City, his fifth goal within the first two weeks of the New Year, and then attention turned to the fourth round of the Cup. City faced a long journey to Essex, having been drawn to play Southend United. The Third Division South side were enjoying their first season at their brand new Roots Hall Stadium, but as the match approached it became clear that the pitch was in a dreadful state, due to torrential rain. In the days preceding the tie, one journalist from Manchester actually witnessed workmen digging up the playing surface and 'installing' new drainage – tons of crushed cockleshells! After City's rather lucky 1–0 win, Roy Paul held that 'most of the lads came off with skinned knees caused by sand and shells. One man got us through this match – Bert Trautmann'. The 25,000 crowd that day certainly saw a legendary display of goalkeeping, and one recorded to this day on the Southend FC official website – it was the day that the underdogs were thwarted by the big German goalkeeper, in what many regard as the finest performance of Bert's career. Joe Hayes nicked the winner for City, and the newspapers dubbed the players 'the Cockleshell Heroes' after a film that was on popular release at the time. Perhaps City's Cup luck was in, after all…

The fifth-round draw saw City given a home tie, against a Liverpool side who were then in the Second Division, where they would remain for some time yet. But before that tie in mid-February, a significant tactical move was made by manager Les McDowall when he played Bobby at number seven, on the right wing, against Chelsea at Maine Road, while Don Revie took the number-nine shirt. This was the first time the two had played together since Revie had been dropped the previous November. Arthur Walmsley, a columnist with the *Manchester Evening Chronicle*, but also then a contributor to City's match-day programmes, described Bobby's display against Chelsea as scintillating. 'He spent as much time cutting inside and carving openings in the middle as he did on the wing. At times, he would pop up on the left wing for a throw-in, at others he would be foraging from the inside-left position,' he waxed. Joe Hayes scored both of City's goals in a draw. The move was seen as firm evidence of McDowall's far-sighted approach to tactical matters; he was further developing ideas that had already been seen as unorthodox.

The following week the fifth-round tie against Liverpool took place, with Bobby and Revie retaining their positions. The match was preceded by a snowstorm, and it ended in a disappointing 0–0 for a crowd of over 70,000, with City perhaps lucky to see a 'goal' from Liddell disallowed. Yet that was nothing compared to the tremendous controversy that followed in the immediate aftermath of the replay, played the following Wednesday afternoon at a snow-covered Anfield.

Bobby played superbly back in the number-nine shirt (Revie was dropped to make way for Clarke), and City equalised when his mazy run created a goal for Jack Dyson. Once again, City had been grateful to an in-form Trautmann on a couple of occasions, but in the final minute Bobby set up Joe Hayes to put City 2–1 up. Then a notorious event occurred. With City on the attack, the ball was cleared from defence and picked up by Billy Liddell, Bobby's Scotland and Great Britain teammate. Racing away into the City half, Liddell reached the edge of the penalty area, and right on the stroke of the final whistle he smashed in what he, the crowd and even Bert Trautmann believed was a Liverpool equaliser. But referee Griffiths had blown the full-time whistle while the ball was in flight, and Roy Paul, City's captain, smartly shepherded the City players from the pitch. The Liverpool players, surrounding the referee, came to terms with that fact that their Cup run was over, although many thousands remained in the ground expecting that extra-time would follow, not believing that the match was over until they were informed by a public address announcement. Billy Liddell graciously accepted the referee's decision, and the following day photographs in the press proved conclusively that the referee had his hands in the air signalling the end of the game before the ball left Liddell's boot. City now marched into the last eight, where they would face the other Merseyside giants, Everton. Coincidentally, the concept of the Wednesday afternoon replay would begin to dim this very day – just a few hours after the disappointed Liverpool fans started to wend their way home, the first ever Football League match to be played under floodlights kicked-off.

The City players were now starting to think that perhaps Lady Luck was on their side and that Roy Paul's promise could be kept. Confidence surged through the team, and they won their next three League games by an aggregate of 10 goals to nil. Bobby netted half of those, starting with a brilliant goal at Preston where he scored twice. Sandwiched into this purple spell was the FA Cup sixth-round tie, where City, with the benefit of another massive home crowd, over 76,000, saw off a spirited Everton performance. By common consent Bert Trautmann and Bobby, who just couldn't stop scoring, played tremendously, though the victory was slightly against the run of play. Everton were leading at half-time, and in Bobby's own words 'they absolutely tanned us. It should have been 4–0.' But after Joe Hayes had equalised, Bobby put City into the lead with a brilliant diving header 'from Roy Clarke's cross. It was one of my most memorable goals.' City held on to win. It was only the second time that Bobby had played in an FA Cup victory at Maine Road, and, strangely, it was the last.

Just two weeks after the sixth-round match on 17 March, Manchester City faced Tottenham Hotspur in the semi-final at Villa Park. As in 1955, this semi-final match was not a classic. City won 1–0, the goal coming just 10 minutes after Tottenham were set back by a disallowed 'goal' following a disputed offside decision. Danny Blanchflower, the Spurs legend, was described as having sacrificed his own game in an effort to shadow Bobby, but it was to no avail as the inevitable Johnstone scored the winner. Once again he threw himself on to the end of a left-wing cross from Roy 'Nobby' Clarke, heading a great goal five minutes before half-time. Bobby had now been at the club a year, and he was making a tremendous name for himself with the press and supporters, scoring lots of goals and justifying his large transfer fee. His latest goal was his 18th, and they seemed to be key goals too. He was in brilliant form; he had scored for the fifth consecutive match, a run that had brought him seven goals. Even though Bobby would score just once more in this 1955–56 season, that goal would create a piece of history.

For the rest of the match, City had to defend under tremendous pressure from the Tottenham assault. Once again there was plenty for the newspapers to talk about after the final whistle, and once again Trautmann, who attracted tremendous publicity by the standards of the time, was at the centre of things. Many newspapers published compelling photographic evidence appearing to show Trautmann holding on to the leg of George Robb, Tottenham's winger, during a goalmouth scramble. Pathé News cameras had recorded similar evidence, and Tottenham, with considerable justification, felt that they should have been awarded a penalty, but City escaped – again. At the time, Trautmann denied being guilty of deliberate foul play, and to their credit Tottenham, and Robb in particular, could not be accused of seeking mileage from the situation.[1] The following week the two sides faced each other again, in a League game at White Hart Lane. One might have expected some pointed references to the events of the previous week, yet an editorial piece in the match programme actually congratulated City on reaching Wembley, while referring most politely to the disallowed goal. On the Robb controversy, the official view was that 'Robb... had his leg impeded by Trautmann so that he could not get his foot to the ball with an open goal in front of him, and this enabled the ball to be scrambled away. Very surprisingly, no penalty was awarded.' The article did concede, however, that Manchester City had played well and had looked like increasing their lead on several occasions in the latter stages of the game. The rather Corinthian conclusion was that their 'Villa Park hoodoo' was to blame – it was the third time that Tottenham had lost a semi-final at the ground. While undoubtedly this was a magnanimous response from the club, Trautmann had been subjected to some upsetting hate-mail during the week prior to the League game, and when he ran out on to the White Hart Lane pitch the crescendo of noise that greeted him was deafening.

With his return to Wembley now seemingly assured, Bobby made his 31st and final League appearance of the season in early April. After the match, a defeat at Newcastle, Bobby left his teammates and headed over the border to report for international duty. During the following week it was announced that Bert Trautmann was to be honoured as Footballer of the Year, beating Birmingham's captain Len Boyd, John Charles and Sam Bartram in the final reckoning. The following day brought the first inkling that Bobby's place in the final side might not be absolutely assured as Don Revie took advantage of his absence, playing superbly in the 3–1 defeat of Sheffield United at Maine Road. Revie was still unsettled, of course – he had played only five League games since the previous autumn, and he was looking at going to play in Australia in the summer of 1956, something it seemed that the club had approved. Eric Todd, writing in the *Manchester Evening Chronicle* after the Sheffield United game, said 'My own view is that it would be fatal to play Revie and Bobby Johnstone alongside each other, as their styles clash. Yet on this showing, Revie cannot be left out.' Perhaps Revie now warranted a place in the team.

On the following Saturday, Bobby earned a fourth cap since moving south when he was selected to face England in the Home International Championship for the sixth consecutive year, this time at Hampden Park. The 1–1 draw secured a share of the Home International Championship for Scotland and Bobby had now achieved at least a share of this trophy for a third time, but this was the last, as he never played for his country again. His international career seems to have been brought to an end by question marks around his reliability, largely because of the increasing effects of his persistent knee injury, and, indeed, according to whichever report one believes, he picked up either an ankle or a calf injury in this, his final international game. It may be entirely coincidental of course, but the new president of the SFA was one Harry Swan of Hibernian. It was no secret that he did not get on with Bobby Johnstone personally, and among the countless others in Edinburgh still disappointed at the break-up of the Famous Five, few were in a position to influence the international careers of those with whom they had crossed swords. Further, the Scotland team contained only one other England-based player, Charlton Athletic's John Hewie, who was making his international debut, and Ken Barnes recalls that this difficulty was one experienced by many Scottish players in England. 'In that era, if you left Scotland to come down to the English League, well... they only wanted to pick players who were playing in the Scottish League. There were a lot of Scottish players who could have quite easily kept their places in the national side, but there seemed to be a funny influence. Bobby had problems with his knee as well... but there was definitely a downer on those that had come south.'

Bobby now ended his international career with 17 caps, a considerable achievement relative to today, when there are so many more international matches played. During his spell in the international set-up, there were 17 further games for which Bobby was not selected, and not all of his absences were due to injury. Nevertheless, he played only half of the games that the national team played, and noticeably seemed to miss out on foreign trips. Lawrie Reilly, Hibs' record cap holder, roomed with Bobby on international duty, and he recalls one transgression abroad earlier in Bobby's international career, following which a complaint was made to the SFA. This may have been a contributory factor, though it is also true to say that pressure for places in the side was intense. Besides the Famous Five, there were men of the calibre of Billy Liddell, Willie Waddell, Bobby Mitchell of Newcastle, Billy Steele and others all vying for places in the team.

The 'all-international' forward line at Hibernian is frequently referred to, and while it is accurate technically, it can also be misleading. In reality, the Famous Five never appeared together in the same Scotland side, and so they didn't get the chance to bring their tactical interchanging on to the international stage. In fact, Bobby did not play alongside more than two of the other forwards in any international game, and never at all with Eddie Turnbull, who had received his fourth cap in the disastrous home defeat by Austria in December 1950. Incredibly, Turnbull failed to play any of the next 47 internationals, spanning eight years, and Bobby's entire international career, before he returned to the fold and picked up five further caps in and around the 1958 World Cup. Gordon Smith played alongside Bobby and Lawrie Reilly in the home defeat to England in 1952, but by the next time those three played together for Scotland, in October 1955, Bobby had left Hibernian. One can only speculate about the impact the full Five might have had, but it would certainly have been interesting because they were so full of ideas. Indeed, in one international game, played abroad, Lawrie actually proposed swapping the number-nine and 10 jerseys with Bobby so that they might '...bamboozle the opposition. The SFA wouldn't allow it though, because the team-lines had already gone in to the referee, and they were worried about any confusion if the referee came to book anybody.'

Back in Manchester, the run-in to the FA Cup Final had begun, and on the day of the Hampden international Don Revie continued in the number-nine shirt, though City lost their final home match to Burnley. As Bobby returned south, the Manchester press reported that he had picked up a calf injury in the international: 'worryingly, this required the attentions of a specialist', and there were now just two weeks to go before the Cup Final. On the eve of the penultimate match, at Luton, the *Manchester Evening Chronicle* announced 'Scot out', as Bobby continued to receive treatment, yet the precise nature of the injury seems to be unclear. While some reports stated that he was now suffering from fluid on the knee, others claimed that the knee was responding to treatment.

On Wednesday 25 April, 10 days before the Final, the club followed the pattern of the previous year when they travelled south by train to spend 10 days on the south coast at their Eastbourne training base, which was handy as the final fixture was at Portsmouth's Fratton Park. At this stage, it seemed that Bobby was 'likely to play on Saturday', as his 'pulled muscle' [*sic*] was improving, but the main concern now focused around Bert Trautmann, who did not travel with the rest of the squad. He had not slept the previous night, having ricked his neck, and so took the later, midday train. With the picture seeming to change on a daily basis, Friday saw the announcement that Bert Trautmann had come through the training sessions on the local Saffron's ground and would play, but after treatment on his pulled muscle, which was still painful, Bobby was certain to miss the last League game.

City won the game 4–2, with Don Revie starring once again in Bobby's absence. Monday's newspapers carried Don Revie's thoughts about his position and quoted him as saying that it would be 'unfair if I play in the Cup Final,' though things were clearly improving and the board of directors had asked him to reconsider his transfer request. Bobby, meanwhile, who still expected to be fit for the Cup Final, had had a dip in the sea, taken some heat treatment, and reckoned he hadn't felt better for weeks. He took part in a practice match at Saffrons and told reporters he was feeling fine. Two days before the Cup Final, Bert Trautmann travelled up to London, ahead of the rest of the squad, to collect the Footballer of the Year award from the Football Writers' Association. Here Bert followed in the footsteps of the 1955 winner Don Revie, but his achievement was all the more notable given the fact that he was a goalkeeper and a foreigner too, and even more so because he was German, with everything that that implied given the cessation of hostilities just a decade earlier. His reward came in spite of some opposition within the FA because of the Robb incident, which was seen as a blemish on his career. On the Friday, the day before the Final, Bobby travelled with the rest of the team up to their Weybridge base, where they joined up with Bert and could congratulate him on his success.

As usual, there were plenty of headaches for the City management team to ponder, and the final line up was still far from settled. Should Bobby fail to make it, the obvious alternatives for his place in the forward line were Revie himself, but also now Johnny Hart. He had reappeared in the Portsmouth match, his first game since the serious injury at Huddersfield a year before – and he had scored. Johnny is insistent that he was fit for the Cup Final but may have talked himself out of a place in the team. 'I'd scored at Portsmouth, and I was as fit as a butcher's dog. All the lads said "yer in" for the Final. We were down south, we used to go to Eastbourne and then on to the Oatlands at Weybridge. A couple of us went for a kick-about on to the golf course on the Friday, supposedly to give Bobby Johnstone a fitness test. Anyway, I'm lathered in bloody sweat, but Bobby's not broken sweat; he's whacking the ball all over the course, and I'm chasing it! I said to Laurie Barnett, the trainer, "What's going on 'ere, who's having a fitness test, me or 'im? I'm finished, I'm not going any further." Bobby had hardly moved when we came off the course, and when McDowall had asked him about his fitness, Bobby had just shrugged his shoulders.' Clearly Bobby had major doubts about his fitness; he wasn't prepared to declare himself fit, though like any footballer he desperately wanted to play and hoped to do enough to make McDowall decide to risk him. He revealed his inner thoughts to Roy Allison over the telephone, when he rang his mate, as planned, around tea-time on the Friday evening to arrange where to meet up. Bobby had promised Roy two tickets for the game, but now Roy's plans had changed: 'Margaret wasn't going, so I was taking my brother instead; Bobby rang as promised, and said he had the tickets OK, but wouldn't be playing. "My leg's like a balloon," he said – it was his knee.' Disappointed, Roy decided to travel down anyway – he was a City fan after all, and so he caught the overnight train to meet Bobby.

This was quite a conundrum for Les McDowall, and the indications are that, much as he wanted to select Bobby, he didn't really feel that the Scot was fit enough. Later that night McDowall told Johnny Hart that he would probably end up playing him instead. 'McDowall and I were the last ones in the hotel lounge, around half eleven, and I told him I was livid about this, who was having the fitness test, me or Johnstone? He was supposed to be having the fitness test… yet it was me doing all the running about. McDowall told me then "you'll be playing tomorrow!" But I knew he hadn't finally decided, and I said "Don't be daft – if you play me, and we lose, you'll never live this down." He took some time to think it over, and then he said "Alright, I'll give him another chance – but if he shrugs his shoulders again, you're in."'

Johnny felt that City supporters would prefer Bobby on one leg than him on two, and it was obvious that his best chance of playing lay with Bobby not being passed as fit. Yet that didn't stop him warning Bobby to be a bit more positive… 'I went and told Bobby, down at the golf course again, look Bobby, if you don't say that you're fit after this, you'll lose your place, don't shrug your shoulders. After I'd done all of the running about again, McDowall asked him, and Bobby just said "I'm fit". That was it, end of story. Bobby played right-wing, these things happen.

I might have talked myself out of it, but it was only fair I told Bobby. They would have crucified me, and they would have crucified McDowall because I wasn't the best-liked person in the team, but McDowall knew, everyone knew, that Bobby wasn't really fit because he hadn't played for weeks.'

On the morning of the match it had also become clear that winger Bill Spurdle would not be able to play due to an unpleasant infection on the inside of his upper arm. Bill wanted to play, in fact, but the medical advisors prevented it: 'they just said no, if you fall down on that there's a chance you might not get up again! There were fewer antibiotics around then, of course, but it was ironic, and I told Bobby "I'm buggered, fair enough, but you're playing with that knee of yours!"' Full-back Bill Leivers also required a fitness test, but in the end he was selected, and McDowall chose to play Don Revie at number nine, with Bobby out wide on the right. At least one favoured journalist, camped with the team at the Oatland Park, was made aware of the changes before Don Revie himself, and the story had already been wired back to Manchester by the time McDowall made his way down to the hotel reception area to inform Don Revie that he was playing in what had become Johnstone's more usual number-nine shirt – with Johnny Hart missing out for the second year running. The Manchester press were delighted Revie was in, with Johnstone switching for Spurdle, but McDowall made it clear that they were not to mention Bobby's injury.

While these arrangements were being clarified, Roy Allison had travelled down, had some breakfast and made his way to the meeting place, a corrugated iron gate between the twin towers. He will have been among the first City fans to hear how the team would line up. 'Bobby had said "dead-on 12.30, don't be late." We got there nice and early, walked up... and Bobby was already waiting for us! He said "Hey, Roy, I was out, but I'm bloody playing! Bill Spurdle's took bad." I think they thought he had an infection, or even pneumonia or something.'

Bobby left Roy and went off to get prepared. Later, in the dressing rooms, some of the players, in trying to calm their nerves, glanced through the match programme, which listed the pre-match entertainment in addition to the team formations. Birmingham's men would kick-off precisely as listed, but the late changes for Manchester City meant that Bobby was incorrectly listed at number nine, the shirt that Don Revie would take. Further in, 'pen pictures' informed readers that Bobby Johnstone was a first choice for the Scotland international team, and that his transfer south the previous year had 'caused a big sensation'. Sadly, the reality was that the very injuries that had threatened his appearance here meant that Bobby would never again play for his country, and today's match would see him appearing at Wembley for the fifth and final time. For the fashion conscious, Manchester City this year paraded a continental-style, maroon, short-sleeved, v-neck shirt, with thin white stripes, another first for an English side, following the ground-breaking tracksuits worn prior to the previous year's Final.

The teams took to the pitch as the community singing came to a close under the direction of the conductor, Arthur Caiger DCM, who led the traditional hymn *Abide with Me*. Les McDowall's team talk will have been ringing in the ears of the City players, at least the ears of those that chose to listen. He had emphasised the importance he always placed upon passing the ball. 'Bring the ball down and use it.

Don't panic, no big kicking. Here, pure football, style and skill always pay dividends.' Up in the stands, among the dignitaries, sat an 82-year-old gentleman, Billy Meredith, the 'Welsh Wizard', a man widely recognised as football's first superstar. He had played for Manchester City in the year the club was formed, 1894, had scored the winner in the 1904 FA Cup Final, and then played in the winning Manchester United side of 1909. Back at City, he played his last game in 1924, while in his 50th year. For him, too, it was a last trip to the twin towers, and he was keen to see Roy Paul become the second Welshman to captain Manchester City to FA Cup success.

Bobby Johnstone was the last man out of the dressing room, his left knee and lower calf heavily strapped. His instructions were to play out wide, on the right wing, for only the third time in his career, though the exact nature of the injury to the upper part of his left leg is unclear, with several sources stating that Bobby had a painkilling injection in his left thigh or left calf muscle, following a strain. In later years Bobby always referred to his long-term knee problems, yet the calf strain story endures.

There was a minor but interesting confusion as the captains tossed the coin in the centre-circle, caused by Roy Paul's determination not to make a public gaffe while shaking hands with referee Alf Bond. The official had lost the lower part of his right arm, and Pathé News film footage shows Paul conspicuously keeping his own right arm behind his back during the brief formalities, and remembering to shake left-to-left hands with the referee. When the Birmingham captain Len Boyd proffers his hand to shake, Roy shakes that with his left hand too! The referee then tosses up, but momentarily loses the coin in the grass before it was revealed that Birmingham had called correctly... and the teams switched ends.

Soon after, the whistle went and the Revie Plan bore early fruit. Don played a long ball out to Roy Clarke on the left and sprinted for the return pass, before feeding Joe Hayes, who smashed his shot past the Birmingham 'keeper, Merrick, to put City into the lead after only three minutes. Birmingham played their way through a poor spell for about 20 minutes after City's goal, but then forced Trautmann into a great save at the expense of a corner. After about half an hour, another good move saw Birmingham equalise from a clean strike by Kinsey, whose shot nestled in the back of the net having first hit the post. McDowall's half-time team talk focused on the positive, rather than the concession of the lead. 'One last push lads. Just keep playing and the goals will come.' In the second half, City began to control the game, with Revie playing exceptionally well. Bobby later told his teammates that his pre-match injection had taken some time to take full effect, and indeed some of the reports of the time describe Bobby, out wide on the right, 'visibly limping' early on, although that is an exaggerated description for a player who was undeniably much less than fully fit. By the second half, his knee felt much freer, and in the 57th minute Barnes laid on a great through ball and Jack Dyson beat the advancing 'keeper and put Manchester City into the lead.

Soon, Birmingham began to push hard for a second equaliser, but this was part of their undoing. After another threatening Birmingham move, Bert Trautmann picked the ball up and launched a counter attack. It reached Jack Dyson, and with the Birmingham defenders rushing back, he played Bobby in on goal; a blink of an eye later, and history had been made. This was how the BBC radio commentary of the time relayed these scenes to the masses '...well Birmingham are completely demoralised this half; they've got no idea at all. Here's a lovely goal-kick, right away down through, to the outside-right, he shoots and he scores! Johnstone! A long goal-kick by Trautmann with the Birmingham defence completely upset, flipped along the ground by Dyson, and Johnstone the outside-right has scored – a lovely goal. Absolutely playing Birmingham at the game they played in the first half – quicker thinking, beautiful goal, only three men touched that ball. Tremendous goal-kick by Trautmann after that lovely save of his, right down, a flip forward by Dyson, and Johnstone ran on to it, and cracked it home. And that is now 3–1 to Manchester City, and I make it now that there are 21 minutes left for play.'

The significance of the goal was probably not understood immediately; it certainly wasn't referred to in the match commentary, but in fact Bobby Johnstone had become the first man to score in consecutive FA Cup Finals at The Empire Stadium, Wembley. That world-renowned venue is the traditional and historic setting for the FA Cup Final, the showpiece of the English game, so there is no little irony in a Scotsman performing this feat for the first time. The commentator does, however, refer to City's domination of the play at this stage, and that is how Ken Barnes recalled it years later... 'we really should have won by about four or five at the finish, we had some great chances. However, when you're 3–1 up with quarter of an hour to go, you say to yourself, we're OK, keep it tight.' Bobby, now a lot more involved in the game, beat three men on one glorious run, before laying a beautiful defence-splitting pass into the path of a colleague.

Yet there was still room for drama, and what drama it was; a story that took Bobby Johnstone out of headlines that should have reflected upon what had been an historic goal. Just as Ken Barnes was thinking that City could play the game out, Birmingham's Murphy latched on to a header and got away from big Dave Ewing, City's stalwart Scottish stopper. Murphy had a great chance to score, but Bert Trautmann, long renowned for his bravery, raced out of his goal and dived headlong at Murphy's feet to nick the ball. There was a 'sickening collision' as Murphy's right knee connected with Trautmann's neck and knocked the goalkeeper unconscious. Full-back Roy Little was on the spot, and this was his eyewitness account: 'it was right in front of me and it was an accident. Murphy couldn't be blamed, he just caught him with his knee as he went for the ball... we obviously had no idea how serious it was.' The referee stopped the game immediately, and all involved quickly realised that this was a serious injury, but how serious? Trautmann came round with the assistance of smelling salts but was in severe pain. Roy Clarke thought Bert would have to go off, and Roy Paul the captain, seeing Bert 'reeling around the goalmouth like a drunk,' had already thought about putting Roy Little in goal, although the removal of Bert's shirt might have presented some difficulty. However, Trautmann, in what is widely recognised as one of soccer's greatest displays of bravery, had decided to try to play on. Lawrie Barnett, City's trainer, had to station himself behind Bert's goal, amid a gaggle of cameramen eager to catch the drama for their newspapers. Later, at the other end of the pitch, and following a great pass from Jack Dyson, Bobby almost made it 4–1 when he shot for goal and forced the England 'keeper Gil Merrick to make a spectacular, if rather fortunate, save as full-time approached. After what must have seemed an age, referee Bond blew for full-time, and City had done it.

The players stayed on the pitch, celebrating in the traditional manner, waving to their supporters, and commiserating with the Birmingham players. Roy Paul led the City team up the steps to receive their medals and the FA Challenge Cup trophy, a procession most notable for the man seventh in line, Bert Trautmann, who was obviously in agony and holding his head at a most uncomfortable-looking angle. Back on the pitch, and led by Don Revie, Roy Little and Dave Ewing, the victorious captain, Roy Paul, was chaired on his colleagues' shoulders, while he showed the trophy to City's supporters. The exhausted players then retired to their dressing room to enjoy that traditional rite of the victors, a drink of champagne from the Cup.

In the evening, the team celebrated at a banquet held at the Café Royal, where Trautmann, who could barely remember a thing after his collision, was told the story of that last quarter of an hour, and how he had made two more great saves. One of these involved a heavy collision with teammate Ewing, who, along with Roy Paul, had been trying to form a protective shield around the penalty area. Their tactics, frankly, had been to 'hoof it' and then re-group for the next advance in the hope that they could see out time. This was achieved, and the 1956 FA Cup Final went down in history as the 'Trautmann Final', rather then the 'Johnstone Final' that it could have been had fates not engineered another script. Yet there was never any sense of envy or spitefulness from Bobby about having had his thunder, or 'his' headlines stolen. He never suggested that he hadn't enjoyed his full share of the glory as that was not his style. He was the last man up the Wembley steps to collect his winners' medal, and, if anything, he is likely to have been grateful that Bert was the exclusive recipient, over succeeding days, of all the press attention, which escalated even further once the 'keeper was admitted to hospital. Bobby was happy to remain in the background, and on the open-topped bus that toured Manchester he was not to the fore, waving the Cup around with Roy Paul and Big Dave Ewing. He was seated toward the rear, smiling and waving to the packed streets of City fans, happy, of course, but not exactly embracing the limelight.

Back home in the Borders, an article in the *Southern Reporter* told how Bobby had overcome the disappointment of 1955, and that 'one of the biggest cheers of the day' at the traditional Langholm sports festival, in Dumfriesshire, was reserved for the announcement that Manchester had beaten Birmingham in the English Cup Final. 'All were asking the same question – was Bobby Johnstone playing? The pride of Selkirk was playing alright, figuring in the outside-right position and notching one of his side's three goals... with his big-game temperament, he rose brilliantly to the occasion to put himself back in the reckoning for a place in the Scottish team.'

Some of the football played by City that day was heralded in some quarters as just about the finest seen in a Cup Final – or in any other match – for a considerable time. Frank Swift, a newspaper columnist, and Bert Trautmann's predecessor in Manchester City's goal, commented that Bill Spurdle's injury had turned out to be a blessing in disguise for the club. 'It allowed Les McDowall to field both Don Revie and Bobby Johnstone in his Wembley attack, and these were the two who, more than any others, upset the form book.' Another commentator felt that 'such a collection of footballers, if kept together, would win pretty well everything for which they were entered'. Yet City's final League position of fourth was the highest they achieved during the 1950s, and the 1956 FA Cup win was certainly the pinnacle during Bobby's time at Maine Road, as well as being the last major trophy that City would win for over a decade. The next few years would see a slow decline, although attendances held up remarkably well. The down-turn accelerated in the early 1960s and resulted in the slide into the Second Division at the end of 1962–63 – but that was seven years away yet, and there were to be many twists and turns in Bobby Johnstone's career before then.

During the Cup run, the goalscoring role had been shared evenly between Joe Hayes, Jack Dyson and Bobby with four each (though Dyson lost one from the records with the abandonment of the first tie against Blackpool). Bobby was now 27 years old, and at the peak of his powers. He had made a significant contribution to the team's success, along with Don Revie and Bert Trautmann in particular, and each had earned their place in history. Bobby had become the first to score in consecutive FA Cup Finals at Wembley – and he'd only been in England 14 months.

Many older football fans remember the 1956 FA Cup Final as their first sighting of live football on television, although TV sets were in relatively short supply for the general populace. There are a wealth of stories about 'dozens of people' being gathered around small screens, within streets where only one or two families could afford the new luxury. Others saw pictures of the proceedings from pavements outside television shops, and it seems that the 1956 Final heralded the age when watching the Cup Final became a major TV event, at least in the north west of England. The following Monday, the team's 'homecoming' was the first outside broadcast by the fledgling commercial television station Granada, but the broadcast did not go to plan. Unfortunately, the team were delayed in departing from London Road (now Piccadilly) railway station on arrival in Manchester, and the crowds lining the streets on the journey to Albert Square were so large that further time was lost. In the end the team arrived at the town hall to meet Lord Mayor Thomas Regan some 30 minutes after the scheduled time, and just as the broadcast was due to go off air. Viewers, therefore, missed Roy Paul's triumphant words for the crowd. After the Lord Mayor's reception the team left for a function at Belle Vue, though Bert Trautmann was unable to take any further part in the celebrations because of the pain he was suffering. A couple of days later, the *Manchester Evening News* announced dramatically 'Trautmann: Neck broken'.

Bobby Johnstone's thoughts on his most famous goal were revealed many years later, in a retrospective radio interview granted to a regional station. 'Trautmann kicked a long ball, and Jack Dyson just flicked it on, and I was sort of in the outside-right position, running through, but, looking at it now on the TV when I actually see the replays, I must have anticipated that he was going to put it in the place where he did, because I was there first and just steered it past Gil Merrick in goals; he was the English goalkeeper at the time. The year before, when we lost, we were favourites, but this year we were second favourites. Birmingham were a big strong team and were doing well. Yet we were never in trouble; we played well. I'd had a lot of knee trouble near the end of the season, and actually played outside-right in that Final, which was a position I'd hardly ever played in my life, but the manager thought it might help my knee if I played out wide, that was fair enough, and I quite enjoyed playing there. Funnily enough, I managed to score the third goal in that game, so, you know, I think his decision was probably upheld at the end.'

* * * *

Bobby spent part of the close season back home in Selkirk before returning to Manchester for pre-season training. For the forthcoming season, Roy Allison could look forward to watching most of City's home games from the relative comfort of the director's box, as he had been given use of one of Bobby's players' complimentary tickets, though he would soon find out that that perk had certain drawbacks. Shortly after Bobby returned to Manchester, he rang Roy and made arrangements for them to go along to Old Trafford to watch Jack Dyson opening for Lancashire against Surrey. It was quite a little party. Besides Bobby and Roy, Ken Barnes and Roy Paul were there with a few others, although one or two players had other things to occupy them... Roy Clarke was busy with his sports shop, and Don Revie wasn't there either; as usual, he went off home straight after training. One social event that Don did manage to attend though was the party that was arranged to celebrate his Man of the Match award in the 1956 Cup Final. The party was held at a social club near Maine Road, and next door to a couple of semi-detached houses owned by City. The Revie's lived in one, and they will have been content to avoid the expense of a cab fare.

City's attractive football and their Cup exploits made them a popular bet to continue chasing the game's major honours, and having finished seventh and then fourth in the two seasons completed since Bobby's arrival, hopes were high that the team would push on and make a strong bid for the League Championship once the new season started. Bert Trautmann and Jimmy Meadows were still injured of course, and Revie remained at loggerheads with the club, but Johnny Hart was back in the side, and Billy McAdams was fit and in contention for a place. The temporary goalkeeping problem was resolved by the purchase of George Thompson from Preston North End, though this must have been a tremendous disappointment for the usual replacement, big John Savage. He had been Trautmann's loyal deputy and had kept goal in the four games that the German had missed during the previous three seasons – yet symptomatically for City around the time, just as he might have anticipated a good run in the side he had a foot injury. Thompson kept goal for 'Blues' in the traditional first team versus reserve team warm-up fixture, and they duly overwhelmed Maroons 4–0, helped by two goals from Bobby.

The season proper opened with a 1–5 defeat at Wolves, with a future City player, Jimmy Murray, scoring four times. The following Wednesday saw a 2–2 draw with Tottenham Hotspur, and Thompson's season ended at that point, 22 August. He had been heavily criticised, and whether he was genuinely injured or simply dropped from the team is not absolutely clear, but in any event John Savage now replaced him and held the spot until the return of Bert Trautmann in time for the Christmas fixtures.

Bobby had an unsettled start too, featuring in three different shirts, numbers 10, seven and then nine, within the first four games. He scored the first penalty of his career at Tottenham in that fourth match, which he took because Don Revie was out of the side. That match ended in a 2–3 defeat, as did the next at table-topping Luton Town, but he then missed six games due to injury and was replaced by Bill Spurdle. Bill had been unlucky to miss the Cup Final, of course, and he had not regained his place in the team as the new campaign had kicked-off. Ironically, Bobby's injury now gave him a chance to reclaim the number-seven shirt, and his first two games were wins, but the next four were lost and, even worse, no goals were scored. It was Bill's last spell in the first team; he had been at loggerheads with Les McDowall since the summer because he wanted to become a part-time player, which would allow him to help with the family business. McDowall declined, and Bill was soon moved on to Port Vale, where he played for just six months. When Vale were relegated to the Third Division South, he moved to nearby Oldham Athletic.

By early October Bobby was fit again and ready to return, but probably wished he hadn't been. He helped rectify the lack of goals – City scored three at Highbury – but the seven that Arsenal recorded rather overshadowed that positive. Another defeat followed, and by mid-October City were in something of a crisis. After 13 League games, only two had been won, and the League table showed that City were above only relegation-bound Charlton Athletic; there would be no sustained challenge for the League title this year. Bobby Johnstone had missed six of those 13 games and managed only one goal so far, and that a penalty. There must have been long odds about Bobby being the club's top scorer by the end of the season.

Late October saw Bobby return to Tyneside, where his previous League campaign had come to a premature end in a 1–3 defeat. This time City's luck changed, and Bobby scored to herald a turn-around in fortunes. City collected their first away points at their eighth attempt, and the following Wednesday night a crowd of over 30,000 turned out in very poor weather to see the FA Cup holders take on the League Champions in a unique Manchester 'derby' Charity Shield fixture at Maine Road.

United, who were technically the home team, offered to play the match at Maine Road given that Old Trafford was still without floodlights. City played well, although United won 1–0 in spite of goalkeeping difficulties. United's goalkeeper Wood was injured early in the game, and for a short spell he was replaced in goals by Duncan Edwards, at least until Gaskell, the young United 'keeper, who was aged just 15, could be summoned from the stands. All of this was in the days before substitutes were allowed, of course, which one might suppose is taking 'charity' rather too far, yet the evening's biggest mystery surrounded Bobby's 'goal', which was disallowed. Eyewitnesses saw Bobby, who was positioned around the edge of the penalty area, back-heeling the ball into the net, on the volley, and direct from a corner-kick! Ian Niven recalled the tumultuous applause in the ground quickly dying away, and that 'nobody knows to this day why that goal was disallowed'. The next night, the *Manchester Evening Chronicle* lead writer said 'I thought City deserved some reward for their storming finish, in which Johnstone was most unfortunate to have what looked like a perfect goal disallowed.' The following

Saturday, Bobby's goal against Sheffield Wednesday – another penalty – wasn't scrubbed from the records, and now both City and Bobby were on better form, though he was soon to lose another colleague from the Cup-winning side. Early November saw the long-threatened departure of Don Revie.

Besides the unfortunate Johnny Hart, Don Revie was another with good reason for apprehension at the signing of Bobby Johnstone in 1955. As a student of the game in the late 1940s, Revie understood how to switch the focus of play, and he believed that this could be devastating if an accurate, long, cross-field ball could be supplied, or, equally, where the shorter type of through-ball could be provided for an overlapping half-back or full-back to latch on to. He was critical (even throughout his later career) of what he saw as wasted passing, and he had no time for players who, however skilful, lost possession cheaply.

After a devastating ankle injury while he was at Leicester City in 1946, his return to first-team football saw him drop back, literally out of the front line, to provide a pivotal link between defence and attack. Arriving at Maine Road in 1951, later Revie was in the first team, while Johnny Williamson, then centre-forward in the reserves, decided one afternoon to lie back behind the other four forwards. This threw the opposition, and City's reserve team capitalised to the extent that they went 26 games undefeated. Williamson was convinced that Revie could adopt this approach in the first team, given his acknowledged passing skills, and he told Revie so. Later, the legendary Hungarian international side also used the deep-lying centre-forward in the shape of Nandor Hidegkuti and were triumphant against England at Wembley in 1953. Les McDowall, a man who had a great appetite for tactical innovation, decided to try this plan out at City, with Revie the focus, though Don himself initially had doubts about how the plan might operate at first-team level. He was concerned that the ball would be knocked over him, straight up to the forwards, and while he could lie deep easily enough, it was critical that the players in supporting roles gave him the ball, to feet, and made runs that he could exploit with his passing.

On the opening day of the 1954–55 season, and with a roll of the drums, City had trialled what became known as the Revie Plan, and they were soundly thrashed by Preston North End, who won 5–0. Revie thought this would be the end of the experiment, but McDowall was persistent, and for the next game Ken Barnes was promoted from the reserves and asked to provide specific support to Revie. He formed a linkage in providing the ball to Revie, in what is termed the 'water-carrier' role in the modern game. This seemed to do the trick, and Sheffield United were despatched 5–2. It seemed that Barnes's stamina and supplementary passing skill was key in support of Revie's role, which later became known as the Deep Revie Plan.

Much later in that season, in March 1955, Revie was the man to make way following Bobby Johnstone's arrival, and he missed the first two games that Bobby played – an amazing situation for a man just two months away from being chosen as Footballer of the Year. He was recalled to the side following Hart's broken leg, so one may quite reasonably take the view that Revie, and not Bobby Johnstone, was the main beneficiary of the serious injury to Hart. In any event, from among the quintet of Johnny Williamson, Johnny Hart, Paddy Fagan, Don Revie and

Bobby Johnstone, no more than three ever appeared together in the same City team. Throughout the time that both Johnstone and Revie were at the club, a period of around 20 months, there were recurring rumours that Revie was unsettled, was seeking a transfer and would be leaving imminently. Bobby's arrival definitely had an impact upon Don Revie's position as the focal point of Manchester City's tactical-based approach to the game, and there were further troubles too.

In the summer of 1955 the Revies had arranged a family holiday, their first for six years. The problem was that Revie's wife Elsie, a schoolteacher, did not start her annual holidays until late July, just as professional footballers were returning for pre-season training. Don believed that he had agreed a workable compromise with Laurie Barnett, City's trainer, who simply arranged for Revie to commence pre-season training two weeks before everyone else in the squad; Revie thought this would be the end of the matter. Les McDowall did not agree the arrangement though, but he did offer Revie the 'escape' option of travelling from his chosen destination (Blackpool) on a daily basis. Revie was unhappy with what he saw as a lack of trust, and so took unauthorised leave anyway, continuing to keep fit with his own training programme. Newspapers were soon full of the details of the episode, and McDowall, needing to be seen to be responding firmly, suspended Revie for two weeks. This meant a loss of pay (some £27) for the Revie family and further speculation about Revie's position.

At the time it was generally thought that McDowall saw Bobby as the better player – and Ken Barnes has said as much – although some of the other City players were not entirely convinced. In any event, the 1955–56 season kicked-off with a 2–2 draw at home to Aston Villa, with Revie playing in the number-nine shirt, and scoring a penalty, though this proved to be one of only four League goals in that season. He played exactly half of the 42 League games, not a good return for such a high-profile player, especially when one considers that this coincided with his reign as Footballer of the Year, and, further, that both Johnny Hart and Bill McAdams were unavailable with long-term injuries. Bobby's view about this state of affairs was that the unauthorised holiday was the main reason that Revie found himself on the periphery. In an unauthorised biography about Revie, published in 1990, Bobby is quoted as saying 'It was the beginning of the end – I don't think he [McDowall] ever forgave Don. I think he felt he had let him down, though Don was always straightforward and truthful about it. From then on, it was only a matter of time before he went. But he never said very much to me, he was quiet, a proper gentleman.'

At the end of the 1955–56 season, Revie had been extremely fortunate to gain a place in the Cup Final team, but he took full advantage of the situation and put in a Man-of-the-Match performance, dummying the ball brilliantly to allow Joe Hayes to put City into the lead after only three minutes. Ironically, by the time he was transferred in November 1956, it appeared that his Cup heroics had re-established him in the first team. He had dropped back into a midfield role and missed only two of the first 16 League games. But Revie was becoming concerned about City's erratic form and the amount of tactical tinkering from McDowall. Another probable factor was the chance of earning some money from a transfer fee. Revie often told Bobby and Ken Barnes that 'There's only one thing that will tell you whether you have been a good player, and that is how much you have in the bank.' Aged 29, Revie now left City for Sunderland for a fee of £24,000, which meant that City recouped practically all of the £25,000 they had paid Hull City some five years earlier.

Mainly remembered by Manchester City fans for his role in what was seen as a quite revolutionary plan at the time, Ken Barnes's view was that the whole business of plans was overdone anyway. 'Centre-halves had been used to playing one-on-one with a centre-forward, but with a deep-lying man they had no one to mark, and many were reluctant to leave their comfort zone to go and seek the centre-forward out. I never believed the Revie system was a great plan really, just something a bit different, though a deep-lying centre-forward and wing-half were involved. To me it was just common-sense football, but after this system came a succession of plans and we got bogged down with them.' Revie had scored 41 goals in 177 games for City, a solid contribution, and he later went on to a very successful career as a manager, a period that is well documented elsewhere.

The week after Revie's departure came a sweet match for Bobby, against the Cup Final foes from the previous season, Birmingham City. Bobby scored twice, but also had a blatant penalty appeal refused. A pitch-side reporter wrote 'he was about to score when he was up-ended on to his nose in the penalty area. No penalty was given, and the Scot spent a good deal of the time ruefully rubbing his knee and his face and glowering at the referee. His footwork in the second half was magical to a degree. Glory and loveliness have not yet passed entirely away from Moss Side. There are still players left who can draw staid, not to say arthritic, members bounding wildly out of their seats.' Bobby scored again that month against Portsmouth in a 5–1 win, but prior to that came another trip 'home' to Easter Road, when City travelled north to face Hearts in a Monday evening Floodlit match. The match was billed as a Cup-holders Challenge match between the Cup holders of the two countries, but it was played at Hibs' ground because Hearts still did not have their own floodlights. This was the second time Bobby had returned to Easter Road, having faced Hibs almost a year earlier, and this time City triumphed 4–3 in front of 18,000. The match programme records that City's form had recently improved: 'coinciding with Bobby's return to the team after his knee injury problems'.

In early December there was a Thursday night friendly match at Maine Road, a most unusual event, but one that Bobby enjoyed because the opposition were the Hungarian side formerly known as Red Banner. These were troubled times for that nation, following the unrest that had begun in Budapest only two months before. That uprising had been crushed by a Soviet invasion, and 200,000 refugees had fled the state, and so naturally the arrival of the soccer team in Britain had generated much interest, and a considerable wave of public sympathy. The club was now called the Magyar Physical Culture Club, or 'MTK' Budapest, and they fielded Sandor and other famous names from the historic 6–3 (Wembley) and 7–1 (Budapest) games against England. Bobby went head-to-head at centre-forward against 35-year-old Nandor Hidegkuti, probably the greatest exponent of the deep-lying centre-forward plan. While the result of this thrilling and romantic encounter is of little consequence, interestingly there are conflicting reports about the end of the game. At least one report records that Bobby equalised with six minutes left, to make the final score 3–3, though most authoratitive sources record the result as a 3–2 win for the Hungarians.

It was quite an eventful time at the club. Both Bert Trautmann and Thompson, the two goalkeepers, were now back fit and playing, and almost 7,700 paid to see Trautmann make his comeback for the reserves. Bobby and Ken Barnes had supposedly picked up minor injuries during the friendly, yet two days later Bobby scored a hat-trick against Chelsea in a 5–4 win, his second hat-trick for City. The following week Trautmann made his long awaited return to the first team. This match, against Wolves, was the first to be televised from Maine Road, with recorded highlights being shown later that night on BBC television. Bobby celebrated with another two goals, although it was quite evident that Trautmann had not fully recovered, and City lost 2–3. The next two fixtures were also lost, yet Les McDowall took most of the flak, with many City fans being critical of him for bringing his man back too early.

The year was concluded with a 3–2 win over one of the season's early in-form teams, Luton Town, who had now fallen off the pace and found City just one point behind them. Bobby didn't score in that game, but he went into the New Year as joint top scorer with Joe Hayes, quite an achievement given the start he had made. While they had scored 11 goals each, Joe had played four games more than Bobby. With the final game of 1956 played on Saturday 29 December, there was now a clear week before the next fixture, an FA Cup tie. There were no Football League games scheduled for the Hogmanay period, a busy time for most Scottish footballers, who were facing games on consecutive days. Bobby headed north knowing that, in this sense at least, he was playing in the right place.

Note

1. In later years, Bert Trautmann did concede that he had effectively committed a professional foul, before that term entered common usage. In his biography, published in 1990, he says 'In a way I was desperate to prevent George scoring. I hoped to get the ball, but as I dived into the ruck of players I knew he would get the ball before me. It was more instinctive than premeditated; I just grabbed his leg and held on. I had a better chance of saving a penalty than preventing a certain goal, so I went for it.'

CHAPTER 7

Downhill and the Low Road

*Bobby had high expectations of a third consecutive FA Cup Final, and 1957
began with what the press described as 'the game of the year'.*

The team travelled confidently up to Tyneside for the third-round FA Cup tie
against Newcastle United, and for the third Cup campaign in a row, Bobby would
have a key role. City played well and dominated much of the match. Ronnie
Simpson, the Newcastle 'keeper, was much busier than Bert Trautmann, who was
still returning to full fitness following a rather shaky spell. Bobby put City 1–0 up,
and soon after Roy Clarke turned away believing that he had made it two, but
Simpson made a miraculous save. Newcastle then equalised, but were grateful for
the replay, especially when Billy McAdams missed another great chance near the
end. In spite of the big billing, and a crowd of almost 58,000 on Tyneside, Maine
Road saw the outcome of the tie, in one of the greatest games ever to take place at
that stadium.

The following Wednesday a crowd just a dozen short of 47,000 assembled for a
2pm kick-off, and they saw City storm into a three-goal half-time lead, with Bobby
scoring the second with a header from a Roy Clarke cross. He later got his second
goal of the game, and his third of the tie, but incredibly by this point the game had
gone into extra-time. Newcastle had fought back magnificently to 3–3 in the second
half, earning the applause of all present. During the extra period Bobby had put
City 4–3 up, this time with a header from a McAdams cross, but Newcastle
continued to excel, and two late goals gave them a 5–4 win, though City almost
equalised when Jack Dyson hit a post almost on the final whistle. The next day the
newspapers declared that this match had demonstrated that the FA Cup was the
greatest sporting competition in the world, but that was scant consolation for City,
who were 'out' – there would be no hat-trick of appearances at Wembley for Bobby
and his teammates. While Bobby will have been delighted to have knocked yet
another three goals past Ronnie Simpson, he will have taken some stick too, with
his pal the one to walk off smiling this time. It had proved an unlucky 13th FA Cup
tie since Bobby had joined City, just before the 1955 quarter-final stage. Newcastle
were still the only side he'd lost to.

City's season, badly affected by FA Cup disappointment, never really picked up,
but Bobby wasn't going to let Cup woes get him down. He had made arrangements
to take Roy and Margaret Allison up to Selkirk for the weekend, and the following
Saturday, just a few days after that momentous Newcastle defeat, off they went.
Roy recalled 'City were at Sunderland, and we went on from there. He had a sporty
car, a red Sunbeam Talbot, and he took us to Selkirk in it.' Bobby travelled up with
the team, of course, while Ian Niven drove the car up to Roker Park. After the
match, Ian and his girlfriend returned home, but Roy and Margaret carried on to

Selkirk, Bobby now at the wheel. 'We met his mother and his sisters, and had a great weekend up there. We all had a night out, at a club, quite similar to a working men's club. It was tremendous, we all came out doing the hokey-cokey, and we had a great night.'

Bobby scored against Charlton Athletic in late January, but the next month began badly when Bobby had a very public and ill-timed fall-out with City. The next fixture brought a chance to avenge the earlier derby defeat at Old Trafford, but in the run-up the *Manchester Evening Chronicle* revealed that Bobby had rowed with the club over the allocation of tickets for the big match. On the day of the game, the *Chronicle* ran a front-page piece titled 'I've not asked to leave City – yet' and quoted Bobby. After the game, Les McDowall said 'I talked with Johnstone before the match, and so far as I am concerned the matter has been settled. It is likely, however, that we shall review the position regarding players' tickets, although we have always tried to meet their requests and have never had such trouble before.' But Bobby was not happy, and reporter Alf Clarke's interpretation was that the row masked the real cause, which was 'Johnstone's desire to play at inside-forward. That seems to be the discontent... he is not quite happy at Maine Road.'

Bobby had tried to buy some additional match tickets and was told that all reservable stand seats had sold out some time before. Clarke outlined how 'Players are allocated complimentary tickets and can buy more for friends... other players I spoke to had no complaints.' Les McDowall, who privately must have been seething, told Clarke 'It's a storm in a teacup but, unfortunately, before one of the most important games of the season.' Bobby played, but the game ended in a heavy home defeat for City, 2–4. Duncan Edwards scored the clincher 10 minutes from time, and Bobby suffered a 'knock' during the game. Over an unhappy weekend, he asked to go on to the 'available for transfer' list.

He recovered sufficiently to be included in the team that drew 2–2 at Aston Villa on the Monday night, before his transfer request was considered at the board of directors meeting on the Tuesday. Alan Douglas, the City chairman, had also spoken to Bobby before the derby, '...and I thought the whole matter was finished. The problem will come up before the board and we hope the whole situation will be cleared up.' Alf Clarke's view was that, if anything, Bobby needed to do some thinking. In an article that smacks of the 'party line', he felt it probable that 'Johnstone will be asked to explain some of his actions. He has stated that he received eight tickets when he in fact had 14, six of which were free. In addition, each player is given a top-priced season ticket.' Any merits that Bobby's stance may have had went unheard as the unsympathetic tones continued. In Wednesday night's *Evening Chronicle* the major debate overflowed on to the sports letters page, under the headline 'City should let Johnstone go'. One correspondent's view was that 'City have been troubled before with temperamental 'star' forwards – Revie, Broadis – and they were transferred. Johnstone is a magnificent player, and if he would put aside these tantrums... the sooner City would be back on the road to success. The club is more important than the individual.' Another contributor pointed out that Bobby was in danger of losing the support of his biggest allies. 'If Bobby Johnstone continues to grumble about playing out of position, and wanting more tickets for his friends, he will soon have no true friends left – the man on the terraces who helps pay his wages. A player of Johnstone's ability should be able to play anywhere.'

Ironically, by the time these letters were published, Bobby had already changed his mind, withdrawn his transfer request, and all was sweetness and light. According to Les McDowall, quoted in the same issue of the *Evening Chronicle*, he had also agreed to continue in the deep-lying centre-forward role! He retained his place in the side and scored the following Saturday, as City lost 1–4 against Blackpool, who were without Stanley Matthews through injury. Afterwards Eric Todd, also of the *Evening Chronicle*, suggested that Jack Dyson should be played as a deep-lying centre-forward – with Bobby Johnstone switched to inside-forward 'Before he forgets how to play there'. Perhaps Bobby did have an ally at the *Evening Chronicle* after all.

After the Blackpool game Bobby missed three games with fluid on the knee, and not surprisingly Jack Dyson was moved to centre-forward, with the transfer-listed Billy McAdams coming into the side for the trip to Sheffield Wednesday. No doubt Bobby was resting up in the warmth as City fans, returning home from South Yorkshire after the 2–2 draw, became trapped in coaches stranded on the Woodhead pass. Bobby was next reported as being 'back in training' according to McDowall, but he failed a fitness test and missed two more games, including Newcastle United's return, another defeat. Having already scored four times against the Geordies that season, Bobby might well have added to his tally. In his absence, Ken Barnes took and scored a penalty-kick and began a long and successful run as the penalty taker.

By now the alarm bells were ringing loudly, and City were grateful when Bobby returned to the team and scored another important hat-trick, this time against fellow-strugglers Cardiff City, though, contrary to McDowall's earlier statement about the deep-lying centre-forward role, Ken Barnes played at number nine. The hat-trick gave Bobby a total of 19 goals for the season, three of which had come in the FA Cup, and for the second time in his career he would end the season as his club's overall top scorer, though this time he scored most League goals, too.

At the beginning of April City left for a 10-day 'pep-up visit' to Eastbourne. The players travelled south by train from London Road station, and the *Evening Chronicle* printed a picture showing 'Bobby Johnstone's fiancée, Miss Heather Roden, of Hawick' waving the party off. This year the trip was not the usual prelude to the Cup Final, though it did embrace the fixture at Portsmouth, which City won 1–0. Returning home to two frustrating defeats, Alf Clarke of the *Evening Chronicle* described City as inept at this point, suggesting that they deserved to lose their First Division status. He had good reason – they had now lost three of the previous four home games, and City's position meant that there was plenty to play for. Points were needed from the last three games, all away from home, and the experiment with Ken Barnes at centre-forward hadn't worked; Bobby Johnstone was moved back to the number-nine shirt for the first of these, at Burnley. A surprising 3–0 win removed any possible threat of relegation, though Bobby aggravated his knee at Turf Moor and didn't regain his fitness in time to play again that season, meaning a third spell of absence from the team. With Jack Dyson now back at Lancashire, Billy McAdams saw the season out at centre-forward, his first game there for three years. The last two games were drawn, and four points from that unbeaten finale meant that safety was secured with six points to spare. This was far from the anticipated conclusion to the season; the signs were worrying. The 1956 Cup-winning side had started to fragment, and the team was not improving.

In May of 1957 Manchester City embarked on a post-season tour, and for the third successive year they played in West Germany. This time the tour started in Spain with a match against Barcelona, and to get things off to a flying start Bobby scored almost straight from the kick-off with a massive lob that soared over the head of Ramallets, the Spanish international 'keeper. Although City lost 2–3, Ken Barnes and Steve Fleet both retain clear memories of his wonderful goal, and also a special trip out. Ken recalled 'I played at Barcelona, at their old ground, but we also got the opportunity to go along and have a look at the Nou Camp being built. Bobby's goal was like that Pele shot, except it went in. They said on the telly, when Beckham scored that goal [against Wimbledon], that we'd never seen anything like it before, but I f****n 'ad.' The itinerary then saw City play three games in Germany, including defeats by a Frankfurt Select and then Borussia Dortmund, either side of a 6–3 win against Werder Bremen. To round off, it was back to the Spanish coastal tourist resort of Lloret de Mar for a 9–0 win of dubious merit, before the return to England. A couple of weeks after the return from Spain, Roy Paul, the captain and one of the key members of the Cup-winning side, left City, aged 37, to return home to South Wales. From there he commuted to his new post as player-manager of Worcester City.[1]

Over the previous few years an important technological advance had been taking place, as players tried out the new 'continental-style' football boots. There were variations, of course, but essentially it was from around the mid-1950s that the traditional style of football boot began to be superseded. More modern, lightweight boots, of slipper-style, had been becoming much more widely available. These featured sides cut to below the ankle, improved support to the lower part of the Achilles tendon, aluminium screw-in studs, and a complete lack of steel toecaps! Back in 1955, Roy Paul had tried some out while away with the Welsh international squad, and he had deemed them '...great. They put yards on my speed, and made ball control much easier.' He had been allowed to wear them while representing his country, and was seen to move with 'a nimbleness not seen from him previously this season'. Though this sounds suspiciously like advertising copy, one journalist felt that the failure to embrace such technology typified the way the British game had stood still. Charles Buchan's authoritative football magazine assessed the situation in one of its famed monthly publications: 'it was only actually seeing the South American and Continental ballet-type [sic] boots that had forced us into changing our ideas... for years our players have trudged through match after match, in reinforced dreadnoughts which took several games to 'break-in'. Speed and ball-control were reduced by this footwear.' Bobby and his colleagues had been fortunate to have access to these new products – boot suppliers were more than happy to be associated with successful FA Cup finalists, and there were further connections, too. Bert Trautmann had an association with the founder of the German-company Adidas, and it is thought that Bert was the first player to wear the new boots in

England. Moreover, Roy Clarke's successful sports shop was the first stockist in the north west of England. By the time of the 1956 Cup Final, several of the City players, Bobby Johnstone included, were seen in boots much more modern that those worn just the year before. Ken Barnes recalls some players bringing back new kit to try out from that Spain trip too, 'As a matter of fact, I was one of the first to bring them back, these boots without toecaps, it was around the time of the Spain trip. We'd all had the hard, steel toecaps to play in, and it's amazing now when you think back to the boots that the likes of Bobby and I used to play in, and the weight of the ball, and the kit we wore. Just think of the great players over previous years, with great skills, playing with those bloody steel toecaps!'

It is not clear to what extent all players benefitted from the improvements, but it is conceivable that better footwear improved things significantly. However, Steve Fleet, who in the late 1950s succeeded John Savage in the monumental task of trying to dislodge Bert Trautmann from the first team, remembers Bobby's incredible ability with a football, steel toecaps or not. 'Being a 'keeper, the thing I always remember about Bobby was in training, when the players would try and chip us; we used to have little bets on it. He was the only one who could do it – he could chip me and Bert from outside the box in a warm-up, he'd even tell you which side he was putting it. He did it against John Savage as well, and he was 6ft 5in, the biggest player we'd ever had at that time.' The newer boots were kinder on the foot, too, but still needed 'breaking-in'. Players used to get juniors and mates to wear boots in for them, and Bobby once asked Ian Niven to help. 'It was the first time I'd played in anything other than the old-fashioned, leather hard-toe type. I was playing for the Rusholme City Supporters' Club, and I remember scoring in a 1–0 win and bragging about these new boots, because I so rarely scored.' Stories about players spending weeks softening new boots by urinating on them and soaking them in Dubbin now began to recede into history.

* * * *

Since arriving in Manchester, Bobby's domestic life had been rather unsettled, and there were concerns that his lifestyle might be affecting his football. After spending some time living in the Lord Lyon pub, in the interests of his football career he moved to a more stable family environment, lodging with the Niven family, at No.165 Hamilton Road in Longsight, around two miles from Maine Road. Ian had been abroad for some time after the war and had settled down to married life fairly quickly after returning to England. He and his wife soon had two youngsters and he recalled that his decision about Bobby was perhaps a little impulsive: 'I never discussed it with my wife, I just went home and told her. That was nice of me wasn't it? Imagine, "we're getting a lodger, dear, meet Bobby Johnstone." She was a City supporter – but not that much!' Bobby actually settled in very well and became close to the Niven family. Ian's son, Ian (Jnr.), a lad of around six or seven at the time, used to enjoy his Sunday morning kick-about with Bobby on nearby Crowcroft Park, and he took his first steps as an entrepreneur by getting Bobby to sign autographs, which he used to sell to his schoolmates for a penny a time.

'When he lived with us at Hamilton Road, he was one of the few players who had a car, he had a lovely Sunbeam. In the summer, he often drove back to Scotland, and one year a group of us went and stayed in Edinburgh for a few days. We stayed on the top floor of a large hotel, behind Princes Street, around the Royal Mile. Henry Smith had arranged it, he knew a lot of the police detectives and it was a really good weekend, you know, gentlemen only. A lot of the party were in the CID, but they were nearly all blues and some of them were freemasons too. It was great when Bobby was here; we had good times, and he was as good as gold as a lodger.'

Bobby had long been aggrieved about his financial lot as a footballer and he still talked about his experiences with Harry Swan in his days at Hibernian. He had now been with City for over two years, and the whole debate about wages had moved on briskly. Then, only around a quarter of professional footballers had been receiving the maximum wage, and many fringe and even some regular first-team players were paid on a match-by-match basis, negotiating their own reserve-match fees and summer contracts. Since then, the players' own agitations had heightened the profile of the issues involved, and now broad ranges of opinions about footballers' contracts, and in particular the maximum wage, were being openly expressed. Things seemed to be improving, but slowly. Basic pay for the previous 39-week season had been £15 per week, but new plans for 1957–58 would see wages uplifted to £17 per week, with £14 during the summer months. These were welcome moves for many players, but the dam was starting to burst – at most Football League clubs, recognised first-team players now invariably earned the maximum, the obvious corollary being a minimal pay differential between the very best and their less-gifted colleagues.

The increased campaigning and publicity from the PFA began to expose evidence that the founding principle of the maximum wage, in place since the inception of the Football League in 1888, was being seriously undermined. While the key focus was around wages, other aspects of the arrangements between players and clubs were, if anything, even murkier. On being transferred between clubs, for example, players had an entitlement to a £10 'signing-on fee', and this in particular was routinely abused. During research for this project, several former professional players freely revealed that it was common practice to agree to transfer between clubs where new employers were prepared to make it 'worth their while'. This was the basis of at least one subsequent career move by young centre-forward Bert Lister, and Johnny Hart recalled an occasion when a south Yorkshire club approached City about his availability: 'Rotherham came in for me, when I was player-coach for the A team at City, but I said I'd only go if there was a few bob in it for me. I was just about the only player that Bob Smith, the previous chairman, called by his first name. He told me once that I could stay at City as long as I liked, so I said "put that in my contract then!"' Among the more creative strategies used to supplement players' wages were devices such as 'programme money', from the sales of match-day souvenirs and brochures, and, in the case of England centre-forward Tommy Lawton, the offer of none-too-taxing employment. It had been quite a surprise when Lawton, who in 1947 was the England centre-forward, transferred from Chelsea to Third Division Notts County. His earnings from an additional job, effectively a sinecure, alongside the pay of a footballer, were the bait.

The Football League established a commission to investigate the proliferation of evidence about illegal payments to players. When it reported the findings in April 1957, the League was hit by scandal. Sunderland, alleged to be among the leading 'payers', were dealt with harshly. Five of their players were suspended *sine die*, and four directors were similarly punished, with the club receiving a fine of £5,000. The PFA's inflammatory response to the League, and the banning of their members, was to ask all players to volunteer information about 'under-the-counter' payments. It was hoped that this would embarrass the League into recognising the extent of the leakage and the clubs' complicity. This was achieved.

For the players, wage increases for the coming season were welcome news, of course. In addition, bonuses were to be doubled to £4 for a win and £2 for a draw, although the League, seemingly alone, were concerned that if bonus payments went much higher, say to £10 and £5, this could be too big an inducement and may lead to unfair tactics. Presumably their concern was that players would agree to draw, with a fiver all round! However, the key change within the improved package was the potential for successful clubs to be able to pay more to pools of players for finishing top of the First Division – called 'talent money'. It was envisaged that, in future, clubs finishing in positions down as low as eighth might be able to make such payments. For reaching the FA Cup Final, awards could be up to £200 per player, with win bonuses for each individual round along the way. In an example quoted in one publication, a Cup-winning player could expect to be permitted to earn almost £300 in additional appearance and talent money during a successful Cup run, while a man playing for a side knocked out in the third round, earning no bonus of course, would collect just one £5 appearance fee.

Bobby Johnstone will have been delighted that the game was moving forward in such a manner; the Manchester City squad had all received £10 17s 6d (£10.87) for reaching the 1955 Cup Final, a basic £12 less tax. No additional bonus fell due because the team lost! The following year the team earned the same weekly wage, but this time they had enjoyed a £20-a-head 'win bonus' that contributed to, if not wholly funded, their celebrations. After the second final, the players learned that the City board had approached the FA asking for permission to present each player with a commemorative gift (an inscribed gold watch was mentioned), but the FA turned this down. It would appear that, having competed in two successive FA Cup Finals, and received a pittance, again Bobby Johnstone would feel somewhat left out financially.

For their part, the League simply wanted to maintain the maximum wage principle in the belief that it was necessary to prevent powerful clubs monopolising the best players. Such a situation would negatively affect the wider game, and they saw themselves as maintaining the integrity of the whole of the League, without favour to any of its 92 elements. Laudable, without doubt, but it is difficult to counter the view that a system in which there was little financial advantage to be gained in moving from a Third Division club to a First Division neighbour was fundamentally flawed. The improved 'benefits' package could be described as a fudge, a sop to the discontent among the players. It apparently solved the intractable problem of retaining the maximum wage as a basic tenet, while conceding some ground in allowing improved rewards for high achievers.

One might be tempted to ask what the point of all this was, and some did. An article by David R. Jack,[2] a columnist for the *Empire News* and the *Sunday*

Chronicle, suggested that the maximum wage ought to be completely abolished. Jack argued that 'Football's number-one headache', namely the 'under-the-counter payment', would be disposed of. Further, complaints from players about unpaid benefits would also disappear, because these issues could be dealt with contractually, and 'star' players could more visibly earn 'star' rewards. There is evidence that this latter point in particular might well have appealed to Bobby, while one can never be certain, it seems that he probably benefitted from the odd 'under-the-counter' transaction himself, and contemporaries believe that Bobby was promised things that didn't materialise during his time at Manchester City. Both Steve Fleet and Bert Lister vividly recall Bobby emerging angrily from a discussion with a City director and giving them some blunt advice: '"Always get things in writing," Bobby said, and he told us that a few times.' If nothing else can be proven, it illustrates that this whole area, fraught with the potential for under-hand activity, jealousies and even bribery, needed to be clarified by openness.

In refuting the League's point about the wealthy clubs garnering all of the best players, Jack's article was quite clear – that happened already. He pointed out that even with the maximum wage in place, Newcastle United had always seemed capable of recruiting better players than Northampton Town. He went on to warn that, while the best players were legally prevented from 'bettering themselves', it was inevitable that illegal ways would be found to cash-in on talents. He concluded that removing the maximum wage would see football 'better off, and without the unsavoury scandals such as the recent Sunderland inquiry.'

Other noted journalists of the time supported the League's view: Roland Allen conceded that while some leading players were underpaid 'Many more are grossly overpaid at £24 weekly' and John McAdam of the *Manchester Evening Chronicle* felt that only the elite deserved more. By his reckoning, 'only three of over 1,000 players deserve more than the maximum wage: Stanley Matthews (of Blackpool), John Charles (Leeds United) and Tom Finney (Preston). Reward the very few... Matthews earns £15 per week – a labourer can earn that!' John Thompson of the *Daily Mirror* believed that 'The players' campaign was undermining the dignity of the national game... ultimately they will probably have the players' paradise of which they dream. Whether any such victory would be for the good of the game is a point we will not discuss.' In support of the maximum wage, the League expressed concerns that its abolition would lead to 'poor teamwork' as, for example, envious colleagues at Blackpool FC would fall out with Stanley Matthews and perhaps refuse to pass him the ball because he was earning more! While these particular views were rather naïve, the League more prophetically questioned the ability of the likes of Blackpool, Burnley and Luton Town, among others, to afford increased costs on relatively small gates, and speculated as to where players from such clubs might gravitate. 'Eventually, around a dozen clubs would dominate English football.' The PFA, now led by Jimmy Hill, were not too concerned about that, and they continued their campaign against the system under which players were usually granted one-year contracts, unless they were unlucky. They demanded the right for players to negotiate fixed-term contracts, at rates of pay agreeable to both themselves and the clubs. Progress was clearly being made, yet the 1950s were to end with the retain and transfer system still in place.

It was always possible to earn additional income from outside of the game of course, and some players supplemented their income with secondary jobs, or even their own businesses. Some of Bobby's less bashful and perhaps more photogenic colleagues enjoyed product endorsement deals. In one case, which seems strange in retrospect, Bert Trautmann was pictured smoking the Co-operative Wholesale Society's brand of cigarette. Bobby Johnstone would have looked less than natural relaxing with a smoke, tobacco being one vice that he always avoided.

While Bobby was still residing with the Nivens, one day Ian was mildly embarrassed on discovering, quite accidentally, what Bobby was earning. 'In the hallway, I found one of Bobby's empty wage envelopes, it was about £14 basic or something in the summer. He said he wasn't bothered because he'd thrown it away, but he told me that he sent £5 of that home to Selkirk. I was earning £7 per week then, which was an average wage, not generous. I kept £2, and gave my wife £5 to run the home. Bobby didn't pay us, but when my wife asked me for more money, I had to halve my £2 to £1! That was my love for City and Bobby Johnstone. I wouldn't think of charging him – I could manage it.'

Life as a footballer was a risky one, and by now Bobby was struggling continually with his legs, and he knew he couldn't last forever. Quite naturally, he wanted the security that a higher wage and a longer contract might bring. But there was little hope of a longer contract. Steve Fleet again 'There was none of this "how many years?" like now. In our days, you might have to start pulling your finger out around March, before the retained list came out. If you'd had a couple of injuries you might not even be on it, unless the club wanted a fee. The club wrote to you, but they waited until after the last game. The letter would come in the post, and it just said "Services no longer to be retained." You'd have to ring Cliff Lloyd up.'[3]

One contracted 'perk' that the players did receive was two complimentary season tickets, and Bobby had given one of his, made out to the non-existent Mrs R. Johnstone, to Roy Allison. Roy had relished this at first, but he soon moved back out on to the terraces during the previous season. He had not enjoyed sitting next to Mrs Revie and Mrs Paul one bit, because he couldn't shout the odds and give vent to his feelings in the same way; he had to watch his language. Roy intended to use Bobby's ticket for the new 1957–58 season, which would prove tremendously exciting but, again, that seat remained empty for most games: Manchester City's erratic form might have driven a saint to swear. City were much in demand and would play a total of 19 friendly fixtures, though most of these were played during the actual playing season. Pre-season, there were a couple of games between the first and reserve teams, and it was usual for City to open their gates to the public for these practice matches. The few thousand who could be bothered to attend had their first sighting of the new roof over the Kippax Street terraces. In the second game Jack Dyson, Bobby's goalscoring partner from the 1956 Final, broke a leg in a collision with Bill Leivers, which kept him out for many months. The only other pre-season fixture saw a short trip to Holland to play Twente Enschede, and Bobby played brilliantly, scoring twice in a 4–1 win. Roy Warhurst, brought in from Birmingham City to try to fill the void left by Roy Paul, made his debut in that match, and he later described Bobby's performance that night as the greatest he ever saw. The new half-back said 'Bobby Johnstone was the greatest footballer I ever played with or against. I saw Britain's best, but there was nobody to compare with Bobby when he felt like turning it on, not even Raich Carter, Peter Doherty, Tom Finney, Billy Steele or Stanley Matthews. They couldn't touch him.'

The season proper was a strange one, even by Maine Road standards. It had been scheduled to open with a home game against Sheffield Wednesday, but this was postponed due to an influenza outbreak in the Yorkshire camp. The season began in late August with a 3–2 away win at Chelsea, and by this time only five of the Cup-winning side were available for selection. The next game saw a 1–4 reverse at Old Trafford, so it was early September before many City fans had a first glimpse of their heroes, as they faced Chelsea again in an evening match. There was disappointment in the crowd that Chelsea's new sensation, Jimmy Greaves, was absent, but the game certainly did not lack incident.

City recorded their first double of the season, but the match is more notable for the fact that Bobby Johnstone was sent off for the only time in his career. Bobby's opinion was that a Chelsea inside-forward was jostling his mate Ken Barnes rather too roughly, and he advised his mate to 'stand off him a bit, then run and hit him!' Apparently, the referee overheard this and sent off Bobby for inciting foul play, although other reports state that the referee despatched him for bad language. He ran from the pitch and passed the bench, with Les McDowall simply assuming that he had come off to change his boots! A couple of minutes later, finding him in the bath, the manager listened as Bobby explained that the referee's decision was wrong, and he was sure that he would try to even things up. At that, they both heard the sound of a Chelsea man's studs (right-back Ian MacFarlane) entering the away dressing room. He too had been sent off. Johnstone was fuming and told the press 'If I am penalised, I shall seriously consider giving up football.' The team didn't seem to suffer too badly though, going on to win 5–2, with the remaining forwards scoring all of the goals. It was noted, 'the speed, enthusiasm and skill of the City attack without ace schemer Johnstone was a revelation'.

In the same month, City made their first award to a player under the new scheme of benefits and bonuses authorised by the Football League. The awards were not compulsory, of course, but Roy Clarke received £1,000, marking his 10 years' service. Bobby played the next three League games, a defeat at Forest in Nottingham, and then a couple of routine home wins against Preston North End and Portsmouth, scoring in the latter game. The 2–1 win was more remarkable for the fact that Bobby's fellow-Scot Big Dave Ewing scored his only goal in over 300 first-team appearances for City.[4] While the results were routine, these games saw the introduction of another plan, codenamed the 'M' plan, that initial referring presumably to either its inventor McDowall or key component Keith Marsden. Initially an inside-forward, the previous season Marsden had enjoyed a successful nine-game spell deputising for the injured Ewing in the centre of defence and this plan developed that theme. Marsden took a much deeper position, playing in a defensive role alongside Ewing, in a manner that was a forerunner of the twin centre-halves concept. After the two home wins, the 'M' show took to the road for two away games. These coincided with Bobby Johnstone's absence from the side through injury (he was not suspended following the Chelsea incident) and both were humiliating defeats, 1–6 at Preston and 2–9 to West Bromwich Albion. In the second game, Marsden was injured, although after two such disastrous results, things couldn't continue. Bobby was now fit to return, and the 'M' Plan was abandoned. Keith Marsden never played in City's first team again.

With Bobby restored to the team, City thrashed Spurs 5–1, with Johnstone and Hayes scoring two each in what was widely acknowledged as a superb performance. The next game was another heavy defeat, 0–4 at Birmingham, and the only game in which City failed to score all season. After that opening day win at Chelsea, the Sky Blues had now lost six consecutive away games and failed to capitalise on their good start. However, in football, just as one door closes another one opens, and after the trouncing at Birmingham Billy McAdams took up the number-10 shirt vacated by Marsden and used it 'up front' where it belongs, and to devastating effect. He scored in each of the next 10 League games, rounding off with two against Everton, a match in which Ken Barnes famously scored a hat-trick of penalties. This extremely rare feat has only been accomplished three times in the history of the Football League, yet, amazingly, Bobby had seen a teammate achieve this once before. Right at the start of the decade, Eddie Turnbull had scored three penalties during a Scottish League match against Celtic, and indeed 'Ned' had gone one better; he had topped off his performance with a further goal from open play. Is it feasible that any other player, or perhaps match official or even a spectator, has twice witnessed this deed in British first-class football?

Throughout Billy McAdams's tremendous 10-match scoring run, Bobby played brilliantly at times, notably at Blackpool in a 5–2 win, yet he failed to score a goal. During the corresponding 10-game spell, Ken Barnes scored seven times, although most were penalties. There must have been something in the water at the time, because Barnes was not a prolific scorer, managing a grand total of only 19 League goals during his entire 12-year spell at City; incredibly it was only the second time that Bobby Johnstone had ever gone 10 consecutive matches without scoring!

City were also busily engaged in a series of Floodlit friendly matches during McAdams's golden spell, and so he didn't score in every match that City actually played. Friendly matches occupied all four of the Monday nights during the November, and on three occasions the opposition was from Edinburgh. Firstly, City travelled north and won 5–3 at Tynecastle (Bobby enjoyed scoring twice there) before they faced Coventry City. On the third Monday, Hibs were the visitors to Maine Road, but Bobby, plus Barlow and Fagan, were rested, and so Bobby missed this chance to play for City against his old team. For Hibernian, Lawrie Reilly and Gordon Smith – again – missed out, with Roy Pheonix, Bobby's replacement, scoring the game's only goal. The following week City were defeated 2–5 at Easter Road, and yet again Smith failed to appear! An article written at the time criticised some teams for offering their fans less than top-class fare, dressed as 'floodlit matches'. The suggestion was that the novelty was wearing off, and clubs needed opponents that were capable of filling the house in 'floodlight, daylight or candlelight'. The moral for those starting to experience low crowds for such events was said to be obvious. 'Attractive football will always fill the grounds. A few lamps on pylons never will.'

Billy McAdams's post-war record of scoring in 10 consecutive First Division matches during a season stands to this day. His story is a peculiar one, pre-dating Bobby's time in Manchester. In December 1953 City became the first club prepared to pay a five-figure fee to bring an Irish footballer over to England, when they paid £10,000 to sign Billy from Distillery. He made his Football League debut early in 1954 and scored against a Sunderland side featuring one of his heroes, Len Shackleton. Later that year, in October, Manchester City accepted an invitation to play a floodlit friendly match against the Third Division South side Millwall as part of a series of games played under the newly improved lights at The Den. Millwall were one of the teams leading the campaign to introduce floodlit football across the Football League, to both excite crowds and help alleviate the sort of fixture congestion that badly affected many clubs. In Scotland at the time, of course, Bobby Johnstone was playing for Hibernian, forerunners in the Scottish version of the same campaign. Sadly for McAdams, during this game he collided awkwardly with the wall around the perimeter of the pitch and twisted his back, though the severity of the injury was not immediately apparent.

In fact, Billy carried on playing for around two months, and on 3 November he played for Northern Ireland at Windsor Park, Belfast, against Scotland. In this match he had his first sight of Bobby Johnstone, and, having put Ireland into a 2–1 lead, he saw Bobby equalise for Scotland with around 20 minutes left. Eventually McAdams was forced to seek specialist help for his back problem, and soon after he had an operation, meaning five weeks lying on it. The specialist felt that the surgical procedure to rectify a 'slipped disc' injury had not been entirely successful, and he advised Billy that his playing days were over. However, the Irishman fought his way back to fitness, and by the beginning of the 1956–57 season, having missed all of the two FA Cup runs, he was back and ready for selection. Perhaps Les McDowall thought that Billy's game was too similar to Bobby Johnstone's, who by now had been at the club well over two years, because during that 1956–57 season Billy McAdams played in only 12 League games, 10 of which were when Johnstone was unavailable. In fact, they lined up with each other just twice in the League, and in the two FA Cup games against Newcastle.

Jack Dyson's injury gave Billy McAdams a way back into the team, and Billy and Bobby began to play regularly together over the next two seasons, scoring 34 League goals between them, although the only time they both scored in the same League game was in a heavy defeat at Leicester. McAdams's best season for City came later, in 1959–60, when he played 31 games and scored 21 goals. Subsequently, he found his chances limited again, this time due to the arrival of Denis Law, and so he moved to Bolton in September 1960. That year he scored a hat-trick for Northern Ireland against West Germany at Windsor Park, before moving to join up with his old playing colleague Don Revie at Leeds. After a short spell in Yorkshire, he finished his football League career at Barrow in Cumbria, although as late as 1968 he was still suffering serious back problems, and had just spent a year out of the game. He continued to live in Barrow after his career ended, and in 1993 Manchester City played a testimonial match for him there, after it emerged that Billy had been struggling against a debilitating illness. He died in October 2002 and his ashes were scattered on the pitch during City's last season at Maine Road. His goalscoring achievement remains in the record books, though it has since been matched by Ron Davies of Southampton and Jermaine Defoe of Bournemouth in the lower Divisions, while John Aldridge of Liverpool also achieved the feat in the top Division, his effort spanning two seasons.

* * * *

Shortly after McAdams's record-breaking spell, Bobby scored twice in a 5–4 win against Wednesday in Sheffield, and then the Christmas fixtures twinned City with Burnley. Naturally, City lost one day and won the next, with Paddy Fagan scoring on both days. A derby draw (2–2) closed the year, and, as usual, FA Cup fever heralded the dawn of a new year. City were to play a strong West Bromwich Albion side, and fans will have been wondering which way things might go for this unpredictable City side; very few would have forecast just how badly this would turn out though, as a 1–5 defeat quickly ended any dreams of another trip to Wembley. Bobby scored the following week, in a 1–1 draw at Nottingham Forest, but to say that form was erratic would be an understatement. The Cup exit, and the fact that there were only two League games scheduled for January anyhow, meant a couple of blank dates, so during the following week City played a private trial game against an England XI at Edgeley Park, Stockport, as part of the national team's build-up to the forthcoming World Cup. Quite how graciously Bobby took part in this less than prestigious event is unclear, but towards the end of the month he received tremendous news about his own nation's intentions for that tournament. He had earned a recall to the Scottish representative scene and was invited to a trial match, at which he might stake his claim for a place in the 1958 Scotland World Cup squad.

February's two away games were at Tottenham and Leicester. Early in the month the *Manchester Evening Chronicle's* Monday night sport page gave equal billing to Bobby's fight to overcome a slight groin strain, which had caused him to withdraw from the Scottish trial game in Edinburgh that night, and Manchester United's preparations for their European Cup tie against Red Star of Belgrade, scheduled for the Wednesday. News of Bobby's recovery, and his inclusion in the now unchanged City side, was totally overshadowed by the appalling news of the Munich air disaster. 'The vast majority of supporters want the weekend's fixtures postponed,' declared the *Chronicle* later in the week, but the FA had announced that fixtures would go ahead. City, who thought they had gone 2–1 up, found the linesman flagging against Colin Barlow and got thrashed 1–5 at White Hart Lane in a match where all players wore black armbands.

In mid-February City's game at home to Birmingham was postponed due to bad weather, and at the same time, according to Eric Todd, City were offering to assist their neighbours' rebuilding efforts by listening to offers from United for Paddy Fagan, John McTavish and Ron Pheonix. Fagan, Bobby's Cup-Final teammate, said he would like to go to United, his chances having been limited since the arrival of Ray Sambrook from Coventry, although in the end he stayed until early 1960. Then came the second February away game at Leicester, and incredibly the outcome was even worse: a 4–8 defeat! Bobby scored an early headed goal on a pitch covered with both sand and snow, but he also contrived to shoot wide from eight yards. Later, as City's fortunes dipped horrendously, Bobby put the ball on to the roof of the stand from a corner by Fagan. Ken Barnes also scored, and this proved to be the only time when Ken and Bobby (with two) both got on to the score sheet in a League game, though it's difficult to picture even those two celebrating too loudly under the circumstances.

Bobby was still a bachelor of course, and he enjoyed the range of social opportunities a large city had to offer. He was still close to Ken Barnes, although some of the other members of the Cup-winning side were now starting to break up. One of their favourite haunts was the Cromford Club, in Manchester's city centre.[5] Ken recalls 'It was down Market Street, a little cul-de-sac on the right-hand side. It was well run, and Bobby and me had our own little spot. The manager there was a United fan, and we used to go on a Saturday night. It was a nice club, selective and properly run, with proper doormen.' One of Bobby's favourite ways to spend a Friday night was to go to the greyhound racing at White City and have a bet with his mate Roy Allison. Margaret Allison recalls the lads coming back to Droylsden together if City were at home; there Bobby could relax and get a good night's rest. 'In the old days they would go to Salford dogs on a Friday night, and Bobby would often sleep over here in Droylsden, and then go in for treatment to his knees the following morning. Roy would take him in. They also liked to go to Belle Vue dogs, sometimes on a Wednesday or a Saturday night.' Roy recalled that they occasionally bumped into Andy Black at Belle Vue, Bobby's boyhood hero, who by this time had retired from football and was running The Tatton Arms, a public house near Manchester Airport.

In late February, City publicly denied that they had virtually refused Bobby the opportunity to play for Scotland in the World Cup tournament in Sweden because they wanted him on their planned close-season tour of Canada and the US. In a rather peculiar denial, Les McDowall seems to claim that, while the club had no problem with the players competing in the World Cup, there was a difficulty in that the players had contractual obligations elsewhere! Quoted in the *Evening Chronicle*, he said 'Obviously we must take our strongest possible side on tour, and so we wrote to the FAs of Scotland, Wales, and Ireland assuming that they might wish to call on Johnstone, Cliff Sear and Billy McAdams for the World Cup.'

Back on the domestic front, and after criticism of the team's defending, Dave Ewing was dropped for the next game, against Blackpool, and Les McDowall was said to be deciding between Bobby Johnstone and Ken Barnes as to who would be made captain. Ken Barnes was evidently more suited to that task, and indeed it was Barnes that led City as they scored four again – and this time it was enough, as Blackpool were despatched 4–3. The team had scored nine goals in the previous three games; unfortunately the 16 conceded meant that just these two points were gained.

March saw the return of Jack Dyson to playing action. He managed a couple of run-outs with the A and reserve teams, before the devastating news of a second broken leg while playing in a Lancashire Senior Cup match against Barrow at Maine Road. At the same time, plans were well in hand for the Jimmy Meadows testimonial scheduled for mid April – stark evidence both of the frailty of limbs and the resultant uncertainty. Footballers simply never knew how or when their career might end. Bobby and Jack Dyson, the cricket-lovers, had both scored in the 1956 Cup Final, but they would never play together again.

The topsy-turvy season continued through March, where a surprise draw was gained at Molineux against a Wolves side that would soon be crowned Champions. This point preceded wins against Leeds United (1–0) and, on Easter Saturday, Bolton, where Bobby had a header cleared off the line early in the game. This was the first time that City had kept consecutive clean sheets for two years, though the achievement may have been aided by the postponement of City's Good Friday match at Newcastle because of a waterlogged pitch.

On Easter Monday the 2–1 home win against Newcastle proved to be Bobby's last game of the season. City dominated the first half of the match, with United 'nowhere' according to the *Evening Chronicle*, but after he pulled a knee muscle during the second half, the visitors came back well, had two goals disallowed, and were unfortunate to lose. The injury kept Bobby out of the next game, against Sunderland, when Johnny Hart deputised in the deep-lying role. Hart, making his first appearance at Maine Road in 20 months, was welcomed on to the Maine Road pitch along with another old favourite, Sunderland's Don Revie. With local newspapers speculating on which of City's two teams might be the first to reach 100 goals for the season (the reserves, on 97, were three nearer than the first team), Bobby was now declared unfit for the rearranged Monday night match at Newcastle, a 1–4 defeat. Bobby didn't recover his fitness and also missed the last two games, including the victory at Everton. Here, characteristically two down in two minutes, City rallied similarly and won 5–2, with Ken Barnes scoring his 11th goal of the season; these included nine penalties, of which four were against Everton! Incidentally, that same day Billy Meredith passed away. Billy, who scored City's first ever FA Cup Final goal in 1904, had seen only four City men manage it since.

This was the story of that most amazing season, when City scored 104 goals but conceded 100,[6] a trick that no other Football League team has ever performed. City managed just four clean sheets all season, and so this meant that *both* sides had scored in all but five of City's 42 League games. Yet City had finished a creditable fifth in the First Division, and it is no coincidence that crowds were flocking to see a brand of football that featured goals in abundance – at both ends of the park. Sadly, defeat on the last day of the season, against Aston Villa, denied City a top four, or even third place, which would have been their highest finish since winning the Championship in 1936–37. More significantly for the players, the opportunity to gain some serious 'talent money' was missed; the amount that clubs were allowed to pay their players had doubled under the 1957 arrangements agreed between the PFA and the Football League. It was now permissible to make payments down to the fifth place occupied by City, but the total in the pool for distribution among the players was just £220.

In reviewing his own season, Bobby will have been pleased with his total of 34 games, and he had contributed significantly to the achievements by top scorer Joe Hayes. With Billy McAdams and newcomer Colin Barlow also scoring well – these three scored over 60 goals between them – Bobby's own total of seven goals was a disappointment. It was the first time in his career that he hadn't made double figures, but we will see further proof later that while he was creating large numbers of goals for colleagues, he often failed to indulge himself. Now in his late 20s,

Bobby Johnstone had so far enjoyed a career full of goals, and there were many more to come, though this freak season could never be repeated.

An interesting postscript to this campaign is the fate of Sunderland, Don Revie and all, who had been investigated and found guilty by the Football League commission in April 1957. Their ever-present record in the top Division, a run unbroken since 1890, ended with relegation in 1958. All rather inconvenient for Bobby, of course, who often used to take advantage of City's trips to the North East and nip home to Selkirk. Things could have been worse, though; Sunderland had finished alongside rivals Newcastle United, also on 32 points, but at least the Magpies survived, on goal average, along with Portsmouth.

Two days after the end of the season, his injury cost Bobby the chance to play in Jimmy Meadows's testimonial match. The event was a rich tribute to the once promising youngster, with Don Revie and Roy Paul returning to Maine Road to encore their City careers and support the man who had been unable to fully regain match fitness since his injury in the 1955 FA Cup Final. Just five weeks before that fateful day, Meadows had made his England international debut against Scotland, and his new teammate Bobby Johnstone, at Wembley. As it turned out, Bobby and Jimmy Meadows were to play together for City just eight times.

Thoughts now turned to the forthcoming club tour to North America. City were finalising playing arrangements and planning to travel without two recognised first-team men. Early in May it was announced that Don Revie would travel with City as a guest player, provided that visas, documents and inoculations were all in place. Revie had been granted permission by the Sunderland board 'but there is no question that this is a prelude to getting Revie back permanently at Maine Road', the press were informed. 'We want to take as good a team as possible with so much prestige attached to the tour.' Les McDowall said 'we will be without two first-team players through injury or the problem of flying...'

Bobby Johnstone was the injured man and Bill Leivers was the other first-team regular not to travel. Yet, initially, it had never been suggested that the knee injury Bobby sustained against Newcastle would mean that he was unable to play again in the immediate future, and in fact he faced a summer trying to regain full fitness. But the obvious inference from McDowall's quote is that Bobby's knee-muscle injury was turning out to be more serious than first thought – or was it? We know that Bobby had been receiving treatment twice a day in an attempt to get him fit for each one of the final four League games. The newspapers clearly record him being in the running for selection but failing to make each deadline. It is evident from enquiries among Bobby's close family and former playing colleagues that he didn't want to travel on the trip, which involved a long voyage and then several flights within North America. Bobby had no ambition whatsoever to travel to the US, or anywhere else, and so he simply told the club that he didn't want to go!

This affected plans to demonstrate the deep-lying, centre-forward plan on tour of course, plans that were saved by Don Revie agreeing to make up the numbers, presumably during discussions at Jimmy Meadows's testimonial. Normal training continued, except for Bobby, until the party left for London on 8 May, from where they travelled to Southampton before sailing to America. For Bobby it was off to Selkirk for the summer once again, while Ken Barnes spent the next week being seasick. The City party played nine games in the States, five against local opposition, all won with embarrassing ease. These alternated with four exhibition games against Heart of Midlothian. These were lost with an almost equivalent ease, although there was a remarkable 7–1 win. In all, the nine tour games saw City score 50 goals, mainly against the hosts, and concede 26, mainly against the Scots.

Over in Sweden, Scotland's World Cup progressed according to form if not to plan, with a sole point gained in the opening game against Yugoslavia – all that the team had to show for their preparations and three matches. Eddie Turnbull recalls that, once again, the arrangements were shambolic, and there was friction in the camp. 'At first Scotland didn't have a team manager for the 1958 World Cup, and the guys said, "Ned, come on, you're the senior player" but, anyhow, Busby was appointed. He and I never got on. He'd tried to sign me two or three times, but I refused, partly because I wasn't going to get paid enough. He didn't like me; I remember when Scotland played England in an Inter-League match, and Busby was our manager and I was the captain of Scotland, Hibs and captain of the Scottish League team. Before the game, Busby was doing the team talk in the dressing room, pointing to the board, we'll do this, we'll do that, this is what's happening, and he comes to a guy, Quixall [Albert], who he'd bought from Sheffield Wednesday, the highest transfer £45,000 – a lot of money in those days. He says "Well Eddie, this Quixall can play..." I said "bah, no problem, you leave him wi' me, I'll sort him out," but he was his player, see! He didn't want me to sort him out, he didn't want me to touch him.'

Brazil won the tournament, with the 17-year-old Pele scoring in the Final, but the Champions' style drew much comment from the British media, with at least one journalist (Edgar Turner of the *Sunday Pictorial*) declaring that their attacking strategy was very nearly a carbon copy of that used by City during their Roy Paul days... 'inside-right Didi adopted the same sort of role as Bobby Johnstone or Don Revie, with the right-half, virtually another Ken Barnes, playing squarely with Didi all the time – a helpmate.' There the comparisons ended, because the Brazilians had conquered one thing that Bobby's teammates in Scotland and England had seldom done – the art of defending. The only goals the South Americans conceded were in 5–2 victories in both the semi-final and Final.

Bobby had missed the chance to earn a few quid in America, but for the 1958–59 season there were to be further improvements in players' wages. The League initially proposed that clubs pay £17 for players aged over 17, with £3 appearance money, effectively £20 per week during the playing season, thinking that this might prove acceptable. In the event, the clubs opted for £20 basic pay for pools of up to 15 first-team players. For first-team players aged over 20, this meant considerable increases of £3 per week during the season and £6 in the summer. There were opportunities to earn additional sums from the very limited number of televised games, and further improvements were made to loyalty benefits (these were now the equivalent of just over £3 per week for a player who served his club for 10 years) and retirement funds. After retirement from a Football League club, a player could now expect to receive a sizeable lump sum (around $\frac{1}{12}$ of his career earnings) on 1 January following his 35th birthday. It seemed that the clubs were now awaking to the desirability of better pay packages.

Having played 19 pre and post-season friendly games during the previous campaign, in contrast the start of the 1958–59 season saw only one overture, the usual first versus reserve team game. Once the season started, City seemed determined to hang on to their 'unpredictable' tag, winning the opening game by 4–3 at Burnley's Turf Moor, having been 0–3 down at half-time. Bobby scored twice to bring City level from 1–3, his first being a 'screamer' from 30 yards out, and Joe Hayes smashed in the winner with just 60 seconds left. The week after that nail-biter, a 3–3 draw with Bolton Wanderers was further evidence that City would plough on as before.

However, results started to go badly. Bobby missed a couple of games, and although he scored on his return to the side it was in a 1–5 defeat against Luton Town. In late September City brought George Hannah from Lincoln City for £20,000, rather belatedly forgiving him for having scored the third Newcastle goal against City in the 1955 Cup Final. Hannah's debut was against Arsenal at Highbury, where he wore the number-eight (inside-left) shirt, with Bobby in his usual number-nine shirt. This match saw young David Shawcross make his debut too, but City lost 4–1. The disastrous result against Arsenal, and Hannah's arrival, were destined to have a lasting impact on Bobby Johnstone's City career, as he now bore the brunt of McDowall's disappointment. For the next game, against Manchester United at Maine Road, a very significant move was made. George Hannah took the number-nine shirt, while both Bobby and David Shawcross were dropped, and Roy Cheetham came into the midfield as part of a fairly wide re-shuffle. The derby was drawn 1–1, and the following week Billy McAdams was recalled, so it was he that played alongside Hannah against Leeds United at Maine Road. Cheetham, then a young player desperately trying to establish himself in the side, well remembers Bobby's reaction to this news. 'He was out of the side – he'd put McAdams in, and Bobby came downstairs and said I hope you get f****n' beat six nowt.' Bobby was to be disappointed; City won 2–1 with goals from Colin Barlow and Joe Hayes.

The following week Bobby found himself playing in the reserves for the first time since his youth at Hibs. He scored in a 5–1 victory against Newcastle United reserves at Maine Road, while the first team, featuring the debutant Bert Lister at Molineux, were failing to score for only the second time in 18 months. McDowall took that cue to reinstall Bobby for the next game against Portsmouth, though not in his usual position; he now wore the number-eight shirt. For once, McDowall's thinking seems to have been crystal clear. George Hannah was the new centre-forward, and after Hannah's arrival Bobby wore number nine on just three further occasions. Johnny Williamson remembered the pendulum swinging in Hannah's favour. 'They brought Bobby in for one game with George Hannah, they'd always said they couldn't play together, but they did OK. Actually, George seemed to always do well at the start of the season, somehow, when the grounds were firmer; he was only a slight man.' City won the Portsmouth game 3–2, though neither man scored, and the next week the combination failed altogether in a heavy defeat at Newcastle. Bobby Johnstone now slid off back into the reserves as another of the Wembley stalwarts, Roy Little, moved to Brighton & Hove Albion. Bobby was far from happy, and he insisted that he was put on the 'available for transfer' list. Over the next six months Bobby Johnstone would play just five first-team games, and in total he would feature in only 11 more games all season. Significantly, on eight of those occasions Hannah was absent.

On the 11 November 1958, still in the reserves, Bobby played in a 1–1 draw at Bury's Gigg Lane. By the following week he was back up in Scotland, from where he sent a rather ironic 'Greetings from Selkirk' postcard to his mate Roy Allison. Bobby had returned to Selkirk supposedly for recuperative purposes, while 'under the doctor', but the sarcastic tone of that communication suggests that Bobby was certainly not bemoaning either ill-health or any ill-fortune. There is more than a hint that there had been a major fall-out in Manchester, possibly related to Bobby's undoubted struggle with injuries, with some inference that he hadn't been entirely single-minded in giving himself the best chance of an early return to the team. Ken Barnes, his closest mate within the club, and his minder if not his mentor during his years at City, said 'He might have thought "I'm not playing because of my knees, I'll have a drink," but I remember threatening to ring his mother to tell her he was drinking too much. He looked up from the (exercise) bike and begged me no... his father was dead by then, of course, but he didn't want to let his mother down.' During the Selkirk sojourn, Graham Bateman recalls the football editor of a national newspaper ringing around in an attempt to track Bobby down. He asked if anyone knew where Bobby was, but unfortunately Graham wasn't able to assist – although he had seen Bobby at the cricket club! Back down in Manchester, after his short break, he played in a couple more reserve games before Christmas, including a 4–5 defeat at Huddersfield. He scored in the draw against Aston Villa reserves, but this was a grim conclusion to the year, and there would be a new one before his first-team place was reclaimed.

* * * *

Bobby reappeared in the first team on 10 January 1959 and began a run of five consecutive games, starting with the replayed FA Cup third-round tie against Grimsby Town. In the first match, a 2–2 draw at Blundell Park, City were well on top, but they somehow allowed the home side to establish a 2–0 lead before the interval. They equalised with 20 minutes remaining, leaving sufficient time for Billy McAdams to miss two 'sitters'; thus Grimsby escaped to earn a replay at Maine Road. That was twice postponed due to the bad weather, and when it took place two weeks later City were given a rude awakening. Bobby scored first, but Cockerill had equalised by half-time, and then with eight minutes left Dave Ewing gave away the free-kick that Cockerill smashed past Bert Trautmann for a surprise winner. Bobby's goal was significant only because it keeps him within the top 10 list of City's all-time FA Cup goalscorers, having scored nine. It was now almost three years since City fans had seen a Cup win at Maine Road – the quarter-final tie against Everton in 1956 – and they would wait for three more.

Bobby and George Hannah were in the same side for the next game, a 1–3 defeat against Everton, but they never played together again. Hannah missed the 0–0 draw with Arsenal and the 1–4 defeat by Manchester United at Old Trafford, where Bobby got City's goal, his 50th for the club. It was his first Manchester 'derby' goal, although he'd previously had two disallowed. There were now just 14 League games left to play, and George Hannah played in the next seven; Bobby's City career was drawing to a close, but there would be a truly memorable finale.

Hannah's run of seven games, during which he failed to score, ended with a groin strain, picked up as City lost 0–2 at home to West Bromwich Albion on Easter Monday. The following day, City faced West Bromwich again in a peculiar Easter Tuesday 3pm kick-off, with Bert Lister now replacing Hannah as City lost again, this time 0–3. During Bobby's spell in the wilderness he certainly hadn't been forgotten, and several City fans, from among the thousands who still idolised him, had written to the Manchester press to try to find out what was happening; they were never going to be told the truth, of course, at least not at that stage. One local journalist interviewed Bobby at Maine Road after a morning training session and was told bluntly 'I'm just waiting to see what turns up, but I'm determined to move, I've made my mind up on that score'. In fact, a couple of clubs had expressed an interest, but Bobby rebuffed them both, in one case allegedly because their trainer was an ex-army physical training instructor who worked his players extremely hard!

Now entering April, relegation was a very serious threat to City. After just five games in as many months, and only because of injuries to McAdams, Barlow, Hannah, and Sambrook, Bobby now reclaimed a first-team place at inside-right. The *Evening Chronicle* seemed to have some faith in his ability, describing him as 'the scheming Scot, who could pull City out of relegation trouble on his own'. He retained his place for the last six games.

His first game since the Manchester derby was at Chelsea, but City lost 0–2, in spite of the fact that Bobby and Ken Barnes worked very hard and produced some great play. The problem was goals. McDowall decided that the players needed a break, and the team left for a few days extra training, staying at the Norbreck Hydro in Blackpool, who coincidentally were City's next opponents – in Manchester! The players enjoyed a break from the pressure, trained on the beach and played golf on the hotel's own course. Fit and refreshed, the party left the coast and headed straight back to Maine Road, where they promptly lost 0–2.

Prophetically, the previous night's press had pointed out that 'City have the schemers, but where are the goals going to come from?' This was now a fourth consecutive game without a goal. Joe Hayes scored in the next match at Blackburn, a 1–2 defeat, before the wheel came off at West Ham United, where City lost to five goals. Ironically, they had played well again, but Dave Ewing was injured after just 25 minutes, and he literally had to limp through the rest of the game. Bobby was reckoned to have had his best game of this season though, and City were still in the game at 1–2 until two quick goals in the 69th and 70th minutes killed them off. Ewing missed the rest of the season.

City had secured just 10 wins from their 40 games. The penultimate game of the season was a classic relegation 'four-pointer', against Aston Villa, who had gained three wins and three draws from their last six visits to Maine Road. There was a tactical change, with Bobby switching to lead the attack in the number-nine shirt. It turned out to be a tremendously exciting game, with Bobby

Johnstone and Bert Trautmann in particular playing superbly. Bobby hit the bar with a lob during a good spell for City, but Trautmann saved the day later as Villa pushed hard for a winner. 'Johnstone gave a great display, but even his master strokes couldn't wring goals from this attack,' was one press comment after the 0–0 draw. That result left Aston Villa third from bottom on 29 points, with City just behind them in a relegation slot, their goal average inferior by 0.014. It was a stage waiting for a hero.

City's final game of the season was against Leicester City, themselves a mightily relieved side. They had won their penultimate game, and news of the draw at Maine Road, with City and Villa each dropping a point, meant that they were now safe. On the day of the game, the evening press carried a damning assessment of the state of affairs at City, with everyone acknowledging that the club faced an historic battle that night. Irrespective of the outcome, the article argued 'The only solution is to buy players. Reconciliation between the club and star inside-forward Bobby Johnstone is impossible. Yet take away Johnstone's brilliance from the City forward strength and there isn't much left... speed is useless without skill.' Billy McAdams was fit to resume at centre-forward, so Bobby was moved to inside-right, and Paddy Fagan was stood down for this titanic match.

The possible outcomes of the match were assessed in a handy 'cut-out-and-keep' table produced by the *Evening Chronicle*. Aston Villa's result in their Midlands derby match against West Bromwich Albion would be key of course, and besides each of those possibilities were listed the response that City would require to remain in the First Division. Essentially, City needed to better Aston Villa's result, so, quite simply, a win for City, and either a defeat or a draw for Villa would do the trick. If both sides got the same result, things would be far more complicated. For example, should Villa draw 0–0, City would survive with a draw, but they would have to score a rather infeasible five goals. City might even get away with a 4–5 defeat, providing Aston Villa lost without scoring.

Playing with the abandon familiar to sides who have little to play for, Leicester took the initiative from the off, and the lead 10 minutes in. Bobby Johnstone then got control of the match, and he began to dictate City's attacks in that central, pivotal manner that was the hallmark of the remainder of his career. He chipped the ball up, and Joe Hayes scored a header. Early in the second half, a mazy run by Bobby set up a chance that Sambrook took well, and then McAdams scored a third. But news from Aston Villa's derby game against West Bromwich Albion was bad. Villa were winning 1–0 at The Hawthorns, and so their goal average (0.6744) remained infinitesimally superior to City's (0.6736). City needed another goal.

Down in the Midlands, the manager of Aston Villa, Joe Mercer, believed that his side had survived relegation, although he had to leave The Hawthorns a couple of minutes before the final whistle in order to get to Wolverhampton for a presentation event marking Billy Wright's 100th England international cap. He missed West Bromwich Albion's late equalising goal by Ronnie Allen and was devastated when, on arriving at the banquet, the news was broken to him. Up in Manchester, where City's game had kicked-off 15 minutes behind Villa's game, news of the equaliser was greeted by a crescendo of noise as delirious City fans raised the roof. They spent the next few minutes watching Bobby and his teammates keeping possession of the ball, so that Leicester were unable to make any headway. Joe Mercer must have spent the next few days cursing both Allen and the orchestrater of City's victory, and thus their survival: one Bobby Johnstone.

City stayed up by one point, but the Allen goal meant that City also had the better goal average. It was the first time that Bobby had ever been involved in a relegation battle, and a classic case of 'cometh the hour, cometh the man'. In spite of the view from some influential quarters that Bobby was incapable of overcoming his injuries, and, worse, was actually past it, he had shown the qualities that can best dig any football team out of trouble; sheer ability, and the nous to retain the ball in areas of the park where opponents cannot hurt you. Thousands of jubilant City fans swarmed on to the pitch to pay tribute to the team, and in particular the genius of Bobby Johnstone. Bert Lister saw the game: 'Ronnie Allen scored for West Brom at Villa to keep us up actually, and we knew their score, but late on Bobby orchestrated the game from the centre circle, it was incredible.' Ian Niven was there too: 'That Leicester game; that was some game, Bobby absolutely saved us. Where he got it from that night I've no idea. It was like he was a young boy again. He operated around the centre circle later on in his career, without moving around the pitch too much, but he was just a genius with the ball.'

The following night Arthur Walmsley, the City correspondent, recalled 'the incomparable Johnstone sweeping down the field with a majesty defying his stocky frame and sending Sambrook through for a goal'. Les McDowall thanked the 46,936 fans that had roared City on, the biggest cheer of the night coming for news of a goal they never saw! They were promised 'It won't happen again. This was truly glory snatched from disaster.' Chairman Alan Douglas confirmed that the club had their eye on some new talent, including a couple of young Scottish players, but 'The position of Bobby Johnstone is unchanged and that presents us with many problems.'

Reflecting on the game a short while later, even Bobby conceded that the occasion had affected him: 'I've played in Cup Finals, internationals, and other very important games, but this is one that stands out for me. There were 47,000 there for a night game, and although the outcome meant it was a fabulous match to play in it was one of the worse I've ever known for nerves.'

Many years later, well-known local radio correspondent John Gwynne nominated this last day of the 1958–59 season as his favourite football memory. 'We marvelled at his magic, but none more so than when he played his finest game for City. We had to beat Leicester at Maine Road and hope that Aston Villa didn't win at The Hawthorns. It was so tight that even if Villa won 1–0, City could stay in the First Division by winning 4–1. Bobby Johnstone ran the show that late April night in Moss Side. The centre of the park belonged to Bobby. The outstretched arm with pointing finger, partly for perfect balance, partly for true direction, conducted affairs. The short pass along the ground to Barnes, or the weighted aerial chip to Barlow, Hayes or Sambrook, they were never more determinedly executed. Bobby ran his little blue and white-ringed socks off, too, that night – and City won 3–1. Thankfully, Albion equalised against Villa two minutes from the end in the Midlands, in a match that had kicked off 15 minutes earlier than ours. When the score 1–1 went up in the letter 'S' slot on the scoreboard, the biggest cheer of the season was heard at Maine Road. City had needed victory, though, and Bobby Johnstone, for 15 minutes more, made sure that Leicester didn't get back into the match. Each time he touched the ball he was cheered. He knew that this was his finest hour. There was only one Bobby Johnstone.'

In spite of the euphoria, Les McDowall had started to make firm plans to replace Bobby, though the signing of George Hannah was more an indication that a solution was required than the solution itself. Bobby's injuries were increasingly problematic and keeping the medical staff occupied. Roy Allison used to take Bobby into Maine Road for treatment from his home in Droylsden, and he knew how bad things were at times. 'I've seen him get out of bed upstairs here and go full length, as his knee gave way, he just couldn't stand up on it. They used to give him these 'gold' injections, as they were called, through into the back of the knee, and it was like a painkiller that lasted about 24 hours. He could play then. City had their own medics, and about 10 o'clock on a Saturday we'd go down to the ground, and I'd go in the dressing room with him while he got it done. He was in agony at times. He used to come here sometimes on a Saturday night, and when it was wearing off he was in real pain.' A further factor was the earnings situation, and the ironies here were not lost on Bobby. In the years since City had reached two FA Cup Finals, significant improvements had been made to the earnings potential of players, yet City had now been knocked out in the third round of the Cup for three consecutive years. 'Talent money' had also entered the dressing room vocabulary, and in the first year Bobby and his teammates missed out on collecting decent sums by failing to win their final fixture. This last season had never threatened to generate any talent money, and financially things were getting worse if anything. Bobby had missed 24 out of the 42 League fixtures, playing only 20 first-team games overall, scoring just five times. He had not scored in a winning City team since the opening day of the season, and his 10 Central League appearances were far too many. As he approached his 30th birthday, this was not what the doctor ordered.

Preparations for the new 1959–60 season included a prestigious pre-season friendly in Scotland against St Mirren, who, rather unexpectedly, had won the Scottish Cup the previous season. It was a chance for Les McDowall to pit his wits against his home-town team and also take a look at Gerry Baker, a future City player. St Mirren won 3–0 in front of a crowd of around 19,000 to collect the Paisley Charity Cup. On 12 August the traditional fixture between the Blues (essentially the first team) and Yellows (reserves) was staged at Maine Road. Perhaps it was an indication about Bobby's intended place in the scheme of things, but he played in the Blues side, which prevailed by 5–3, while George Hannah was in the 'stiffs', though both scored.

The reason for the unusual evening kick-off for this fixture was that at short notice an invitation to West Germany had been accepted, and on the Friday morning a party of 20 players flew to Berlin, where they played against Sporting Club Tasmania 1900, winning 2–1. Officially, Bobby Johnstone and Ray Sambrook both dropped out of the party 'owing to injury', though, again, Bobby's aversion to flying is a more likely explanation in his case. News that the aircraft carrying the City party had run into an electrical thunderstorm on its way through to the beautiful city of Berlin will have been upsetting even for the more relaxed travellers among the party, and things were no less calm once on the ground, with Billy McAdams being sent off by an over-zealous official, leading to a busy time for the diplomats.

Bobby was quietly back in Manchester, and in the run-up to the new season Cardiff City contacted Maine Road with a routine enquiry about Bobby's position – and a speculative £5,000 offer. Bobby was still available for transfer, though Peter Slingsby's view, in the *Evening Chronicle*, was that Bobby 'would soon ask to come off the transfer list, four and a half years after his £25,000 transfer'. Slingsby was correct in one sense – the position with regards to Bobby's availability would indeed be resolved, and soon, though publicly at this stage the club declared 'the offer was well short of Les McDowall's valuation of a highly-talented player'.

On the opening day of the season City beat FA Cup holders Nottingham Forest by 2–1, and Bobby scored City's first goal. Having finished the previous season on such a triumphant high, and beginning the next where he had left off, there was considerable confidence that Bobby was 'back' and in a position to make a big contribution. But the next two games were away, and both were lost, at Fulham (by 2–5) and then Sheffield Wednesday, where the players sported the new amber and black change strip. By the time the team played again at Maine Road, against Fulham in early September, further changes had been made – Bobby was out of the team and soon out of the club. Ironically, City had just announced that Dave Ewing, the loyal Scottish centre-half, had also been awarded a £1,000 benefit to mark his decade of service to Manchester City. In contrast, Bobby Johnstone was dropped, and Hannah came back into the side for a long run.

Bobby played just two more reserve-team games at Maine Road, the first a Monday night draw (2–2) against Huddersfield Town played on his 30th birthday; not what Bobby had in mind for that milestone, and one suspects that Les McDowall didn't bother with a birthday card. Bert Lister was carried off the park in that game with a suspected broken ankle, though the injury turned out to be no worse than severe bruising. He missed his pal's last game in a City shirt, an unspectacular 2–3 defeat at home to Stoke City on Saturday 12 September, witnessed by a crowd of around 3,000. The following week saw the big Manchester derby at Maine Road, but Bobby Johnstone was nowhere to be found. George Hannah celebrated a year at the club as City gained their first victory in a 'derby' match since 1955, but Bobby could not have cared less.

A leading authority on the history of Manchester City records that City had been looking to replace Bobby for some time, although George Hannah had failed to cut the mustard. 'Johnstone made only 18 appearances the previous season, and although he was vital in a number of games, City had begun to look to a future without him. Les McDowall had already viewed a 19-year-old striker playing for Huddersfield, but the problem was price... his name was Denis Law.' Roy Cheetham had joined City as a star-struck junior professional in 1955, making his debut three years later when Bobby was out injured. They were at the club simultaneously for almost four years, and Roy played together with Bobby in six first-team games. He remembers the Scot with affection, and was around when things went sour. 'I remember him leaving, but I don't really know why... I'd played in the draw with Villa and the 3–1 win against Leicester; and I'll never, ever forget either of those games... but he was always falling out with McDowall, his knees weren't right, and he was a bit cheesed off.' Steve Fleet feels that Bobby was largely the architect of his own demise. 'Bobby fell out with McDowall; he wasn't the fittest lad. He was often very quiet – almost introverted, but he could be very cutting and critical at other times, and he said one or two things that went against the grain. That's why he moved on.'

Bobby had decided to leave City; his time in Manchester had been eventful, but he had never really settled. On his last day he went around saying his goodbyes, but he could not bring himself to shake hands with Les McDowall. Worse still, he told him pointedly that 'there's a better set of donkeys on Blackpool sands than what you've got 'ere'. On that note, he walked out, safe in the knowledge that he would never cross McDowall's path again.

Notes

1. In 1959 Paul led his non-League side to a famous FA Cup win over Liverpool.
2. The name David Jack appears alongside Bobby Johnstone's in many record books. David B.N. Jack was the first man to score in two FA Cup Finals at Wembley. He scored in the first to be played at Wembley, the famous 1923 'White Horse' game, since which FA Cup Finals have been all-ticket affairs. Three years later he scored for Bolton Wanderers once again, this time the only goal against Manchester City. Jack later played for Arsenal and managed Middlesbrough. He died in hospital in 1958.
3. Cliff Lloyd was then secretary of the Professional Footballers' Association.
4. Big Dave Ewing holds a record that may never be beaten, having scored 10 own-goals against City. He was later manager of Hibernian for a short period, prior to the appointment of Eddie Turnbull in 1973. He returned to Manchester City and coached the reserves to the Central League Championship in 1978. He passed away in 1999.
5. The Cromford Club was a top-class cabaret nightclub and casino at the time, located close to the Market Street/Cross Street area. At the end of the 1950s the manager of the nightclub, who was well connected in football circles, assisted with the transfer of a couple of players to help Manchester United over the immediate difficulties following the Munich Air Disaster. The Cromford was situated within the area devastated when the massive bomb exploded in 1995, though the nightclub itself had been demolished around 25 years before, when the major shopping centre development known as the Arndale Centre was constructed.
6. The record is 105–105 if one includes the single FA Cup defeat by West Bromwich Albion.

CHAPTER 8

Hame and the Baker Boy

'Disastrously from a Scottish point of view, the road south has almost always been a road of no return. There are few instances of a player, once having gone to England, returning to Scotland at anything approaching the height of his powers.'
R. Crampsey

In spite of interest from some English clubs, including Leicester City, who had so recently seen him in top form, Bobby opted to return to his former club Hibernian. He signed on Tuesday 22 September 1959, for a fee usually recorded as £3,000 or £4,000, though at least one newspaper claimed that City had received as much as £7,000. This latter figure is most unlikely, not least given that this was the first significant fee that Hibs had paid for any player since the late 1940s!

Having left Hibernian as they conceded supremacy in Edinburgh, Bobby moved to City just as it seemed that they might assume the leading position in Manchester – but that hadn't worked out as planned. The Edinburgh club had not progressed too well during Bobby's four and a half years away, and their supporters had long got used to Hearts having the upper hand locally; in fact, the Jambos had now finished higher up the League than Hibs for six consecutive years. Around 20 years later, in an interview given to Radio Tweed, Bobby revealed publicly how disappointed he had been at the way things had turned out at Maine Road, quite unlike what he had known previously at Easter Road. 'It was a different type of game there. I didn't have the same players around me that I had at Hibs, in the forward line especially. I was very disappointed with the forward line at Maine Road when I went, it was a different ball game altogether. They played a deep-lying centre-forward, with the two inside-forwards pushed up, and when I first went there I played inside-left quite a lot, which I wasn't too happy about for a while. But eventually, you know, we got things ironed out and we did alright, we got to two Finals, but otherwise it wasn't that successful.'

After some years of what could be described as 'unsettled' domestic arrangements, Bobby moved back into the Johnstone family home at Raeburn Place, in Selkirk, where he could be nearer to his fiancée Heather.

Bobby and Heather had met in the early 1950s at a local dance hall, and by now they had continued their courtship for the best part of a decade. Heather made many trips down to Manchester while Bobby was playing for Manchester City, though she continued to live and work in Selkirk. Later, when her own family moved to Hawick, around 12 miles away, she had moved into Raeburn Place to live with Bobby's mother for a short time, though she had moved out well before Bobby came back north in 1959.

While the Famous Five had broken up when Bobby left for Manchester in 1955, the remaining four played intact for a further three years, until Lawrie Reilly decided to retire at the age of only 29 in April 1958. Though he now accepts that this might have been somewhat premature, Lawrie, as ever, took decisive action at the time, largely because of his knee problems, and in spite of the fact that Hibernian invited him to carry on. 'When I packed it in, the manager Hugh Shaw said we'd like you to stay, and they actually offered me £18 a week, a two-pound rise, to play on. The biggest wage I ever earned was £16 a week, and now I couldn't play they were offering me more than ever! But I was having trouble with the left knee; it's twice the size of the right one even now, look. I said no, I'm not going to be a one-legged wonder out on the park, fiddling aboot and just going down and down, I'm going to pack it in. It was 1958, but I'd bought a pub in Leith about six months earlier, so I had something to fall back on. Now there were no substitutes in these days – if there'd been the substitute thing, I could have played maybe 45 minutes or something like that, but I didn't want to be known as a bloody cripple, or carried as a passenger.' After retirement, Lawrie lost interest in football and never pursued a career in the game. 'I just concentrated on building up the pub, and I didn't see much football at all. The chairman Harry Swan phoned me once at the pub, wanting to see me. I went up to his house and he said "How would you like to become a director?" I said, err, obviously I was quite interested in becoming a director of the Hibs, he said "OK, there's a publican at Easter Road, just across from the ground, and if you can get him to give over his shares, you can come on the board." But the shares were going to go to Harry Swan and not me. I made an arrangement to see the guy, and he said there's no way I'm giving my shares to him [Swan]. Anyway, I was lucky to achieve success with the pub, we got many Hibs supporters in, and I'll always remember a branch of the Rangers supporters bringing their bus to my pub for a drink. They would stay right up until kick-off, and there was never, ever a bad word said or any bother, because the older guys told the younger ones "Now we're going to Reilly's pub, and we hope to keep on going – any of you boys that cause trouble won't be on the bus again." The Bowler's Rest it was called, because it was next to a bowling green. Bobby came to the pub once or twice after he came back to Hibs, but it was the wrong direction for him really, heading away after games.'

Lawrie's boyhood hero Gordon Smith continued to play, though he was no longer at Hibs. After some 18 years as a professional, Smith had begun to suffer from serious ankle problems. He had missed most of 1958 while recovering from an operation, losing the chance to compete in that year's World Cup Finals, not to mention the Scottish Cup Final, which Hibs lost to Clyde a few days after Lawrie Reilly retired. Halfway through the following season, as Bobby's time in Manchester was drawing to a close, Gay Gordon had come back into the Hibs team, and brilliantly so, but his 364th goal, in a replayed Scottish Cup tie at home to Raith Rovers, proved to be his last – for Hibs. He picked up another injury as the season drifted to a close, and at the end of it Eddie Turnbull announced his own retirement, at which he was offered the post of club trainer.

Hibernian had publicly expressed some concern that Smith would never regain full fitness, and they 'granted' him a free transfer, purportedly in his own interests, stating that they didn't believe a further operation was wise. Smith promptly paid for his own treatment, and then spent time negotiating with the dozen or so clubs that had expressed interest in his services. He plumped for Hearts, almost inevitably as they had been favourites to sign him in 1941, and around 10,000 turned out to welcome him to Tynecastle on his debut for the Jambo's reserves. Many years later Smith declared himself 'Sick, I was absolutely shattered that Hibs didn't want me. I tried to put on a brave face, but it was hurtful to be released after what I had gone through.' So Bobby returned to a Hibs team that had been shorn of three members of the Five over the previous 18 months, though Willie Ormond was still a first-team regular.

The re-signing of Bobby Johnstone was not met with universal approval among Hibs supporters, a number of whom were not sure that his rejoining the club was sensible. Their apprehension was based mainly around fears that his style may not blend well with the prolific Joe Baker, who had been a sensation since arriving on the scene two years earlier. Baker had scored 30 goals the previous season and was about to become the first man ever to be capped by England while playing in the Scottish League. Bobby's first game, as he strove to regain full match fitness, was to have been a reserve match against Hearts. Around 8,000 fans turned up to welcome him back, but they were let down when he was unable to reach Easter Road in time following the completion of the transfer formalities, and so they had to satisfy themselves with a 5–2 win. Bobby met up with his new teammates the next morning, but it wasn't until the following Saturday that Hibees got an opportunity to welcome Bobby home, when he made his second 'debut' in a Scottish League game at Easter Road. Hibs' opponents that day were Kilmarnock, coincidentally the team Bobby had last faced back in 1955, though that game had been played at Rugby Park. An appreciative crowd of over 24,000 were there to greet him, and they had been led to expect big things by the comments of manager Hugh Shaw, who went public hoping 'that he will impart to the young lads alongside him that touch of know-how that could be of great benefit not only to his forward mates, but to the team in general'. The team had been struggling and had made a poor start, so there was a sense of relief as Hibs now gained only their second League win of the season. Bobby didn't score, though goals would come in time, but he made a good start and was influential in a 4–2 win. After the game, the *Edinburgh Evening News* noted that the supporters' doubts had lasted 'only until Johnstone got his first touch of the ball, killing it stone dead, before sending it with laser-like precision into the path of its intended target. All was sweetness and light after that.'

The Hibernian supporters, with just two or three chances to see Bobby during his four and a half years' 'exile', will have noticed two things on this reappearance. Firstly, his game had changed in that although he was still notionally playing at centre-forward it was more the deep-lying 'schemer' type of role, favoured during his time under Les McDowall in England. Secondly, the first change had been brought about partly because of his more generously proportioned figure, which lent itself more naturally to the pivotal, less frantic kind of role. One of the first tasks that new trainer Eddie Turnbull undertook was to put Bobby through a training and fitness regime that apparently removed around a stone in weight, and this was later credited with having restored some of his sharpness. Two days after the Kilmarnock game, Bobby's first competitive game for a month, the club took a party of over 30 players and staff down to the Borders, where a reserve team overcame Selkirk by 4–0 in an afternoon game at Ettrick Park, before journeying on to North Berwick for five days by the sea. There, Bobby got down to some serious training, enjoyed some links golf, and got the chance to get to know some of his younger teammates.

Any advantage gleaned from the break was not immediately obvious on the football fields, because the following week Hibs lost at Clyde, a match that they dominated, with Bobby's promptings setting up a host of chances. On the following Monday, Bobby scored in a floodlit friendly match against the British Army, his first goal since his return to Edinburgh, though he would have some time yet to wait before managing the feat in a full first-team match. The next day the benefits of the seaside trip became clearer when Bobby won a club golfing competition at Longniddry, with a 74 (net 68). In the middle of October Hibernian thrashed Dunfermline Athletic by 7–4, with Joe Baker scoring only the second hat-trick by a Hibs man in 1959. The following week Bolton Wanderers were put to the sword, 5–2, in a night-time friendly, and then on Saturday 24 October Hibs finally managed to win an away League game by 11–1 at Broomfield, home of Airdrieonians FC. Tommy Preston got four, and Joe Baker, who scored a hat-trick, took particular pleasure in the suffering of Airdrie centre-half Doug Baillie, who had given the youngster a torrid time on his debut a couple of years earlier.

All of this had occurred within a month of Bobby's transfer, with the Airdrie result in particular leaving an indelible mark. This is still Hibernian's record score for any League match, and it remains the British record score by any away team in a League game.[1] It also meant that Hibs had scored 23 goals in a week. Amazingly, Bobby failed to score any of them, and he had to wait until the following week for his second 'first' goal for Hibs, which came on the last day of October at Easter Road. Hibs came back from two goals down at half-time to draw 3–3 against Celtic.

It is worth recording that this was the second time that Bobby and Willie Ormond had been part of a Hibernian team that had scored so heavily. It had occurred previously over the week of Gordon Smith's benefit match against Manchester United in 1952, and *The Scotsman's* reporter had hailed their 22 goals that week as a 'feat most unlikely to be repeated'. In fact, on the previous occasion Hibs had been somewhat dilatory in requiring four matches and eight days!

Bobby was now off the goalscoring mark, and he was demonstrably fitter. Trainer Eddie Turnbull had been credited with getting a little weight off him, and there was even some newspaper speculation that Bobby might force his way back into the Scotland side, perhaps to play alongside Joe Baker, who had earlier played for Scotland Schoolboys. Meanwhile, the goals continued to fizz in, and early November saw a notable friendly game, a 6–6 draw against Middlesbrough, who featured their centre-forward Brian Clough. Baker got a hat-trick for Hibs (Bobby scored two), but in fact Baker and Clough were chief rivals for the *England* spearhead role,[2] and two weeks later Baker was capped against Ireland. In doing so, he became the first Scottish League player ever to feature at full international level for England – an incredible achievement for a man who, after all, was with a Scottish provincial club.

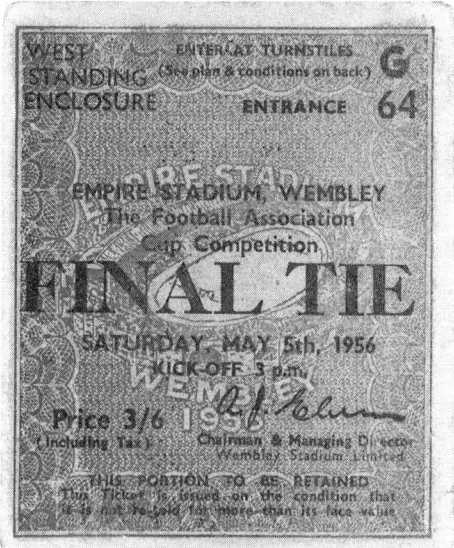

Used tickets for the 1955 and 1956 FA Cup Final matches at Wembley Stadium. Bobby scored in both games, of course, and gave this 1955 ticket to his friend Roy Allison. Courtesy of Phil Noble

An autographed picture of Bobby's national service pal the late Ronnie Simpson, who kept goal for Newcastle in the 1955 Cup Final and played against Bobby many times both north and south of the border.

The proposed line up for the 1956 FA Cup Final pictured at Maine Road, Manchester. Note the exclusion of Don Revie.

Courtesy of Manchester City FC

The moment history was made. Bobby Johnstone shoots past Birmingham City goalkeeper Gil Merrick to become the first man ever to score in consecutive FA Cup Finals at Wembley.

Images of Sport, a MCFC book by David Saffer

1956 FA Cup winners. Note the way the forwards now line up, alongside the victorious captain Roy Paul (holding the football).

Images of Sport, a MCFC book by David Saffer

An oil painting of Bobby, which hangs in the Director's Lounge at Easter Road in Edinburgh. The source for the work is thought to have been a photograph of Bobby in a Manchester City shirt.
Courtesy of Hibernian FC

Bobby at Maine Road in 1957.

One of Bobby's two players' season tickets. This one, which was often used by Roy Allison, appears to have been made out to a 'Mrs R. Johnstone'.
Courtesy of Mr R. Allison

Block C Row W Seat No 419
MANCHESTER CITY FOOTBALL CLUB LTD.
Name Mr R. Johnstone
Address
(Please Insert Your Name and Address)
GRAND STAND—CHAIRS
(Not Transferable)
Season Ticket 1957-58
Complimentary
Secretary

MANCHESTER CITY FOOTBALL CLUB Ltd.
Registered Office—
MAINE ROAD, MOSS SIDE, MANCHESTER, 14
Tel. MOSs Side 1191
SEASON 1957-58
Directors—
Chairman - A. DOUGLAS
E. GILL R. SMITH
D. P. HAMER F. R. JOLLY
W. SMITH
Manager—L. J. McDOWALL
Secretary—W. GRIFFITHS

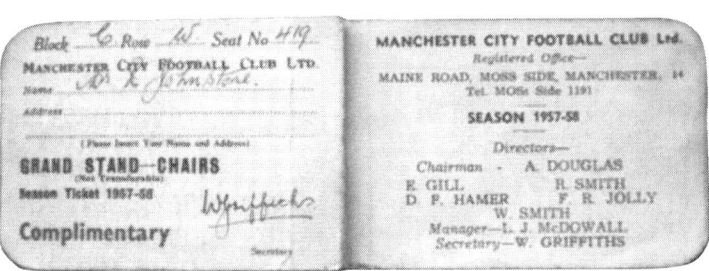

Hold it! Bobby in training with fellow forwards Fagan, McAdams, Dyson and Clarke before the 1957 FA Cup match with Newcastle United. In spite of Bobby's three goals, City's attempt to reach Wembley for a third consecutive year failed at the first hurdle.

Courtesy of Mr R. Conner and *Manchester Evening Chronicle*

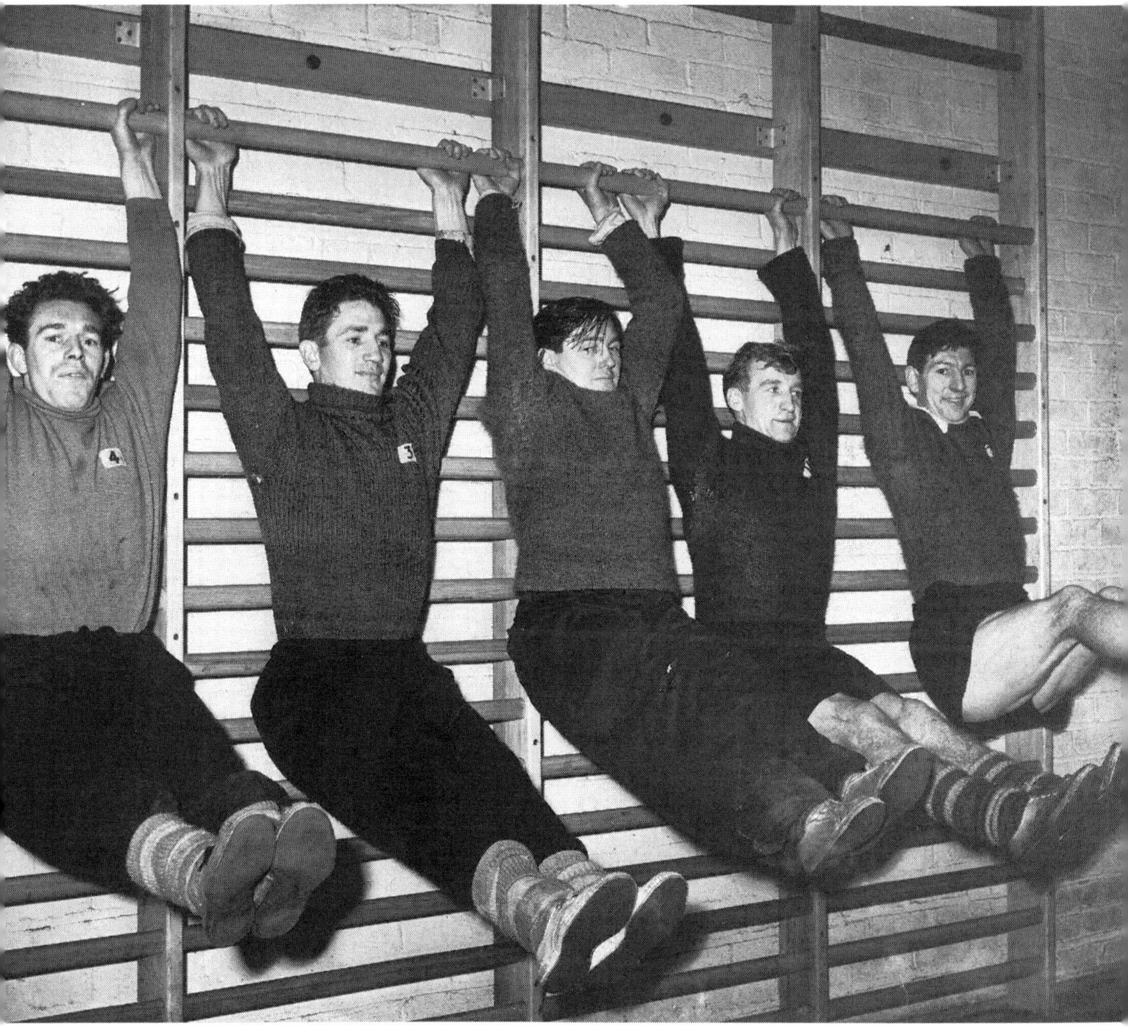

An oil painting that hangs on the wall of the Director's Guest Lounge at the City of Manchester Stadium.

By kind permission of MCFC, photograph by Ed Garvey

Tel. MOSs Side 1191

MANCHESTER

CITY

Directors:
A. DOUGLAS (Chairman)
A. V. ALEXANDER
D. F. HAMER
F. R. JOHNSON
A. P. LONGSHAW
W. SMITH

Manager:
L. J. McDOWALL

Secretary:
W. GRIFFITHS

Football Club Ltd

PRICE TWOPENCE

Vol. 1 No. 5 (New issue)   SATURDAY, SEPTEMBER 12th, 1959

Sky blue shirts   **CITY RESERVES**   White knickers

DOWD, H.

2		3
MacDONALD		SEAR

4	5	6
PHOENIX	TAYLOR	SHAWCROSS

7	8	9	10	11
PENNINGTON	HAYDOCK	JOHNSTONE	FAGAN	FIDLER

Referee:
L. STONE (Sheffield)
Kick-off 3.0 p.m.

Linesmen:
K. P. DANIELS (Red Flag)
J. C. POPE (Yellow Flag)

11	10	9	8	7
WALLACE	ANDERSON	HOWITT	THURSFIELD	CONWAY

6	5	4
REYNER	ASPREY	SKEELS

3		2
WILSON		ANDREWS

HALL

Red & White
Striped Shirts   **Stoke City Reserves**   White knickers

THE TEAMS ARE SUBJECT TO ALTERATION

NEXT MATCH AT MAINE ROAD

FIRST DIVISION

LUTON TOWN

Wed. next Sept. 16th 1959. Kick-off 7-30 p.m.

KEEP THIS
COUPON
and watch for
ticket match
announcements

MANCHESTER
CITY F.C.

No. 7   12.9.59

TICKET COUPON

Bobby's final appearance in a Manchester City shirt came shortly after his 30th birthday, in a reserve-team fixture against Stoke City. An undistinguished City team also featured a future FA Cup winner in Harry Dowd, the goalkeeper.

153

Bobby is back. Bobby's second debut for Hibs was against Kilmarnock in 1959. Here he attacks the Killie defence in a match that Hibs won 4–2.

Team line ups for the Scottish League Cup fixture between Hibs and Kilmarnock in August 1960. The names Bobby Johnstone and Willie Ormond have been deleted and replaced by substitutes.

Opposite: Programme cover for Bobby's last appearance in Scottish football. Newly-promoted Dundee United overcame Hibernian FC rather too easily in the view of manager Hugh Shaw.

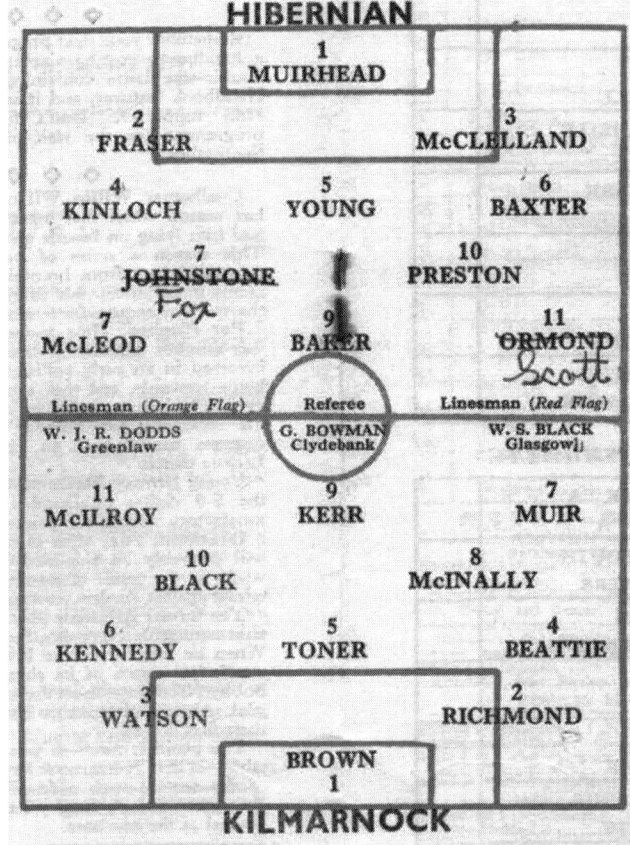

154

DUNDEE UNITED

FOOTBALL CLUB LIMITED

Directors—Mr E. S. ROBERTSON (Chairman)   Mr JAMES LITTLEJOHN   Mr G. F. FOX (Treasurer)
Mr DUNCAN HUTCHISON   Mr J. J. GRANT
Manager and Secretary—Mr J. KERR   Registered Office—TANNADICE PARK, DUNDEE

| Vol. 1, No. 3 | Wednesday, 24th August, 1960 | PRICE, 3d |

SCOTTISH LEAGUE

DIVISION

ONE

KICK-OFF 6.45

VERSUS

HIBERNIAN

155

In April 1961 this Doncaster Rovers defender was left facing the wrong way, looking back to try to catch a glimpse of Bobby.   Courtesy of *The Oldham Evening Chronicle*

The Oldham Athletic team line up for a pre-Christmas fixture against Chester at Boundary Park in 1961. Bobby went on to score in a 4–1 victory.   *Soccer Star*, January 1962

The Johnstones at their home in Royton, near Oldham, in October 1964. Courtesy of M. Johnstone

Opposite: In 1972 the Famous Five reunited in honour of Jimmy McColl, who by then had given 50 years' service to Hibernian. Pictured here are, left to right, Gordon Smith, Bobby, Jimmy McColl, Lawrie Reilly, Johnny Halligan (a teammate of McColl's from the 1920s) and Eddie Turnbull.

Courtesy of J. Rafferty

The Famous Five assemble at Easter Road in the 1970s.

Courtesy of J. Mackay

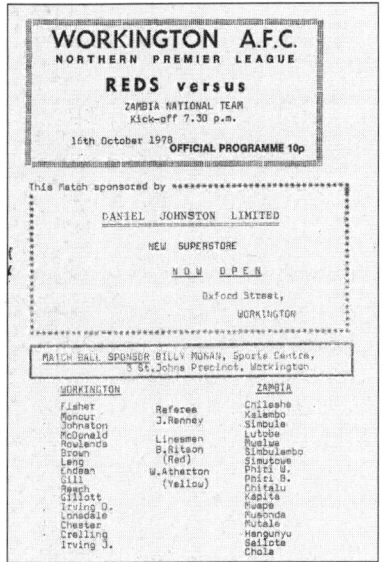

In 1978 Bobby had a brief and unproductive spell as manager of ex-Football League side Workington FC.

Courtesy of S. Durham, Workington AFC

WORKINGTON A.F.C.
NORTHERN PREMIER LEAGUE

REDS versus

ZAMBIA NATIONAL TEAM
Kick-off 7.30 p.m.

16th October 1978 **OFFICIAL PROGRAMME 10p**

This Match sponsored by *****************************

DANIEL JOHNSTON LIMITED

NEW SUPERSTORE

N O W   O P E N

Oxford Street,
WORKINGTON

MATCH BALL SPONSOR BILLY MONAN, Sports Centre,
3 St.Johns Precinct, Workington

WORKINGTON		ZAMBIA
Fisher		Chileshe
Monaur	Referee	Kalembo
Johnaton	J.Renney	Simbule
McDonald		Lutobe
Rowlands	Linesmen	Mualue
Brown	B.Ritson	Simbulembo
Leng	(Red)	Simutowe
Endean	W.Atherton	Phiri W.
Gill	(Yellow)	Phiri B.
Reech		Chitalu
Gillott		Kapita
Irving D.		Muape
Lonsdale		Musonda
Chester		Mutale
Crelling		Hangunyu
Irving J.		Sailote
		Chola

Bobby's last-ever game in professional football was this game between Workington FC and Zambia. Immediately after the game, the board accepted his resignation from the manager's post at Borough Park.

Presentation of a painting by Hibernian FC Supporters Association in 1998.

On the day of the opening of the Famous Five stand at Easter Road in 1998. Bobby, accompanied by Mrs Ormond and Lawrie Reilly, watches the start of proceedings. By kind permission J. Jeffrey

Bobby Johnstone and Graham Bateman ensure that the Selkirk FC club crest is in safe hands as it leaves Ettrick Park for the short journey to the new ground, Yarrow Park.   Courtesy of G. Bateman

Bobby Johnstone's funeral was held at Selkirk's Shawfield Cemetery in August 2001. Among the large number of mourners were Gordon Smith, Eddie Turnbull and Lawrie Reilly, pictured here paying last respects to their pal.   Photographer Alastair Watson, *Southern Reporter*

Bobby scored four goals in the four League games during the remainder of November, including a brace against Dundee at home. Early in December, Ayr United were beaten 5–1 at Easter Road, but an important point here is that Bobby took and scored with his first penalty-kick for Hibs. The following week, and only eight weeks after the Airdrie romp, Hibs put 10 past Partick Thistle at Firhill Park, and they had two disallowed to boot. Believed to be only the fourth time that an away side had reached double figures in a League match, the press were full of praise for the team: 'Hibs – out of this world' was the opinion of the *Sunday Mail*, while Jack Harkness of the *Sunday Post* felt that the team had now 'truly emerged from the wilderness, in all their glory'. Johnny McLeod got three, and notably Baker did not score a hat-trick, though he did score for a 10th consecutive Scottish League game, still a Hibs record, and no doubt an achievement that put Bobby in mind of his old colleague Billy McAdams, who had done likewise for Manchester City.

'Who can stop these Easter Road gluttons?' Asked Stewart Brown in the *Evening Dispatch*, and the answer came quickly – Aberdeen. The festive period was not kind to Hibs, who followed up that astounding Partick result with a Boxing Day blow (4–6) at Pittodrie, and then a New Year's day defeat at home to Hearts, who featured Gordon Smith in handing down a 1–5 defeat. Bobby will have taken small consolation from having scored in both games, and more from the fact that his billiards was as good as ever. His prowess on the baize was undiminished, and once again he assumed the mantle of club Champion, winning a clock after beating Joe Baker in the Final of the players' tournament. The following day Hibs collected a point in a 1–1 draw at Ibrox Park, their first point there for five years. Without Bobby in their side, Hibs had avoided defeat there just twice since before World War One, yet he maintained his incredible personal record of just one League defeat (in 53–4) at Ibrox, a stadium that had often seen him perform at his best. Later in January, he scored twice in a 5–5 draw with Clyde, his ninth and 10th goals since returning to Scotland, and then Hibs headed south to play a floodlit game in Manchester, against City. On leaving Maine Road the previous autumn, Bobby had been rather unkind about his former colleagues, and in the run-up to the friendly he was quoted as saying 'If City aren't playing better than when I last saw them, I can't see them holding this Hibs side.' Manchester fans were warned that Hibs had returned to free-scoring form and were top scorers in the Scottish League with 82 already. In the four months that Bobby Johnstone had been back with Hibs, improved supply to the strikers had already seen seven hat-tricks recorded – only 10 had been registered during the entire four and a half years that Bobby Johnstone was 'away' in Manchester. In the event, the match ended in a rather mundane 1–1 draw, but Joe Baker got two further hat-tricks before the end of the season, achieving a club-record 42 League goals and an overall total of 46.

February's Scottish Cup campaign began successfully against Dundee, and Bobby's goal in that second-round match began his spell of seven in nine games. The next round brought an opportunity for Bobby to play a first-class match at Firs Park, East Stirlingshire's home in Falkirk – they had joined the Scottish League just as Bobby left it in 1955. He failed to score there, but did register a penalty against Rangers in the fourth round at Ibrox Park. The game ended 2–3, and this proved to be Bobby's last tilt in the Scottish Cup, a trophy that was greatly coveted, and in many senses more so than the League Championship flag. Lawrie Reilly summed up the feelings of his teammates and supporters when he reflected on Hibs' inability to claim the Scottish Cup during the Famous Five's heyday. 'My only regret is that Hibs never won the Cup. God just didn't want it. It was such a big thing to do then, to win the Cup. The League was not as important as it is today, what with the European Cup. But with the Cup, you could come back and parade through the streets of Edinburgh. We got close on many occasions, but kept failing…' Sadly, it is now over a century since the name of Hibernian FC was engraved on to this trophy.

The statisticians now had to put in extra hours, and on 2 April 1960 Bobby scored his 100th and final Scottish League goal for Hibernian in their 3–2 win at Stirling Albion. After a 5–0 win against relegated Arbroath,[3] Hibs picked up some silverware when they triumphed 3–2 in an Easter Monday derby at Tynecastle, retaining the East of Scotland Shield. Bobby scored twice there, but it was small beer compared with former achievements. At the end of what was nonetheless a truly remarkable season, Hibs could look back on having scoring four at Aberdeen in a defeat, five in a draw at Clyde, but a finishing position of only seventh in the League. Yet, inevitably, they were the League's top scorers. Bobby scored 17 League goals, including that 100th, and in doing so became the last member of Hibs' Famous Five to reach that milestone. His seasonal total was supplemented by a League goal in England, and with two goals in the Scottish Cup his total of 20 was a mark he only ever otherwise reached during the halcyon days of the Famous Five. Joe Baker, who later left for Torino, became the fastest Hibs player ever to reach 100 goals. It's no coincidence that this was the club's record goalscoring season too, with 106 goals scored, eclipsing the Manchester City total of two years earlier. In conceding 85, though, Hibs finished with only 35 points, 19 points behind the Champions Hearts. Kilmarnock scored just 67 goals yet managed 50 points and finished as runners-up! Bobby Johnstone's career was beginning to sound like a storyline from a boys' comic-strip. His previous three seasons had now seen Manchester City score 104 and concede 100 in 1958, the last-night drama of the Leicester game in 1959, and now the move back to Hibs, where once again the goals had been flying in from everywhere. It was a plot that would continue for some time yet.

As the season was concluding, details of an extensive club tour to the continent were announced, and Bobby was among a list of 15 players to be accompanied by Hugh Shaw and Eddie Turnbull. The initial intention was to leave a few days after the end of the season and head to the south coast of England. In an itinerary familiar to Bobby at least, there would be a friendly match at Portsmouth before the players were to watch the FA Cup Final. Thereafter, the party were to go on to Holland for a midweek friendly. After games in Germany and Italy, the trip was scheduled to conclude in Switzerland. However, the tour turned out rather shorter than planned, and took in only three games. The party headed straight for Germany, and began with a 3–2 win against Bayern Munich. From there, it was on to Yugoslavia, where Bobby scored Hibs' goal in a 1–1 draw with Dinamo Zagreb before facing Rijeka, then a considerable force in the Yugoslav First Division.

The night before the game in Zagreb had seen a very famous European Cup Final tie played back home in Scotland, when Real Madrid scored seven against Eintracht Frankfurt in a 10-goal bonanza at Hampden Park. Alfredo Di Stefano scored three in this match, and Ferenc Puskas, two years older at 33, scored four. Being abroad, Bobby missed the opportunity to see Puskas in the flesh, though he subsequently referred to having seen the game – presumably he was later able to view film of the match. Bobby reckoned that Puskas was the greatest player he ever *saw,* let alone played against, although by 1960 he was considered to be past his best. Having defected to the West following the Hungarian uprising of 1956, Puskas spent a year in Austria while hoping to get clearance to play in Italy. He failed to get a playing permit, started to put on weight and drifted for some time before moving to Real Madrid. By the time of the 1960 European Cup Final, many experts considered him too old and too large, yet he turned the clock back, producing a scintillating performance. The comparison is compelling. Bobby Johnstone had played for clubs that had adopted the deep-lying centre-forward plan made famous by the Hungarians. He had heard suggestions that he was too old, and rather too rotund. Might he yet emulate the great Puskas and produce more magic as his own career moved into its autumn?

* * * *

During the summer break it was cricket and relaxation, and there were plenty of mates in Selkirk who were glad to see him back, and indeed quite a few with whom he had stayed in touch with anyway. Naturally, he began to lose touch with several of his friends in Manchester though, including the Niven family. Ian (Snr) recalled 'It was when he went back to Hibs that we lost contact with Bobby… it wasn't that we weren't friendly, we just lost track. I'd never been a drinking or social buddy of Bobby's anyway, and when he moved back up north things moved on for all of us.' Bobby's sister Jenny and her family came through to visit for a few days. Bobby's young nephew Robbie, then aged nine, was beginning to get more interested in football generally, and Hibs in particular, in spite of the difficulties keeping up to date. The family lived on a rather isolated farm at Duns in Berwickshire, and Robbie's father, a shepherd, had little interest in football. Up until that point, the youngster's involvement in the game had extended no further than listening to the scores as they came through on the wireless, though he knew his uncle was a famous footballer. His earliest realisation of that came earlier, in the summer of 1956. Bobby had put him in the back seat of his car and taken him down to the Market Square in Selkirk, where he bought the youngster a toy: 'Obviously, I didn't understand what fame was as such, but even then I realised he was special, with people stopping him in the street. At first I didn't stay closely in touch with his football career though, and the families seldom spoke; there was only one phone on the farm in those days, and that belonged to the farmer! I'll never forget one time, though, when my Uncle Bobby came through to the farm. I was still at primary school, around eight or nine, and Bobby had come back to Hibs. One of my mates, Denny, he was older than me and already at high school, he was a Hibs fanatic. I told him my uncle was coming through, and when he saw him he was shaking like a leaf. I know that years later Denny had a season ticket for Easter Road, but I've not seen him since those childhood days. It's a powerful memory, and I'll never forget Denny's face – but it was just Uncle Bobby.'

The 1960–61 season kicked off as usual, with the League Cup the initial focus of attention. Hibs were grouped with Kilmarnock, Dunfermline and Airdrie, and the six fixtures began badly with a defeat at Rugby Park by 2–4, though Bobby did score from a penalty-kick. Midweek came a routine 3–0 home win against Dunfermline Athletic, and on the next Saturday Bobby got his second goal of the season and Joe Baker scored four times in a 6–1 stroll against final League Cup group opponents Airdrieonians. That last goal, scored coincidentally against an ex-Hibee and, indeed, Newtongrange Star teammate Lawrie Leslie, would prove to be Bobby's last for Hibs.

The following Wednesday the Scottish League campaign opened, disastrously, at Tannadice Park, the home of newly-promoted Dundee United. A 1–3 defeat was not only an inauspicious start, but, more significantly, it was Bobby's last appearance in the green of Hibs. The fourth of the League Cup group games came next, against Kilmarnock the following Saturday, but both surviving members of the Famous Five were dropped for that game. It might have been coincidental, but manager Hugh Shaw's usual column in the match programme was replaced by an editorial piece. That article speculated about which of the two sides would progress to the League Cup quarter-finals from a group that remained wide open, and also bemoaned the 'great disappointment... that the boys had failed to match the furious spirit of the promoted Tannadice side, and paid the penalty. Manager Hugh Shaw has been absent from his desk this week due to a bout of tonsillitis. Two points today is the best tonic that the boys can give the boss.' It is inconceivable that Shaw remained in his sickbed while the decision to dispense with the services of a legend such as Bobby Johnstone was being finalised, but, whatever the behind-the-scenes goings on, there was no going back. Desmond Fox, who took the number-eight shirt, replaced Bobby, while Scott replaced Willie Ormond. Eyewitnesses confirmed that Bobby was present at the ground, and he started watching the Kilmarnock match from the trainer's bench. But he was then seen to leave the ground sharply, having summoned a taxicab – there had been a terminal fall-out. The following Monday, Hibernian FC issued a statement to the press, stating that Bobby Johnstone was not to report back to the ground until contacted. 'Don't call us...', in effect. The Dundee United game formed a most unsatisfactory end to what had been a glorious career for the club.

The precise reason for this state of affairs is unclear, but one authoritative source, who discussed these events with Bobby many years later, sheds light on the matter. 'When Bobby left the club the second time, it was under a cloud. They had lost at Dundee United, and the following Saturday Willie Ormond and Bobby were dropped from the side. Nobody likes to get dropped, but I think there may have been some transgressions on the Dundee trip during the week, and of course the match result was bad. In any event, Bobby didn't like Harry Swan, the chairman. He told me himself – it was one of the reasons he had left in the first place.' Disagreements with directors about money is a theory almost ubiquitous whenever Bobby was involved, and this time there was also speculation that Bobby was an unsettling influence on Joe Baker, who was in tremendous goalscoring form. 'Joe Baker was very hot property then; there were some suggestions that he was being advised to get down south, to get more money.' These factors may all have been contributory, but the deciding issue appears to have been the relationship between Bobby and chairman Harry Swan. Informed sources state that the two had a public row, for which Bobby was effectively sacked. Ironically, a couple of months after the Johnstone business, it was Joe's brother Gerry who moved south when he left St Mirren for Manchester City. In 1961 Gerry moved back north to Hibernian, but by then his brother Joe had made an ill-fated move to Torino, in Italy, where he lodged with Denis Law, who had just left City. It seems that Bobby might have made a decent living as a football agent in today's game!

The acrimonious split between Hibs and Bobby Johnstone was symptomatic of a difficult spell for Hibernian. They failed (for the seventh consecutive year) to progress into the knock-out stages of the League Cup, and no points whatsoever were accrued from their first eight League games, stretching well into October. Yet even this predicament was not sufficient to make Hibs summon Bobby Johnstone. Indeed, new players were brought in, one being Sammy Baird, a wing-half from Rangers, who was brought to fill Bobby's former role. Another incomer was Bobby's old friend Ronnie Simpson, who was generally felt to be past his best as he, too, was over 30. By the time Hibernian finally collected the first point of their season, Bobby was well ensconced at new employers, and he had once again scored in the Football League, having endured around seven weeks out of the game.

The achievements of Bobby Johnstone and his Hibernian contemporaries seem unlikely to be equalled in the near future, and for this reason the club and its supporters have never allowed the acrimonious nature of their final parting to cloud the memory of those glorious years. To this day, Bobby Johnstone is revered at Easter Road, and a wonderful oil painting of him is a feature of the director's hospitality suite in the main stand. He remains the sixth-highest goalscorer in the club's post-war history, the five men above him being the other members of the Famous Five and Joe Baker. That is some record for a man who was not a recognised goalscorer as such, and who played less than 200 League games for the club – at 30 games per season, Bobby played the equivalent of less than seven full seasons for Hibs.

An embarrassing difficulty that arose from Bobby's departure concerned a friendly fixture that had already been arranged between Hibs and Manchester City, which was scheduled for 26 September, a Monday night. Shortly after Bobby's suspension from duty, the club programme provides an 'explanation', if that is the correct phrase, implying that the match was in jeopardy, though seemingly not for any reason related to Bobby Johnstone. Apparently, having initially agreed to play the Inter-Cities Fairs Cup tie against the Swiss side Lausanne Sports in Edinburgh on Wednesday 28 September – two nights after the proposed friendly – 'subsequent events' had now made that night unsuitable for the game, and Hibs had agreed to travel to Switzerland to play the away leg on that Wednesday night instead. This meant the City friendly would probably have to be postponed; otherwise 'this would mean Hibs playing three games in five days'. A more accurate explanation would refer to the additional travelling under these altered arrangements, because three games in five days was plainly the initial intention. Subsequently, Lausanne Sports withdrew from the Inter-Cities Fairs Cup competition, and a 2–0 win was awarded to Hibs, their first 'win' for some weeks. In spite of the unexpected gap in the football calendar, the friendly game was never played, and the two clubs did not meet again until 1979.

Notes

1. Co-incidentally, Gordon Smith won a League Cup-winners' medal with Hearts that day, and so became only the second of the Famous Five to collect a senior Cup-winners' medal. At Easter Road, Hibs reserves won 8–0 against Airdrie reserves.
2. Though he had been brought up in Lanarkshire, Joe Baker was not qualified to play at international level for Scotland under the rules that prevailed at this time. He was born in Liverpool, while his father was stationed there during the war, and the rules that would subsequently have allowed him to opt to play for Scotland did not come into effect until 1967.
3. During this season Bobby faced Arbroath and Dunfermline Athletic in the Scottish First Division for the first time; they are the only two sides that he failed to register a career goal against at that level.

CHAPTER 9

Resurrections in Oldham

The Football League had formed into four Divisions in time for the start of the 1958–59 season, with the inaugural Division Four comprising those teams that had finished the previous season in the bottom halves of the old Division Three North and Division Three South. Although Oldham Athletic were close to earning a place in the new Division Three – a win in their last game would have seen them finish 10th – defeat meant that they finished in 15th place, joining the sides that were technically relegated into the new Fourth Division. They performed poorly during the first season under these new arrangements, finishing fourth from bottom, and so were ranked 89th in the 92-strong League – dismal, undeniably, and as a result Latics were forced to make a first-ever application for re-election to the Football League.

They were successful, but by April of the following season things were even worse. Bobby Johnstone was now playing at Hibernian as the 1959–60 season drew to a close, blissfully unaware of the adversity threatening his next club. Their bleak situation prompted this gloomy article from the sports editor of the *Oldham Evening Chronicle*: 'Any responsible person who could help the club over its crisis period would be more than welcome at Boundary Park. Being blunt, the days of life-saving appeals by Athletic are finished. The general public cannot come to Athletic's aid with donations. I am not being pessimistic, therefore, when I say that unless some responsible help can be found, Athletic are on the brink of closing down. For the club's sake, and for the sake of soccer in Oldham, I hope something will happen. I hope help will come forward. I hope a solution can be found. The coming weeks could decide whether football is played at Boundary Park next season.'

The article hardly galvanised any dramatic improvement because the season fizzled out, but this time with Oldham Athletic occupying 91st place, a mere point in front of the hapless Hartlepools United. Once again, this meant a humiliating application for re-election to the Football League, but this year there was cause to worry. Where previously the re-election process had been almost a foregone conclusion, this year candidates knew that Peterborough United were making an impressive claim to join the League, and this would have to be taken into account. Having knocked on the door of the professional game for some time – this would be their 19th application to enter the Football League – the Midlands League side had just embellished this year's claim with a run to the fourth round of the FA Cup. The League needed a fall guy. That fall guy, luckily for Latics, was Gateshead FC, in what came as quite a shock at the time. The north-east side, having finished third from bottom, and above Latics, were applying for re-election for the first time since the war and could consider themselves extremely unlucky on being unsuccessful. They believed that, unjustly, geography was the primary consideration in the League's decision to oust them. They immediately applied for membership of the Scottish League, but, ironically, were turned down on the grounds of distance: only Berwick Rangers' ground, which is also in England, was comfortably within 100 miles of their Tyneside home. Oldham Athletic, after a major scare, had lived to fight another day as members of the Football League.

* * * *

In July 1960, during the close season, Oldham appointed Jack Rowley, the former Manchester United and England forward, as their new manager. It was a start. Then new players started to arrive: George Greenall from Southampton, Johnny McCue from Stoke City and Jimmy Frizzell from Greenock Morton. There was new confidence within the revitalised camp, yet the season started as disastrously as ever, and by the end of September, Oldham's playing record was won 1, drawn 2, lost 9, those 12 League games rendering a sorry total of four points. Six home games had yielded one solitary point, and if that were not sufficient evidence of the new depth of the old crisis a 1–5 defeat away to Accrington Stanley most emphatically was. Stanley would fold and go out of business within 18 months, and, frankly, Latics were no better. Further reinforcements were called for, and at that stage Ken Branagan and Bert Lister came from Manchester City, in a £10,000 package deal.

Meanwhile, ex-City player Bill Spurdle, now in his fourth season at Boundary Park, knew that Bobby was not getting a game. 'He'd kept in touch from Scotland, and when I heard that he was not playing after a fall-out with the Hibs directors – I think he'd said something in the papers – we worked to get him down to Oldham. We were struggling, and I told Fred Williamson, one of the directors, you know, come on we're struggling here, let's try and get him down.' Recent upheavals had seen seven new directors join the board at Oldham, and one of them was Vic Gledhill, a City supporter. Vic knew Bobby from his time at Maine Road, and Bobby had promised that if he thought about moving back to the North West, he would let Vic know. While there were long odds against Oldham's board being capable of enticing Bobby to Boundary Park, at least Vic could put it to them. It would have to be some deal though; a club struggling to hold it's own in the Football League would need to look very creatively at funding the acquisition of a famous Scottish international, enticing him, if that is the correct word, with the prospect of assisting their fight for survival.

On the playing front, October began more brightly for Oldham, with a victory against York City, a game that Bobby watched from the stands. Then there was a relapse against Crewe Alexandra, before a morale-boosting win, away to top-of-the-table Stockport County. On 13 October came the best news of all. Oldham Athletic announced one of the major transfer coups in many a long year, the signing of 31-year-old Bobby Johnstone, with a transfer fee of £5,000 being paid to Hibernian. Bobby hadn't played since his August fall-out with Hibs, and his best days were clearly now behind him, but he arrived at Boundary Park to find plenty of familiar faces waiting, in particular several of his old mates from the

Manchester City days. Bobby already knew the manager, Jack Rowley, too. They had faced each other when England overcame the Scots at Hampden Park in April 1952, and there had been other 'friendly' occasions, most notably Gordon Smith's legendary testimonial, when Rowley had scored twice. Within a few days of signing for Latics, Bobby stated publicly that he was quite happy to be under his leadership. He even went so far as to suggest, tongue-in-cheek, that with so many ex-Manchester City players around it might be a good idea to consider adopting the Revie plan! This would be a matter for the manager, of course, but he 'was willing to play any scheme that Mr Rowley wants'. All very homely then, yet any suggestion of a comfort zone should have been quickly dispelled by a glance at the League table. Latics were at the bottom again and attracting crowds of only around 5,000 to 6,000.

Many years later Bobby recalled the scale of the challenge that faced the whole club at the time of his arrival in the autumn of 1960. 'When I arrived at Athletic, there was everything to play for with the club rooted to the bottom of Division Four, and the real possibility of dropping out of the League altogether. At the time there were a number of ex-Manchester City players at Boundary Park, Bill Spurdle, Ken Branagan, Peter Pheonix, and Bert Lister, and we all helped each other out in our new surroundings.' A couple of days after the transfer was completed, on Saturday 15 October, Bobby made his debut for Oldham against Exeter City at Boundary Park. A massive attendance of 17,116, the highest crowd that Latics had attracted for over six years, turned out to see if it was true. It was.

Bobby Johnstone gave a majestic performance, treated the crowd to a goal and played the leading role in a 5–2 win. As early as the 12th minute, he created a chance for John Liddell, who scored. After just under an hour, Peter Pheonix knocked the ball through to Bobby, and he calmly slipped the ball wide of the 'keeper and into the net.[1] In the 62nd minute Bobby dummied a centre from the left, and Bazley made it 4–1. Although Exeter City pulled another one back, a further goal three minutes from time re-established the three-goal cushion and sent the bumper crowd cheering on their way. The success-starved home fans hadn't seen their side score four times in a match for two and a half years, but that feat would be replicated on five further occasions before the New Year. Picking up on the sense of a new beginning, the local newspaper described Bobby as 'The Pied Piper', referring to the way the crowds had flocked along Sheepfoot Lane to see their new hero. The authoritative *Oldham Athletic – Complete Record* book described this match as one of the most critical in Latics' history; it was Bobby's debut, certainly, but it was also memorable for the way the team had played, with Bobby giving 'a virtuoso performance, thrilling the huge crowd, and paving the way for a new era in the club's history'.

The *Oldham Evening Chronicle* ran a lengthy piece that day, headlined 'Bobby Johnstone tells the story behind his signing'. In the article Bobby revealed that he had been 'put out of football for seven long weeks, but I don't want to be bitter about that'. He was making public that there had been difficulties, though he was careful not to elaborate, and he actually denied that he had left behind any ill-feeling in Edinburgh. The article goes on to mention several other factors that threw light on his decision to return to the North West, and these points are rather more convincing. Chiefly it seems that Oldham had simply been the first club to offer him a chance to return to the game, and his evident affection for that area was in their favour. He knew that 'Lancashire folk are naturally friendly', and the presence of several of his former playing colleagues from Maine Road must also have been of some comfort. Perhaps the most illuminating remarks centre upon what Bobby describes as the deciding factor, namely his own well-being. 'One thing that four and a half years at Maine Road taught me is to look for comfort and security when signing for a new club. Finding suitable lodgings is the single footballer's most important job.' Here Bobby is patently referring back to the somewhat nomadic existence he had led while at City, involving him in several changes of address, including some places better known by their name rather than a number. In fact, one of the key factors attracting him back up to Scotland and Hibernian was the opportunity to return to the stability of life at home in Selkirk, once again. Happily for Latics fans, with this move there was to be no such concern – Bobby reveals that he was going to be lodging with his friend and playing colleague Bill Spurdle. Bill had known Bobby since he first came down to Manchester five years before, and they had both scored against West Bromwich Albion on the day the Scot got his first goal for City. Bill and his wife, Marjorie, had agreed to Bobby lodging with them while more permanent arrangements were made. Marjorie remembers 'he moved in with us at Glen Thorne, on Rochdale Road, Royton. We had a lovely big house on a corner; it was like having four children, rather than just our three! Heather came down from Hawick on a regular basis, and she'd stay with us too.' With the immediate problem of suitable lodgings resolved, Bobby was confident that he was in a position to get his Oldham career off to a good start.

Bobby rounds off the newspaper article by praising the club's directors, who successfully conveyed their 'sheer enthusiasm and determination', leading Bobby to conclude that the set-up at Boundary Park was different to anything he had seen before, 'they strike me as men with their heart and soul set on rebuilding this club. I am honoured to think that they want me to play a part in that reconstruction. With this background, I think Athletic can, and will, see better days in the none-too-distant future.' These would prove prophetic words. Results picked up dramatically, and the week after his debut Latics visited newcomers Peterborough United, and gained a creditable draw. The next game had the bean-counters rubbing their hands even more vigorously, as Southport were despatched 3–2, with Bobby scoring again. After an FA Cup first-round win at Rhyl, it was back to League action, and this time Crystal Palace were the victims in a 4–3 thriller that saw Bert Lister score his first hat-trick for the club in front of 18,500 spectators. In late November Bobby got his first FA Cup goal for Latics in a thrilling 4–4 draw at Third Division Chesterfield, yet, having apparently done the hard part, Oldham inexplicably lost the replay 0–3. A disappointing result, but overall Bobby had settled back in the North West, and his football was going well.

Much of this could be attributed to his improved discipline off the pitch. The Hibs denouement came as a severe jolt, and coupled with the fact that there was little interest from the upper echelons of the game, it seems that Bobby had realised that he needed to settle to a more sensible way of life and give himself the best chance of extending his career in the game. Certainly while he lived with the Spurdles, he eschewed the opportunity for midweek socialising, and Majorie recalls Bobby 'sitting quite happily, watching television with one of the kids on his knee, and he'd have a glass of Ribena. He definitely never drank alcohol in the week, in fact he never touched a drop while he was in our house.'

This was a golden period for Bobby and Latics. The balance was right both on and off the pitch, and during an eight-match winning streak he even found time to marry his long-time girlfriend Heather Roden. The couple were married on 7 January 1961 at St Aidans and St Oswald's Roman Catholic Church on Vaughan Street, Royton, near Oldham. For some while, Ken Barnes had been standing by to be best man, but on the day he was out of the country – playing in a third-round FA Cup tie at Cardiff – and so it was Heather's brother, Peter, who presided over the nuptials.

The ceremony preceded Oldham Athletic's match against Hartlepools United at Boundary Park, and Marjorie Spurdle recalls the celebration continuing as the party made their way up to the Flying Horse, a public house in Rochdale, before the players had to dash off. Ken Barnes was quite surprised when he heard, though not at the apparent fixture congestion, 'In those days you would get married and play the same day, why not? I did. These days, it's all this "I can't play because my grandfather's died, or something," in them days that never came into it. You just got married and got back for 3 o'clock for kick-off!'

Bobby also moved out of his 'digs' at the Spurdle's house, the marital home being at Eskdale Avenue, Royton, which was just a little further to the north of Oldham, and a place provided by the football club as part of the transfer deal. 'It was a lovely place, I went there a couple of times. They were nice and cosy there' Marjorie recalled. It turned out to be quite a time for weddings, because the previous year Bobby's mother Elizabeth had re-married. She married a gentleman called James (Jimmy) McDonald, who coincidentally had played football for Jedburgh and, indeed, against Hopey on a couple of occasions.

By the February, Oldham Athletic were safe from the clutches of relegation, having gone on a run of 20 League games yielding 30 points, with just two draws and four defeats. The scale of Oldham's transformation is demonstrated by a quite serious remark from the editor of the official programme, when in early March he bemoans the fact that the ball has not run their way recently, and this has put paid to any promotion chances! The entire atmosphere at the club had been miraculously transformed. The reserves were 'doing well, with five wins in a row, and the third team were enjoying their best spell for many years'. That same month saw Latics' biggest crowd for seven years, 28,000, watch them play the newcomers Peterborough United, who would go on to be crowned Division Four Champions, and score 134 goals in the process. It was a titanic match, and the crowd that day was just 1,600 behind the attendance at an all-Lancashire First Division tussle seven miles away at Maine Road, where Manchester City faced Everton.

Since Bobby had joined the Latics they had played and won 10 successive home League games, scoring 38 goals, and they had enough chances to win this one too. However, the run came to an end, but with a creditable 1–1 draw. Oldham's goal came from a penalty, earned after a Peterborough defender had handled the ball to prevent Bobby advancing through on goal. This most volatile of seasons ended with Oldham Athletic safely located in 12th place. Twenty-eight players had been used in total, and over a dozen of them had arrived during the campaign. At the end of the season, 12 men were given free transfers, and for those leaving Oldham at the time it appears that there was nowhere else to go – only one of those released managed to secure a position with another League club.

Bobby Johnstone had played a major part in pulling things around, and crowds averaging well over 12,000 were testament to the directors' judgement and courage. They had invested wisely, brought a renowned star of British football back to the Lancashire hotbed and been richly rewarded. On a personal note, Bobby, now playing a deeper, pivotal role, had played 30 League games since his autumn arrival, missing only the December defeat at Northampton. He had finished as the second-top scorer with 11 goals, behind Bert Lister, who managed 14.

Bert, who would remain a lifelong friend of Bobby's, had joined Manchester City as a junior in October 1954, several months before Bobby arrived at Maine Road. His headmaster, Jimmy Mulligan (himself a City player during the 1920s), made arrangements for Bert to sign for City, and so he was allowed to leave his school in Blackley earlier than usual. It seemed that young Bert had a great future ahead; he had scored plenty of goals in junior football around Manchester, and he'd captained the Manchester Boys side. He spent six years at Manchester City, turning professional in November 1957 and making two first-team appearances in season 1958–59 when aged 17. Though he didn't play alongside Bobby Johnstone at first-team level, the pair played several reserve games together, particularly during Bobby's troubled last season with City. Bert's second game for City's first team was at inside-forward during the 1959 Easter holiday programme. 'I played for the reserves against West Bromwich Albion at Maine Road on Good Friday, and then again the next day away at Sheffield United. On Easter Monday I travelled down to West Bromwich for the reserves return fixture. We got back to Manchester late that Monday, but I had to report back to the ground at 9am on the Tuesday, and when I got there Lawrie Barnett told me that my boots had been called for... the first team were playing that day, also at West Bromwich. I told Denis Fidler what I thought of him, actually, because McDowall had been in and seen me, but he hadn't said anything, so I thought they were all taking the mickey, especially as Bobby had played for the reserves over the weekend, and was available. Later George Poyser came in, smoking his pipe, and asked why I was still here, as I was playing for the first team. It was a 3pm kick-off on the Tuesday, so I had to get my skates on. When I got down there, McDowall said "give me 100%, but don't worry, Colin [Barlow] will be fit for Saturday!"' After facing West Bromwich three times in five days, and Sheffield United too, Bert was rewarded with the drop, and Bobby Johnstone then took the number-eight shirt for the next first-team match, and he kept it for all but one of the remaining games that season.

Bert stayed with City after Bobby left for Hibernian the following September, but 18 months later, with no further appearances in the first team, he decided that enough was enough. He moved to Oldham on 28 September 1960 in the £10,000 deal that also included Ken Branagan. Two weeks later, Bobby Johnstone walked through the door. 'It didn't come about through me,' Bert says, 'but Bill Spurdle suggested Bobby to the new Oldham directors. One of the directors was Vic Gledhill, actually they were a great board. Maybe Jack Rowley mentioned it to Bill Spurdle, and Bill spoke to Bobby? Anyway that's the influence, not me. But Bobby and I were pals together at City, and of course I was delighted. We used to go to the Cromford Club together, and we'd had some good days in the reserves at City.'

Having previously seen Bobby Johnstone's ability at close-quarters, did he hope that Bobby's arrival at Boundary Park would be the spark to set his professional playing career off? 'It wasn't that I thought the partnership would be good for me, I never gave it any thought. I never looked at who their centre-half was anyway, tactics and all that. Bobby knew what was going on, he was the one who looked around the park. If I saw he had the ball, I'd run out to the wing, then double back to try and escape the centre-half, and the ball would arrive.' As testament to Bobby's wit on the ball, Bert believes he has a justifiable claim to the fastest goal ever scored in the Football League. 'One day, around Easter time in 1963, I scored against Chesterfield after... it must have been less than five seconds. Bobby was thinking about what was going on before we even kicked-off, and he told Bob Ledger to belt down the wing from the kick-off, while I just rolled the ball to Bobby and ran. Bobby launched it wide out to the right, Ledger played it first time into the middle, and I just volleyed it in. A year after Bert's goal, in April 1964, Jim Fryatt was at Bradford Park Avenue, and he scored a goal against Tranmere Rovers that was supposedly timed at four seconds, and so officially Fryatt holds the record. 'Jim Fryatt's goal went via three sides of a square in effect, but when I scored against Chesterfield it was just two moves. You'd obviously need a camera to sort it out, but I don't see how anyone could beat that.'

The partnership between Bobby and Bert proved a fruitful one for Oldham, as Bert went on to score 83 League goals in four seasons from just 135 appearances (overall his total was 95 goals in 152 appearances), before he left Latics for two years. Later, during a short spell at Stockport County, he scored some vital goals and earned a medal as part of their Fourth Division Championship side in 1966–67. In December 1967 he left to join non-League Altrincham, enjoying a spell there as a semi-professional.

Today, having retired as a businessman and sometime taxicab driver based in Blackpool, Bert is an active member of the Manchester City Former Players' Association and spends time at his homes in Manchester and Enniskillen, Northern Ireland. His summary of his close friend Bobby Johnstone, perhaps somewhat biased, is quite blunt: 'The best player I ever played with.'

* * * *

Quite naturally, with the club now revitalised, the following season kicked-off with some expectation that Latics were going to make a strong bid for promotion to Division Three. It seems that Bobby initially rejected the new terms offered to him by the club, but he eventually agreed to them, and though there doesn't seem to ever have been any genuine doubt that he would re-sign, again the issue of money had raised its head. Out on the pitch, Bobby started in great form, scoring three goals in the first four games, but only one of these was won, and it was the end of September before Oldham secured their second win of the season. Early in October, Boundary Park became one of the last Football League grounds to have floodlights installed, though the still precarious finances saw them funded by voluntary donation. The club celebrated by 'switching on' their new lights in a game against Burnley, which attracted a crowd of 15,500. The game ended in a 3–3 draw, both Bobby and Bert Lister scored, and it was around this time that Bert remembers seeing Bobby looking around the crowd during a pre-match warm-up; Bert asked him who he was looking for, and was surprised to hear the answer... Bobby was 'guessing the bloody crowd, because he didn't think they'd been getting all of their bonuses!'

Bobby maintained his goalscoring form with a goal in a 3–1 defeat at Holker Street, Barrow, the following Saturday, his fifth of the season, and results then took a definite turn for the better, though the first 'win' in a good sequence was notable. On 11 October 1961 Latics thrashed Accrington Stanley 5–0. Later, when Stanley were unable to complete their fixtures, the League erased the results of the 33 League games they had managed. Outside of Accrington, few will have been more disappointed than Bert Lister, who had his four goals in that match crossed off. But the win was useful nonetheless as a platform for Oldham, and they became further encouraged by achievements in the FA Cup. During the home victory against Shildon, a Northern League side from Co. Durham, Bobby converted his first penalty for the club. Although he was now a senior professional, he had hitherto played in teams that already had expert penalty takers – notably Eddie Turnbull and then Ken Barnes, and so Bobby's prowess from the spot had rarely been called upon. Why he started to take penalties for Oldham at this particular point is a mystery, because the usual penalty taker Ken Branagan was on the pitch at the time, yet Bobby took, and scored, the kick anyway. Two weeks later, at Workington, when Latics were awarded their next penalty, Bobby was absent, so it was Bill Spurdle that took on the responsibility, although again Branagan was present.

Bobby's three-match absence (due to injury) began with the previous match, at home to Mansfield, and this turned out to be Oldham's first home League defeat of the season. He also missed the second-round FA Cup game, when Latics once again travelled over to Chesterfield and earned a draw. He was fit for the replay though, which this year proved successful. The Derbyshire men were despatched 4–2, with Bobby scoring from the spot again in front of almost 21,000. The reward was a trip south to face Bristol Rovers at Eastville, a tough task, as although Rovers were struggling they were nonetheless a Division Two side.

The team continued their tremendous run, winning six of the next eight League games. Bobby notched three more goals before the New Year, taking his tally to 10, more than creditable by that stage of the season, and a pattern that, peculiarly, seemed to recur throughout the latter stages of his career. On New Year's Eve, in a 5–0 stroll at Southport played on two inches of snow, Bobby scored and pulled all the strings. One newspaper report referred to 'the masterful performance and skill of a man who has played on every type of surface – by the time he set up Oldham's fourth goal, it was noticeable that half of Southport's crowd had returned home to their fires'. In the New Year, the town warmed to the gallant 1–1 draw earned in the third-round FA Cup match at Bristol. That match had to be postponed from the scheduled Saturday kick-off and was held over until the Monday night, but Bristolians were warned in the match programme that 'the small but brilliant Johnstone has proved one of the best bargains ever, and his influence has often worked miracles'. The Oldham townsfolk responded in droves to the prospect of a replay at Boundary Park, and a crowd of over 27,000 turned out to see the Latics triumph 2–0. The fans then gleefully awaited the draw for the fourth round, and they were not disappointed; a 'plum' tie against Liverpool was scheduled for late January.

A massive crowd of 41,733 turned out to see a tremendous Cup tie against the Reds, with Latics having an opening 'goal' disallowed when Bobby put Bert Lister through on the left. He shot first time across goalkeeper Bert Slater, netting from outside of the area, but his delight turned to dismay when he realised the linesman had called offside. The referee later told Lister that Peter Pheonix, out wide on the right, was in an offside position. It seems strange today, but it appears that the officials had simply applied the rules, with little, if any, regard for the intricacies of passages or phases of play, or interference with this or that. Latics held Liverpool until the 73rd minute, and, with the crowd spilling over from the terraces and on to the perimeter of the pitch, Ian St John scored a goal that was hotly disputed. His shot hit the underside of the bar and bounced down, at which it was hacked clear by John McCue. The referee awarded a goal though, and six minutes later St John added Liverpool's second. John Colquhoun then scored for Latics, but in spite of their brave effort the Merseysiders held on and went on to a fifth-round tie against Preston North End. They also won the Second Division Championship by a good margin, entering the First Division, where they still remain well over 40 years later.

After the heroics of their FA Cup run, Latics were unable to maintain their form, and the season petered out disappointingly. Bobby scored only one more goal, in a 1–3 reverse at Rochdale, though he did have the satisfaction of completing all but two of the remaining League fixtures, coincidentally missing the away game against Mansfield too, which was also a defeat. There was a short burst of winning form at the end of the season, with three meaningless victories, but these served only to leave Latics in a disappointing 11th spot. Their downfall had been inconsistency away from home, with only five wins and five draws from those 22 games. At Boundary Park they were far more successful: 31 of their 46 points total were gained at home. Bobby managed 46 League and Cup games, and 12 goals, but his scoring pattern mirrored the team's problem – he scored just three times away from home. Jimmy Frizzell, the new hot Scot, led the goalscoring effort with 24, and Bert Lister got 17. In spite of everything, the official club view of the season was disappointment that the promotion dream had faded away, although attendances had held up magnificently. Latics were now the best-supported team in the Fourth Division, attracting higher crowds than many Third Division clubs. There was some regret, but a determination that next year things would improve further.

The following season got off to a great start, and after 16 games Latics looked to be making a real surge for promotion. They headed the Fourth Division with 26 points, and there was only one defeat in this excellent opening spell. The only time Latics had failed to score was in the 0–0 draw at Newport County, and in some ways this was now the problem. It was the only game that Bobby missed. His prompting from a position behind the strikers was a vital part of their success.

This point in Bobby's football career saw a definite watershed. Jack Rowley had brought yet another Scot down to England, Jim Bowie, and early on in the season Bobby and the new man linked up twice. Soon though Jim effectively became Bobby's understudy in the number-eight shirt, playing only whenever the senior man was unavailable. As Rowley was well aware, injury was indeed taking a greater toll on Bobby's availability, and he would play in only 13 of the remaining 30 League games. Latics' form began to take a turn for the worse, and it is no fluke that this coincided with Bobby's increasing absence.

After that tremendous opening spell, Bobby missed two drawn games, at Aldershot and Doncaster, coming back into the side for the 2–5 defeat at Bradford City in the first round of the FA Cup. At this stage of the season, now into November, Latics had still to lose an away League game, but they would not wait long. The following week saw Latics' 10th away League game, and defeat, 3–4 at Gillingham. Latics had two 'goals' disallowed, including a long-ranger from Bobby, and it seems almost incredible to record that without Bobby Johnstone the team would muster just one single point away from home during the rest of the season – yet still they achieved success.

The following week Bobby faced Dave Ewing, who had just signed for Crewe Alexandra, and the honours were even at 1–1. Latics now began a run of mainly home fixtures, and they went the next eight games with just one defeat, at Brentford, the only match in this sequence that Bobby missed. On 26 December there was a truly notable achievement, when Southport were thrashed 11–0 on a snow-covered pitch. This is still Latics' record victory, and an occasion warmly remembered for one of the greatest of goalscoring feats by Bert Lister, who grabbed a bagful in front of the Bank Holiday crowd of 15,000. Bert recalled 'The whole forward line scored, and I got six. But honestly, Bobby's was the best of the lot, but it was disallowed! The 'keeper punched it out, and Bobby volleyed it back in over his head, but I was given offside.'

The *Oldham Evening Chronicle* recorded that Athletic had been trying hard to better their 11 goals against Chester in 1952, when they recorded an 11–2 win, a result that remains in the record books as Chester's record defeat. For Latics, the Southport victory replaced that achievement, though a 12th goal evaded them. The *Oldham Evening Chronicle* reported that 'no one tried harder than hero Lister, who hit four of his six goals in that final 45-minute period. In the closing minutes, Athletic raged even fiercer than the driving snowstorm, which threatened to wipe out the game. But they couldn't make the dozen. Disappointment number two was for schemer-in-chief Bobby Johnstone. While he watched his fellow forwards take large helpings of the goal feast, Bobby just couldn't get his name on the score sheet.[2] One blockbuster of a goal disallowed, and two great saves from goalkeeper Joe Harris, almost added up to a conspiracy to cheat Athletic's top-class architect. But if Bobby didn't get among the goals, he had his share of the glory. Like an impudent snowman, he was all over the snow-covered pitch, prodding and probing, reducing the shattered Southport defence to a state of total collapse.[3] Prior to the game, Harry Massey, the club chairman, had rather unwisely offered the Latics players a £5-per-goal bonus. To his credit he paid out – Latics were top of the League after all – but it had been a fit of seasonal generosity that he probably regretted, and he certainly didn't offer again!

It is worth recording here that the overwhelming majority of professional footballers go through their entire first-class career without ever being involved in a match where *either* side scores 10 goals. For Bobby Johnstone, this was the third time in just over three years that he had played in a side that had reached double figures in a League game, an astonishing fact that the author believes is without equal.

In many respects, it was fortunate for Latics that the Southport game was even started, never mind completed, given Boundary Park's position among the highest grounds in the Football League. This was the winter of the great freeze, and Bobby and his colleagues played no more football for almost a month. On 12 January 1963, with Athletic's game at Torquay United postponed, the *Oldham Evening Chronicle* ran a light-hearted article about Bobby, but throwing little new light on what was now a substantial playing career. It did enlighten readers about his other sporting loves, including cricket, of course, golf (his handicap at the time was 8), badminton and snooker. Presumably desperate to fill its otherwise empty sports pages, the article was accompanied by a photograph of Bobby and Heather supposedly cleaning their car outside their bungalow in Royton, near Oldham. There is more than a suspicion, though, that the Johnstones were actually engaged in no such thing, unless one is inclined to believe that the two of them routinely cleaned their vehicle in several inches of snow while wearing 'smart-casual' attire.

With games few and far between for most clubs, Latics actually managed to play three more home games, but no away fixtures, by the middle of February. Some clubs went well over two months without being able to complete any home fixtures at all, so Latics hadn't fared too badly, and for Bert Lister the 'whiteout' coincided with an incredible purple patch. He had scored 12 goals in Latics' previous five games. Later in the month, the weather was improving to some extent, particularly in the south, and Oldham were due to visit Exeter City. Officials hastily agreed to rearrange the previously postponed game against Torquay United for the preceding Wednesday night, and thus Bobby played for the only time on the English Riviera. If he was seen wearing sunglasses, though, it is less likely to have been related to the weather and more to do with the fact that he was taken out of the game by an over-physical Torquay United side. That game ended in defeat, as did the Saturday fixture against Exeter, and back in Lancashire the following week the programme editor, ruing the defeats in Devon, could barely contain himself. 'We lost Bobby Johnstone to what I really and truly thought was an over-vigorous way of going into the tackle... their officials made no bones about it, one saying that this would be how they would stop us taking away the points. There is no doubt about one thing – Bobby was made a TARGET, and as a result he could be out of the game for many weeks to come.' Bobby missed nine consecutive games.

On the bright side, there was satisfaction that the club had not fallen too far behind its programme, while other clubs had many fixtures to make up due to the weather, which it was hoped would be to Oldham's advantage. In spite of the two defeats, the League table showed that Oldham, with 41 points, were still at the top, with Brentford (the eventual Champions) in second place, some seven points behind, but with four games in hand. The next clubs, both 10 points behind Latics, were Mansfield Town, albeit with six games in hand, and Torquay, who could only realistically look to kick their way to second spot at best.

Of the nine games that Bobby missed, only two were victories, and this took Latics rather unsteadily through to the beginning of April. Now locked into a run of very poor away form, a defeat at Haig Avenue, Southport, meant that they had now lost eight of nine away games. When Bobby came back into the side for a five-match spell towards the end of the season things turned around immediately, and his comeback came at an absolutely crucial point, the 3–2 win in a genuine four-pointer at Crewe Alexandra. Two further wins at Boundary Park helped to steady the ship. Thankfully, home form had held up remarkably all season, and Latics reached the end of the season having suffered just the one home defeat, against Exeter City in late October. Latics finished in second place, behind Brentford, having scored 95 goals. From what had seemed a strong position as the teams entered autumn, Latics had rather stumbled over the finishing line, and in the race for the runners'-up spot, and talent money of £400, they had held off the challenge of Crewe Alexandra only on goal average. The rout against Southport and the thrilling win at Gresty Road on Bobby's return to the side had proved critical. Tellingly, Bobby had missed 18 games, of which Latics managed to win only five, all at Boundary Park. In the 11 away games he missed the team picked up a paltry four points, scoring only nine goals. Jim Bowie, the young Scot, deputised for Bobby 12 times, and Bobby was asked what he thought of the lad. His reply was not disrespecting his colleague, but it did put things in perspective: 'he's a good lad... but at his age I'd been capped eight times.'

Of the 28 League matches Bobby did play, Oldham won 19 and drew five, and he played in all six away wins. For a promoted side these statistics seem rather peculiar. In fact the 1962–63 season was one of the most peculiar in the whole of Bobby Johnstone's career – he scored only five goals all season, and the fifth and final of these was a spectacular overhead kick against York City way back on 1 December. It was clear now that Bobby's role was almost solely that of a provider. The club's top scorers were Bert Lister with 30, and Colin Whitaker, who managed 17, between them scoring half of Latics' total. According to the club's young assistant secretary Bernard Halford, the chief reason for Oldham's success was simply the number of goals they scored when Bobby Johnstone played. 'Most of the goals were created by Bobby, and if he didn't play we struggled.'

While Bobby's career was now starting to go into decline, one contemporaneous point concerns Bobby's old Famous Five partner Gordon Smith, who had played his first game for Hibernian when Bobby was aged 11. Smith was still playing at the top level in the Scottish League, and while Bobby was gaining a first-ever promotion, Smith actually played in the semi-finals of the European Cup, his side Dundee losing only to the eventual winners AC Milan.

In May 1963, just after the topsy-turvy but nonetheless successful promotion season, something very unusual in football occurred: Oldham Athletic manager Jack Rowley lost his job. Rowley had many fall-outs with Bobby Johnstone over what might charitably be called 'lifestyle issues'. In fact, he was convinced that Bobby was breaking club rules by socialising and, more specifically, actually drinking on Thursday and even Friday nights. On occasions, Rowley had been known to tour around the pubs of Oldham himself, checking for miscreant players, most notably Bobby Johnstone – though he never actually found him. Bernard Halford recalled 'He'd go up and down Union Street and Yorkshire Street, into the Oldham Hotel, The Friendship, Royal Oak, the Mess House, checking all the pubs – he'd stop his car outside and dash in, leaving the car doors open – checking that Bobby wasn't out drinking after a Wednesday.'

It is important in any team game to maintain discipline, and for senior players to set a good example to the younger ones; it is football lore that no man is bigger than the club. Against this background, the 10 directors of the Oldham Athletic board had to decide upon an improved contract for Rowley. With his authority reinforced, there was some suggestion that Rowley might take the opportunity to move Bobby out of the club. There remained significant support for the player among board members, some of whom believed that he had almost single-handedly earned them promotion. Prior to their meeting, it seemed that the 10-man board would go 6–4 in favour of awarding Rowley a new contract, and, in doing so, bring to an end Bobby's time at Oldham. On the night, with Alan Crook, Vic Gledhill and a couple of others firmly in the pro-Johnstone camp, it required at least two more directors to change their minds. One such director was George Howarth, a confectioner from Duchess Street, Shaw, but somebody else must have been persuaded beyond second thoughts too, because in the end it went 6–4 against Rowley, and he was asked to resign, and by 11 May. Bobby Johnstone stayed.

With any uncertainty gone at least for the immediate future, Bobby was a happy man, and two weeks later, on 26 May 1963, there was even better news as Bobby and Heather's only child, their daughter Nicola, was born. With Heather temporarily indisposed, Bobby had an evening meal at Bernard Halford's that night, courtesy of Bernard's mother, but the two were unable to 'wet the baby's head' together: 'I had a bowling fixture, so I couldn't go out with him. After his tea he went off in his car, and a couple of people rang my house later, but, of course, I had no idea where he was.' Bobby was delighted with one departure and one arrival, but football is a very strange game, and when

Oldham Athletic's new manager was appointed, Bobby's heart must have nearly hit his boots. In walked Les McDowall, his old boss from Manchester City! As Oldham Athletic were being promoted, the 'donkeys' at Maine Road had been relegated, and with that the manager had lost his job. Bernard Halford commented 'I thought what a mess the directors had made of it, they'd sacked Rowley after gaining promotion, largely because of a spat with a player, and then appointed McDowall!' Bert Lister's first thought when he found out was 'That's me gone', even though he'd scored over 30 goals the previous season.

A couple of months later, a momentous decision was made, and it changed the face of football. Just as many lawyers had predicted, on 4 July 1963 the High Court decided that 'The retain and transfer system was unlawful, because in effect it was a restraint of trade.' The case had its origins in 1959, when George Eastham of Newcastle United requested a move south for personal reasons. Newcastle refused to countenance Eastham's request, and so he raised a test case. As with many of the other advances that players made in the post-war years, this came too late in Bobby's career for him to benefit to any great extent.

Oldham Athletic had been promoted for the first time in a decade, and prior to the first game of the season a tannoy message announced Nicola's birth during the close season, then her father's dedication, 'Bobby's Girl', which had been a hit record for Susan Maughan the previous winter, just at the time the Johnstone's realised that they would have to start planning for their new arrival. Bobby enjoyed popular music, and in the old days back at Hibs it was a tradition for the players to take turns choosing a record to be played over the PA during the half-time break. Bobby often chose something by his favourite singer Nat King Cole: he particularly liked his version of Mona Lisa.

The season kicked-off with manager Les McDowall's bold statement making his intentions clear: 'Give the fans a winning team, and they'll turn up.' Hardly rocket science, but by October Oldham were top of the Third Division table with 17 points from 11 games, a superb start for any newly-promoted club. Bobby Johnstone missed the first three games of the season, including a couple of long-distance away games at Bournemouth and Bristol Rovers, but he then had a good run in the side until he missed two more away games at the end of October. One highlight was the 4–0 win at Wrexham in September, Ken Barnes being their player-manager. During November and December, while results generally were inconsistent, Bobby himself hit some goalscoring form, with six in six games, although the latter four were from the penalty spot.

Things went fairly well as Christmas came and went, though Bobby can't have guessed that he would score only once more in his career. As the year turned, Latics crashed 2–4 at Notts County, and the following week, in the third round of the FA Cup, they proved no match for an Ipswich Town side that had won the League Championship two years before, losing 3–6, though their manager Jackie Milburn was impressed enough to suggest that Latics would 'skate out of the Third Division'. But three away League games in January yielded just one point and no goals, though a home win by 2–0 against an emerging Coventry City brought a welcome two points. Coventry, who were correctly nominated as certainties for Second Division football (they were promoted as Champions) lost just their fourth game of the season at Boundary Park. The victory helped Oldham retain second position, at least until the end of January. The last of the three away defeats though, at Crewe, heralded a remarkable collapse, and only one point was earned from the next six games. By the time the rot was stopped, Bobby was again out of the side due to knee problems.

By early April, when he regained his fitness, any chance of promotion had gone. Two points from the previous six home games had seen Latics fall to 11th place in the League table. Bobby made a goalscoring return to Boundary Park in the next home game, a 1–0 victory against Mansfield Town, but this goal, on 4 April 1964, proved to be his last in first-class football. He stayed in the side to complete the League programme, but even with two further wins from the last four games, a total of only 12 points from the last 17 games, meant that Latics had finished ninth, a tremendous disappointment given the start they had made.

On 15 April, a Wednesday night, Bobby returned to Maine Road to play in Bert Trautmann's testimonial match,[3] in front of a crowd seriously under-estimated at over 47,000. Playing alongside Stanley Matthews in a reprise of the 1955 Great Britain side, once again the great man scored as Matthews looked on! Although the score didn't matter, for the record Bobby's International XI 'suffered' a 4–5 defeat to Bert's combined Manchester XI, with Bobby's future Oldham colleague Albert Quixall scoring twice, and their other goal coming from a true comedy moment when Maurice Setters, playing for Manchester XI, ran towards his own goal and smashed the ball past Trautmann. Setters later explained that it was something he had always wanted to achieve, and he knew he wouldn't get another chance! Bobby was always forward with his opinions on the merits, or otherwise, of playing colleagues, but he was proud to have been associated with Bert Trautmann. After a match at Chelsea, just a few months after joining City, he had said 'there is no one better. With this chap, you win when you should have lost,' although ironically City had lost 1–2 that day, though Chelsea might have had 10. Years later, more thoughts on the goalkeeper were revealed in a radio interview, when the main subject had been the 1956 Cup Final. 'Bert Trautmann, the big German goalkeeper we had then, was the best goalkeeper I ever played with in my life. I've never played – I've never seen – anybody catch the ball as cleanly as he did, he was a marvellous goalkeeper.'

By the end of the season, Bobby could look back upon 16 full seasons since his Scottish League debut for Hibernian. Now aged 34, he had actually managed six games more than in the previous season, though he was struggling badly with his knee. He had improved his scoring ratio too, with nine in total, although this was assisted to a large degree by his continuing with penalty-taking duties. Bobby scored five times from the spot, in what was effectively his last 'full' season. Again, though, the curious goalscoring pattern of previous years was evident, with Bobby only scoring once after Christmas.

Bobby failed to start the 1964–65 season in the first team because of an injury received while playing a pre-season friendly. Now approaching his 35th birthday, he was getting weary with his knee problems, which were certainly not getting any better, and for Latics the disappointing performances of the previous season continued into the new one. An opening day 1–5 home defeat to relegated Grimsby Town was swiftly followed by a 0–5 drubbing at Peterborough, just 48 hours later. Bobby was recalled to the first team for the next game, but he had no obvious effect in a 1–4 defeat at Field Mill, Mansfield, and sadly this was the only one of the first nine League games for which Bobby was fit. Les McDowall had obviously realised that he must manage without Bobby, although it was less than clear whom he had in mind as a replacement because in the first six games of the new season the number-eight shirt was occupied firstly by Bob Craig, then Bert Lister, Johnstone himself and Jim Bowie (for two consecutive games!) before Albert Quixall arrived. By this time McDowall was starting to receive criticism from the Latics faithful, who were aggrieved, not unnaturally, about results. To this end, Latics made a bit of a splash to try and move away from the foot of the table, most notably by signing Quixall, the former England international. Perhaps Oldham were hoping that the 'famed former international' recipe would work for a second time. However, for many Oldham supporters a secondary cause of terrace hostility towards McDowall was because their favourite was out of the side – whether or not Bobby's physical condition actually justified his inclusion was a side issue!

Throughout the majority of this opening period of the season, Bobby had actually been playing regularly in the reserve team, and he later referred to the enjoyment he had gained from playing a role in the development of younger players, many of whom were just starting out in the game. The reserves were then part of the Northern Regional League, and Bernard Halford, now in his mid-20s, used to enjoy watching their home matches. Many of these were played on Saturdays while the first team were elsewhere. Bernard recalls several occasions when Les McDowall would stop to give him a lift up to the ground as he passed Bernard's bus stop on the following Monday morning. McDowall would then be forced to listen to rather subjective descriptions of Bobby's feats for the second team – in common with many Latics supporters, Bernard too felt that Bobby should be back in the first team. McDowall would noticeably blanch at hearing this, and Bernard goes on: 'McDowall just didn't like it, he went quiet. The reserves won their League that season. This one lad, Albert Jackson, was full-back in the reserves, and they tried him at centre-forward, and he started to score goals for fun, with Bobby putting him through. Meanwhile, in the first team they'd tried Bert Lister, Bob Craig, John Colquhoun up front, and none of them could score goals, they all got dropped. Anyway, around the end of September we'd lost a load of games, and we had a midweek match against Exeter, and he put Bobby back in the first team and played Colquhoun at centre-forward. Bobby turned it on, juggling and all that for the crowd, but I believe it was also contempt for McDowall, and we won 2–0, Colquhoun got them both.' In fact, one of Colquhoun's 'goals' was recorded as an 'o.g.', but the point is well made. The depth of feeling among Latics supporters was tangible, and one supporter, who occupied a regular spot on the terrace steps just by the players' tunnel, wasn't slow to vocalise this. He went by the name of Foster Crickitt, had a booming voice, and was a renowned 'blaster' of match officials. That night Bernard saw him walk down to the front of the terracing where the dugouts were located, turn around, and sarcastically bawl up to the directors, squirming in their box, '10,000 are wrong, and one bloody man's right'.

Bobby Johnstone played another half-dozen times after that memorable game, but it was clear to all, Bobby included, that the magic had gone, and by mid-October he was out of the side again. The team struggled badly for much of the season, with both Bobby and Albert Quixall out for long periods. Only Jimmy Frizzell, who played most of the season at wing-half, reached double figures in the goalscoring charts – and he needed three goals playing as an emergency inside-forward during the last four games to achieve that paltry total.

Bert Lister left the club not long after Christmas, having scored only twice all season; he sensed change in the air once again. The club were struggling financially, crowds were not turning up in numbers, and the days of five-figure home gates had gone, in spite of the fact that Third Division football remained on offer. Bert learned that he 'could go if he was happy enough with the back-hander! I got nearly two grand, so I went to Rochdale'. At the end of March, with his playing career now almost at an end, Bobby came back into the side for three final appearances. The circumstances for Latics were desperate, and with only eight games left relegation was more than a possibility. Surprisingly, Bobby, who hadn't played in the first team for five months, was recalled for a home game against Walsall, taking the injured Jim Bowie's number-10 shirt, which he retained for two further games because of the subsequent absence of Jimmy Frizzell. But he was no longer capable of conjuring up one last hurrah, and in fact all three games were lost. His final appearance, only his 11th of the season, came against Workington in a 0–2 defeat, before a dismal 'crowd' of just 5,500.

Once Jimmy Frizzell was fit, Bobby dropped out, and Frizzell then replaced Bobby in the forward line for the final five games, moving forward from his now usual wing-half position. The three goals he scored were chiefly responsible for creating the three-point margin by which Latics survived to fight another day in the Third Division. It was time for Bobby to retire. The knee injuries that had plagued him for so long, and prematurely ended his international career almost a decade earlier, had now overwhelmed him. Bobby had completed this final season as a non-contract player, and Oldham offered Bobby a similar arrangement for the 1965–66 season, probably with an eye to him continuing the sterling work that had been put in at reserve and junior level. Many of his associates of the time, and indeed some members of his family, felt that he could, and should, have stayed in the game in some capacity. Yet Bobby declined; he had played for Latics for almost four years and scored 35 goals in 143 League games, but it was time to draw a line under his career.

In essence, Bobby did not see a future for himself inside the game. When asked how he had felt, Bobby later described this period as very moving because he knew he couldn't carry on playing. 'I knew I was finishing. I'd had trouble with my knee nearly all season. I hadn't played many games, I'd been helping the youngsters quite a bit in the reserve team, and we had one or two decent youngsters. But it was very sad, and I hated having to give up playing. I'd played for so long it was the only thing I knew. I found it very difficult.' Bobby also had firm views about the way the game itself was heading – and they weren't positive views. 'I don't think I would have liked to stay in football though, because the game, even then, it was going backwards. They were teaching young players to mark you out of the game. I actually played a game about three weeks before I finished, and we played Watford, and there was a young left-half playing, only a kid about 17, and he was marking me tight, standing up my back all the time, and his manager kept shouting to him "Mark him, never mind the game, mark him." I said to this kid before the end of game "You've not had many kicks at the ba,'" and he said "No, I've only had about two"... That's how the game was going, that was the beginning, marking players out of the game instead of playing. When you've got the ball you've got to play yourself, but this kid, as soon as he got it, he just knocked it, and then came back and stood behind me.'

Thus the curtain came down on a fabulous football career that had spanned 19 years, 17 full Scotland international caps and three major Cup Finals. Bobby Johnstone had represented the Scottish League six times, played for Great Britain and collected two Scottish League Championships with Hibernian, and he had made history by becoming the first man to score in consecutive FA Cup Finals at Wembley Stadium – and he was a Scotsman! He left the football arena at a time of great change, as a new era began.

A few months earlier, 1965 had opened with the knighting of Sir Stanley Matthews, the first footballer to be so honoured. There can be no doubt that if any player deserved it Matthews had the most compelling claim. Here was a football hero that had provided entertainment to the masses for over 30 years. Yet in contrast that same month saw 10 players found guilty of match fixing. Around three or four weeks into the New Year, the whole nation had gathered around its television sets as the state funeral of Sir Winston Churchill took place. Considerably fewer than millions had watched the new, regular broadcasts of football on BBC2's *Match of the Day*, but nonetheless, the regular televising of Football League matches began at the start of this, Bobby's last season as a player. Was this the time when we began to see the beginnings of a broader media interest in the game of football, and its combatants? It was the beginning of an influence that would later have a massive impact in popularising the game across all sections of society, and four years on, colour television would generate a further surge. The debate about the benefits (or otherwise) of televised football continue to this day, but 40 years after these initial events, one thing is clear. The most dramatic change to affect the game is directly traceable back to those early, crackly television pictures of football matches.

Sir Stanley Matthews retired at the same time as Bobby, the end of the 1964–65 season, although Matthews hadn't actually played in the first team since February. Now aged 50, Sir Stanley Matthews had made his Football League debut in 1932, and in 1933 played a famous FA Cup tie against a Manchester City side containing Matt Busby. The same Matt Busby who, tired of reserve-team football in 1928, had decided to go home to Lanarkshire and his kin. However, he battled on and gained a wealth of experience. A crowd of 84,500, still a provincial record, watched that FA Cup tie in 1933, and Matt, by now manager of Manchester United, the League Champions, would later win the European Cup, and earn his own knighthood. But what could these characters teach the new breed? Within 12 months, El Beatle had arrived, and that was the future: George Best became the reticent standard-bearer as football moved into the showbiz age of fast cars, new houses and the international jet-setters with a champagne lifestyle. In Matthews's final match, when he played for Stoke City against Fulham, it was surely fate that saw Rodney Marsh, a future glamour boy of the new soccer era, give Fulham the lead.

Another player who retired at the same time as Bobby was Arthur Rowley, the younger brother of Bobby's old boss, Jack. He ended his career as Shrewsbury Town's player-manager having scored an amazing 434 League goals. Will figures like this ever be seen again? Perhaps it doesn't matter, but again, it is a reflection of changing times as these players, many of whose early careers had been affected by the war, came to the end of the line just as the Churchill age became history. It was the passing of an era.

* * * * *

Bobby Johnstone played alongside and against some of the greats, but who in his mind was the greatest? 'The player that I really remember being privileged to play against was Puskas of Hungary. Without a doubt he was the finest player I ever saw. He was such a clever player. Some of the tricks that he could pull, even before the ball had reached him, he was unbelievable, and, honestly, I've never seen a player like him in my life. Tommy Docherty was right-half the day we played against Hungary – and Docherty was known for his pretty-hard tackling, 'no ceremony' and all this, but he didn't get near Puskas that day, he was so brilliant a player that it was impossible to catch him with the ball at his feet. That is the hallmark of being a good player: being in the right place at the right time, and showing it, you know.'

Many sources record Bobby Johnstone as having gone on from professional football at Oldham Athletic to play semi-professionally for Witton Albion of the Cheshire County League. The connection with Witton, who play in the Cheshire salt town of Northwich, was Ken Barnes, who was then their player-manager. Bernard Halford certainly recalled the proposal being discussed, most particularly during one get-together at the Free Trade public house in Chadderton, near Oldham, and Ken himself confirms that Bobby did turn out for Witton, though his appearances were limited to pre-season 'friendly' fixtures. 'He definitely played a few games for me at Witton Albion. I can't remember whether he signed anything, but he played alright. I've no idea how many games he played, it was a bit of fun, but can you imagine a club like Witton getting a player like that?' The intention appears to have been that Bobby would play on a semi-professional basis, but the records from the start of the 1965–66 season make clear that Bobby did not make a full first-team appearance, primarily because, by now, he was not up to it. This view is substantiated in the authoritative book *Manchester City – Cup Kings 1956*, which states that, realistically, the signing could never have come to fruition simply because of the condition of Bobby's knees.

Notes

1. This was the 200th goal of Bobby's senior career; his first for Oldham followed 138 goals for Hibs, 51 for Manchester City and 10 for the full Scottish international side.

2. A theme recurrent during Bobby's career was his failure to register a goal on the occasions when teammates scored heavily. While he evidently scored a good number of goals himself, he was chiefly a goal creator, and he almost invariably missed out when really big scores were achieved. He failed to score the first time that the Famous Five played together, in an 8–1 win in Belfast, and did so again when Hibs defeated Stirling Albion 8–0 in January 1952, in spite of the fact that he was then in the middle of the most productive scoring spell of his entire career. He also failed to register a goal on all three occasions that teammates achieved double figures in League games. The only example of Bobby scoring when colleagues hit more than seven was in the Scottish Cup match against Stenhousemuir in early 1953, when Hibs won 8–1. Bobby scored once that day; one can only imagine that he was erroneously credited with a deflection.

3. Some eight years after the George Robb incident, Bert Trautmann received a marvellous accolade, truly demonstrating that Tottenham Hotspur fans bore him no ill-will. The treasurer of Tottenham Hotspur's Supporters' Club sent a cheque for £5 in favour of Bert's testimonial fund, and the accompanying letter stated that the donation had been authorised by their executive committee. Their view was that 'his conduct as a sportsman and a footballer has been of the highest order. It seemed to us he saved some of his best performances for whenever he played at White Hart Lane.'

CHAPTER 10

Life After Football

'I would advise every boy who wants to take up the game professionally to follow my example and finish his apprenticeship or training in some other job before becoming a full-time player.'

This sound advice came from Billy Liddell, and perhaps Bobby now began to have cause to regret the decision he had made almost two decades earlier. Liddell scored the final goal against England at Wembley on Bobby's international debut, and not only was he an exceptional footballer, but he was a qualified accountant too. He usually trained two mornings a week, but even at the height of his career, during the 1950s, he would regularly work in the office on Saturday mornings before playing for Liverpool. In contrast, Bobby had no obvious 'trade' to turn to, having abandoned his painting and decorating apprenticeship in 1946 to sign for Hibernian. Around the late summer of 1965, when it became apparent that Bobby wasn't capable of a valuable contribution at Witton, he began to focus more clearly on the future. He started looking to his next move, knowing that he had to find a way of providing support for his family.

The latter half of the decade became a period of great transition in Bobby's life. Whatever the views of others about his staying in the game, Bobby did not see himself in a coaching or management role. There had been some mention of the Johnstones buying a small business, perhaps a shop, but in the immediate future, at least, this option was not pursued. Over the next few years Bobby settled to working life in the construction industry. He was always able to find and retain employment.

Naturally, Bobby's social circles were very different from his playing days, as he settled to a more typical way of life. He lost contact with many of the friends he had made through football, though he remained in touch with Bernard Halford, still the assistant secretary at Oldham, and they would bowl together from time to time. The family continued to live on Eskdale Avenue for some while after Bobby finished playing, though the bungalow belonged to Oldham Athletic, of course. After a while the chairman, Harry Massey, asked Bernard Halford to tackle the delicate issue of getting Bobby to make some alternative arrangements. While this was not a pleasant task for Bernard, the club needed the house to accommodate a new signing, Frank Large, and so early in 1966 the Johnstones left their home of five years. They remained in the area though, moving to Withins Road, Hollinwood, a couple of miles south of Oldham town centre, and into a maisonette provided by the local authority.

Times were changing for Bernard too... 'Bobby was my best man when I first got married in 1966. I had my reception at the Free Trade, a pub in Chadderton. I married the landlord's daughter! We were still in the pub at three in the morning on the day I got married, and Bobby was on the tables, leading the singing: *Donald Where's Yer Troosers*, I can still see him now with his antics. I went to work the following morning, and, just like the players, got married in the afternoon. I didn't have a day off, and I didn't have a honeymoon or anything.' Within days of his wedding, Bernard got a promotion and became acting secretary at Oldham Athletic. A new chairman had taken over the reins at a club that once again was struggling badly, and it wasn't long before he started making changes. 'Ken Bates, the chairman, sacked the previous secretary and came and threw me the keys. He said there you are Bernard, it's all yours. A couple of months later, in the June, he confirmed my appointment as secretary. Bobby was really pleased.' Bobby's former landlord Ian Niven had also changed direction. In 1965 he left his job as a buyer to begin a successful career as a publican at the Fletchers Arms at Denton. While he might have thought that his new profession could encourage a good number of visits from Bobby, in fact Ian saw him only once or twice.

By the early 1970s Bobby was working for M.W. Kellogg Ltd, an international engineering and construction company, who were engaged in the construction of a chemical plant at Carrington, near Manchester. Bobby's role, as a materials expeditor, largely involved checking-in goods received at the site. In May 1972 the company published an article in their staff magazine informing colleagues that he had once been a footballer, and part of a forward line reckoned to be the best in the world – not something that Bobby himself suggested. He also gave some trenchant views about the game, of course, some seven years after his retirement. 'The game has altered so much, and I think that the teams are over-coached, with many players losing their individual flair.' He advocated a couple of things designed to improve entertainment – firstly, the abolition of the offside rule, which 'players never bother with in training', and a reduction in the number of players to 10! It is pretty clear that Bobby was disillusioned with the direction in which he believed the game was moving. The year after his retirement, England's 'wingless wonders' had won the World Cup, and most Scotsmen at least would argue that this alone made his point. While manager Sir Alf Ramsey's predecessor, Walter Winterbottom, had been a great admirer of Bobby's ability, it is doubtful that Ramsey would have given him a look-in even had he and Bobby been born on the same side of Hadrian's Wall. In the late 1960s and early 1970s Don Revie had taken Leeds United to great heights, almost conquering Europe – but the football fare from these two admittedly successful sides was not going to get Bobby reaching into his wallet. No, Bobby's clearly stated view was that the game had moved into a different era – and it had not improved.

He had referred in the article to seeing some football, and he did take in the odd live game. In August 1971 the Famous Five received a great cheer from the Easter Road faithful when they made a brief appearance on the pitch before a pre-season friendly against Schalke 04. The Five had played against the German side 21 years earlier during the Hibees unbeaten tour of West Germany, overrunning them by 3–0. The activity that Bobby really preferred though was his bowling, and this took up a good part of his leisure time. The Allisons had hardly seen Bobby and Heather since his move back to Scotland in 1959, though they had stayed loosely in contact. Roy had always continued to bowl, and he would occasionally bump into Bobby at tournaments and meetings. 'He'd bowled on the flat greens in Scotland as a youngster, and when he came to the Dargai Street club in 1955 he didn't know what crown green bowling was, he'd never seen it. But he soon became a fair player! After he left City we lost touch, as you do, but we took up again with the bowling after he retired from football. He played for Hollinwood Bowling and Cricket Club, and then at Hollinwood Institute, and at a number of clubs up on Broadway. It was all crown green down here, and Bobby did very well.'

Bobby took Nicola and Heather over to Elland Road, Leeds, to watch a UEFA Cup tie between Leeds United and Hibernian in 1973. It was a match that involved two of Bobby's closest former playing colleagues, because while Don Revie still managed Leeds United, Eddie Turnbull was now in charge of the Hibees. After the match Bobby surprised Eddie, asking him up to the boardroom, where he had been enjoying a chat with Don. Eddie could still recall that meeting more than 30 years later... 'I couldn't believe it, we'd been down and played extremely well, we played them off the park really, but only drew 0–0. After the game, I was in the dressing room, and the commissionaire came... "Mr Turnbull, there's a gentleman who'd like to see you, knows you very well – it's a Mr Bobby Johnstone." "Oh Christ," I says, "where is he?" And I went to see him. We were very close Bobby, Ormond and I, we were really close. I remember the first thing he said to me was "Hey Eddie, where did you get that big inside-forward?" He meant Tony Higgins, who was playing for me, he was six-foot odd, and this night he had been fantastic, and Bobby wanted to know where I'd got him. It was grand to see him – we'd had such great times together.' Bobby had been very impressed by the Hibs performance; they had held their own against one of the top sides in Europe, although they were later unlucky to lose the tie on penalties.

The following year, Bobby had a nasty shock when he unexpectedly lost his mother Liz, who passed away while on holiday in Australia. Liz had been visiting Sheila, Bobby's youngest sister, and the family in April. The following month Bobby, now in his mid-40s, played for one last time at Maine Road. The occasion was a testimonial match awarded to Johnny Hart, who by now had given over 25 years of loyal service to Manchester City. That spell had only recently culminated in a short term in the manager's seat, but, typically, illness had forced him to stand down. Hart's luck around the time of the two mid-1950s Cup Finals had been in stark contrast to Bobby's, and the Scot now joined the queue of football luminaries wanting to pay tribute to this most dignified of men. Names like Revie, Mercer, Busby, Bell, Law, and Crerand were all personal friends of Johnny's, of course, and Bert Trautmann and Gordon Banks both played in the main event. During the half-time interval, Bobby played in a seven-a-side game, alongside elder statesmen such as Roy Paul, Ken Barnes and Roy Clarke, enjoying a knockabout in which Tony Book and Paddy Fagan scored for the 'Blues' in a 2–1 win over the 'Whites'.

While the footballing skills might have waned, Bobby still got a lot of pleasure from his sport. In addition to his prowess on the bowling greens, he continued to play cricket for Hollinwood Cricket Club in the Central Lancashire League, and with some success. Bobby was in Hollinwood's second team, and they claimed their League Championship at the end of a fantastic run. Having lost five of the first nine, there had been a miraculous turn-around in form, with only one further defeat in their last 21 matches. The previous season Hollinwood had lost in the Moore Cup Final, but this year they collected that trophy too, with a comprehensive win. Batting first, Hollinwood made 167 (Hibbard 45, Johnstone 31) and then bowled out East Lancashire Paper Mill for 83, claiming the trophy for the first time since 1948. It was a great double, and the circumstances of the Cup win brought back some happy memories of 1956!

In the mid-1970s Bobby worked for a poultry supply business and this job saw him dropping in regularly to one of his old haunts, Maine Road. Bobby would pop up to the offices to see Ken Barnes, by now chief scout, for a chat and a cup of coffee. Ken's office was quite an intriguing place then, and because of the number of ex-professionals that passed through to chat with Ken, it developed a reputation as quite a learning ground for young players and budding managers.

It seemed that Bobby had settled into the routine of family life without football, yet he was soon to spring a surprise. All but three or four of his colleagues from the 1956 Cup side had gone into football management posts, with differing degrees of success, though it always seemed that Bobby had no inclination to follow suit. Over 13 years after retirement from the game – a period in which he had had no active involvement at a professional level – he was appointed as manager of ex-Football League club Workington. However, this was only on a part-time basis as he still had a full-time job in the Workington area. Here he followed in the footsteps of his Cup-winning teammate Bill Leivers, who had managed the club in 1966.

Bobby had played just once at Workington's home ground, Borough Park, way back in 1962, and, coincidentally, he played his final League game against Workington at Boundary Park. Bobby told Ken Barnes about his plans, and Ken expressed his astonishment at the news... 'I said to him Workington... where the f**kin 'ell's that? You know, how the hell did you come to get in there? I never really knew how, or why – what the link was. In some ways Bobby was like that. He didn't always discuss things with you, he was very laid back. But if somebody contacted him about going there, and he decided that was what he was going to do, he did it, and he stuck to it. If he made a decision, that was it – done.' So it was quite unexpectedly that Bobby turned up to take over the reins at the club, amid considerable excitement from those who knew about the achievements earlier in his career and quite a fuss in the local press. But it would prove to be no easy ride...

Having finished in the bottom two of the Fourth Division in each of their last four seasons in the Football League, the west Cumbrians had failed to be re-elected at the end of the 1976–77 season and had been replaced by Wimbledon FC. Their first season as a non-League outfit had not been a success either, and during the next close season Bobby's appointment was confirmed, but in plenty of time to gear up for a second season in the Northern Premier League. The venture saw Bobby also continue developing the Oldham-based junior side Mount Pleasant FC. One of the earliest fixtures arranged by Bobby, in July 1977, was between Mount Pleasant and Cumberland Star, a junior side from the Workington area, with the Cumbrians travelling south to play in Chadderton, near Oldham.

Bobby's influence was clear to see from Workington's pre-season fixtures, a five-match programme that opened with a game against Manchester City and also included a visit from Selkirk FC, who at that time were a dominant force in the East of Scotland League. The game against City was organised through Dave Ewing, Bobby's former teammate, who was City's reserve-team trainer. Unfortunately, the fixture was set for 2 August, and the previous night City's first-team squad had commenced a two-week tour to Belgium, Denmark and Holland. The team that turned out at Borough Park did feature many of the Central League Championship side from the previous season, but it was well short of a full-strength City side, and didn't prove too great an attraction to the Cumbrian townsfolk, a few of whom saw their side win 2–1.

The Selkirk game was a 1–2 defeat, and on 19 August the season itself kicked-off with a tremendous win at Buxton by 4–0. All seemed well, though behind the scenes things were far from positive. The groundsman, Billy Watson, who had been at the club since 1951, recalls that Bobby was seldom seen and never heard... 'He came up to Workington twice a week, Tuesday and Thursday nights, and sometimes he would stay over. On training nights you couldn't see him, he hardly came out of his office. The players would say "Where's the bloody manager?" but he was in his office! On the odd occasion that he came out, he would just stand there, watching...' The next two home games saw no goals for Workington, though a point was gained from a draw with Gainsborough Trinity, and the League Cup was little better as Workington drew 1–1 at home to Netherfield (a Kendal side), won the replay 1–0, but then lost 2–1 at Northwich Victoria.

The team were looking for some inspirational leadership, but it quickly became clear that they weren't going to get it from Bobby. Although he did make some efforts to settle into the locale: 'He asked me once, "where are the good pubs round here Billy?" So I told him "I usually go down to the docks, there's nice people and pubs down there," and he said "We'll have a run down then." After I'd locked up and all of the lads had gone, we'd go for a drink. He used to drive down to the harbour. The trainer would come sometimes too, a lad called Ted Cushin, who'd played for us just after the war. We'd go down to this pub, and after two or three bottles he'd open up with his own reminiscences about football; I recall him talking about his home town of Selkirk, and he actually gave me a pennant from the football club – but he never talked about our game. Sometimes we'd be in the pub until midnight, but he never looked any different, he could handle it. He was no different except for the conversation – he'd start to talk a bit. On a match day, he would sit in the dug-out, and there was no excitement at all with him. I don't know why they gave him the job... it must have been because of his name.'

Bobby's assistant was Peter Foley, an Edinburgh lad, who knew the lower Leagues well, having spent his playing career at clubs such as Workington, Scunthorpe, Chesterfield, and also several non-League sides. He had come back to Workington in the mid-70s, before they got relegated from the League, and he was a natural for the job as assistant to Bobby. 'I'd actually retired once, but started to play again with the club dropping out, and the next season Bobby came in. I knew of him as a player already; I grew up in Edinburgh and saw most of the Famous

Five play, so I was excited when I heard he was coming. But it was obvious almost as soon as he came – he didn't have a clue. I've no idea how he got the job; he hardly communicated with the players at all, he just wasn't a manager. He couldn't put the game over to people, describing what he wanted them to do; he wasn't that type of person. I'd heard stories that even in his days at City, 20 years before, he didn't take part in team talks, he left all that to Revie; Bobby just did his own thing.'

After a few more games, Workington defeated Stafford Rangers 1–0, giving them a second League win of the season, but things were far from settled, and the following week the situation deteriorated further. 'We were playing Morecambe, and Keith Newton was playing left-back for them. Bobby's got me playing right-back, and admittedly there was a bit of a clash between Keith and me, but I was OK. But Jimmy Irving was struggling badly with half-an-hour to go, and I shouted to Bobby to make a sub, as Jimmy could hardly walk. But what does Bobby do? – he subs me! I came off and said, "What are you doing, look at Jimmy!" It was down to poor communications... it was just chaotic.'

Bobby remained in charge for only 14 full first-team matches – 11 in the League, of which only two were won and seven lost. Most surprisingly for a side with Bobby involved, there was a paucity of goals: only eight were scored and 16 conceded. The final straw came on a Monday night in October when Workington played another 'friendly', beating the Zambia Under-23 side by 3–2 at Borough Park. This proved to be Bobby's final game in charge and his last involvement with professional football. Even then, it seems he was heavily reliant upon Peter Foley: 'When it came to the team, I had to do all the organising... the sheets had to be handed in to the referee half-an-hour before the kick-off, and I was having to write the team out. The night he quit, we played the Zambian national side in a friendly here, and Bobby Moncur was guesting for us. We asked Johnstone what our team was, but he never sorted it out. So I had to pick the team, and tell people what they were doing, and straight after the game I went to the chairman and told him "that's it, I can't handle this anymore." Bobby didn't seem to have a clue what he was doing, and I couldn't be there every game, particularly some of the away matches, I just couldn't get there; it was becoming a bit of a mockery.' Within about 45 minutes of the end of the Zambia game, the board of directors had met and effectively forced Bobby to resign. Peter Foley immediately took over the reins as caretaker manager, but with regrets about the way things had turned out. With memories of their Football League days still so fresh, everybody connected with the club hoped that Bobby would be the man to lead them back. Peter too had desperately wanted things to improve, and initially he thought that Bobby would prove himself capable of picking Workington up again. 'I liked him as a bloke, I loved him as a footballer, and he was one of my heroes when I grew up, he could make the ball talk. But it was all his own stuff. It was amazing that he'd been part of City and all of those tactics, because if you told him to do something he couldn't do it, it would just have to come out his head, naturally.' The following Wednesday, Workington lost at home to Southport, another former League side, by 0–2, but by then Bobby had gone, ending this rather peculiar and unhappy chapter in his football career. It was his last ever attempt at a career in the game he loved – playing.

The following year, in the August of 1979, Bobby was present as a guest and judge at the Skol Festival, a four-cornered football tournament played between Manchester City, Coventry City and the two senior Edinburgh clubs. The matches were scheduled over three days, and the sponsors of the Skol Festival Trophy, Ind Coope, hoped that the four-team idea would take off. Sadly the crowds did not turn up in sufficient numbers for what was effectively a pre-season warm-up tournament. Willie Ormond, manager at Hearts at the time, was absent, having become ill while on holiday in Tenerife, but with Eddie Turnbull managing Hibs, no doubt the other two took the chance to toast his good health. Up to this point, Bobby had not kept closely in touch with many of his former colleagues from the old days at Hibernian, though he had been saddened to hear about Willie Ormond, who passed away on 4 May 1984. Some time later Bobby had the chance to give his views about Willie in an official film released by Hibernian FC '...he was fast, and had one of the best left foots I've ever seen, and he could cross the ball. They talk about Beckham nowadays, but Willie could cross the ball as well as anyone you'll ever see. His left foot was deadly; I always said he should have had a licence for it, because it was like a gun goin' off when he hit a ball.'

The four surviving members of the Famous Five still got together on the odd occasion. Coincidentally, in 1990, the four were just about to get together for one of their golf days just as Hibs entered a particularly stormy period in their history. Wallace Mercer, of city rivals Heart of Midlothian, staged a controversial attempt to take-over the Leith club, and then close it down, leaving just one senior club in Edinburgh. The crisis was dominating sports pages, and not just in Edinburgh, and the newspapers were quick to stoke passions by evoking memories of the Famous Five. Before heading up to Scotland, Bobby was quoted in the *Edinburgh Evening News*, declaring his great sadness at heading north under such circumstances 'I can't believe it. Only last year we opened the Famous Five Lounge in the supporters club. They can't let it happen. I was a Hearts supporter when I was young, but since I signed for Hibs at seventeen, I've been a Hibs man. Just being part of the Famous Five were the greatest days I can remember.' Lawrie pointed out that he would suffer the greatest wound should the 'merger' progress: 'I was the only one of the Five to be born a Hibs supporter, and it would be especially bad to be taken over by Hearts rather than have a new name like Edinburgh United, though I don't think it would make a lot of difference. I don't think the fans will switch allegiance to a new team anyway.' Perhaps most poignantly, as most Hibees would be well aware of Lawrie's love for the club, even as a schoolboy, he rounded off his quote with a thrust aimed directly at the very crux of a supporters passion for his team, a passion that invariably crosses the generation gap: 'I will become a strict neutral if this goes ahead, and so will my son. My father will be turning in his grave.' Eddie Turnbull, who at the time was running a bar in North Leith, not far from Easter Road, was pointed as ever. While he was sad that Hibs had gone downhill, he felt that 'Economics governs everything these days'. In the end, Sir Tom Farmer CBE saved the club the following year, when its owners, Forth Investments plc, went into receivership.

In the late 1980s BBC Radio had interviewed Bobby, and many of the issues he refers to have been covered elsewhere in this work. But in addition to talking about his sporting life at that time, the interviewer asked Bobby about his views on the game in general, and how things had changed some 30 years on. Bobby started to reminisce about how the Famous Five team had approached the game: 'The Hibs set-up was marvellous at the time, they were an attacking team. Most of – all of – the players were attacking, not only the forward-line, which... I mean, we'd five internationals in the forward line, but it was just an absolute treat to play wi' the Hibs at that time. It lasted for about 7 or 8 years, and we had a right purple patch. We didn't win the Cup, but entertainment-wise, I think we must have been the most entertaining club in the country.' Selkirk journalist Graham Bateman was present in the studio, and he commented that Hibernian had revolutionised the Scottish style of forward play... 'It was their interchanging... prior to that, a right-winger kept to his right wing, a left-winger was more or less contained down the left touchline, but those chaps, they switched backwards and forwards, so that they completely bemused the defences, and their inter-switching really set a new pattern in Scottish football, and it was just brilliant to watch.' Earlier in the interview Bobby had expressed firm views about the way the game had gone, and here was another chance. 'I was lucky to play in the era I did, I think, because, all-round it was an attacking sort of game; it was before the coaches got in to try and stop other players from playing, rather than coach players to play themselves, which is a different thing altogether....'

Around the turn of the decade, in an article for the Oldham Athletic match magazine, Bobby was compared to the great Peter Doherty and Wilf Mannion by interviewer Tony Bugby. After enlightening readers about what he was up to, he rather grumpily declared that he had 'turned off' most of the games played in the 1990 World Cup. Scotland had preserved their record of failing to progress beyond the opening rounds, and while that won't have helped, Bobby's views actually centred upon the players rather than particular teams. 'No individuals and no skill' was his indictment. 'Flair was encouraged in my day. Peter Beardsley is the only player who excites me today.' Bobby's 'peculiar feat' of scoring a hat-trick of headers against Portsmouth in 1956 was also mentioned, and Bobby conceded that it had been rather 'unusual for one as small as myself'.

Around the time of Bobby's 65th birthday, in 1994, the *Oldham Evening Chronicle* published an article celebrating the milestone with their readership. Even though he had reached retirement age, with the business still going well, Bobby made it clear that he had no plans to retire: 'I may be 65, but I am carrying on with my job,' he said defiantly. He continued to live in Hollinwood, and was still heavily involved in competitive bowls and occasionally picked up trophies. He played at Hollinwood Institute during the summer and also played for Springbank. He won the Coronation Cup at Springbank in July 1994, and during the winter he would play indoors with Coalshaw A team. He also played for the Oldham indoor team, with his friend and bowls partner Stan Boston, who later described Bobby as 'A very good skip, and we won the Lancashire over-55s pairs together.'

Soon after, Bobby had cause for a re-think about continuing to work. The business, which he had initially taken over when his former employer had died, had over time become a working partnership, and at some stage Bobby agreed to cede ownership to his colleague. Now, roughly 30 years after quitting football, Bobby did decide to retire, and he returned north to live in Selkirk. Bobby and

Heather had divorced in 1987 and he had been living on his own in Oldham since then. Initially he moved in with his younger sister, Betty, at Shawburn Road, though in the longer term he intended to secure his own accommodation, so that he wasn't imposing.

Looking back to that time, Betty knew that Bobby was still rather unsettled, 'I think he sometimes regretted coming back, it was as if he didn't seem to know quite what to do, but he wasn't too worried about it. He brought boxes and boxes of stuff with him. He was also courting a lady called Maureen, from Oldham, she was here for Sheila and Tom's ruby wedding, and she came up a couple of times. He didn't tell me a lot, he kept it inside himself, but I think he'd had a bit of a fall-out with Maureen.'

As a man of leisure for the first time in almost 50 years, Bobby was able to take advantage of his free time to do some serious bowling. He had always remained a 'town member' of Selkirk Bowling Club throughout the years that he was away, and he now found himself just a short walk away from their flat green, where he found some new mates and picked up with some old acquaintances. As he approached his 70s, he could still be found playing competitive bowls in the Border Bowling League. His passion for the art of bowling was something that never left him.

He also started to see more of his former playing colleagues, one being Lawrie Reilly, and the advancing years and old football injuries were beginning to take more of a toll on both of them... 'He used to moan about his knees too when he came back and played golf. It was a good opportunity for us all to get together, and Gordon would be there too, even though he was a shy man, maybe a bit of a loner. He was married to Jo, and kept himself quiet. It wasn't that Gordon would nae mix, after the fitba' he became a key member of the golf club, he came to every outing, but he was really a shy bloke – he wasn't really a guy that should have been captain at all. They were both decent golfers, but Bobby especially was never as interested as I was. I was club Champion three times at my golf club and got my handicap down to three. I won the Longniddry Club Championship, and played in the Scottish Amateur and things like that, but Bobby never got as keen. He'd play a round, but he borrowed clubs, he couldn't even be bothered with his own clubs, you know. He was so keen on the bowls, and the two didn't go together.

'We had learnt to play golf at the Hibs, they used to take us golfing, and we would go away to North Berwick for two or three days and have an hilarious time with the boys, they'd really enjoy themselves you know. But it shows he was a real ball player, Bobby; he was more than reasonable at golf, without ever playing very much, he was good at the bowls, he was very good at the snooker, cricket, all ball games. We were out of the same mould, because I was good at ball games, too, table-tennis for one, but I was never that good at snooker – Bobby was different class at snooker, he always did very well at the Hibs club competition each year.'

In 1995 Hibernian FC had unveiled their brand new North Stand at the Easter Road Stadium, and in 1998 they announced plans to name it 'The Famous Five Stand'. In late July Hibs staged a prestigious friendly fixture against Barnsley, who had just been relegated from England's Premier League. Prior to this match, a formal naming ceremony took place, and the four remaining members of the

Famous Five were welcomed on to the pitch alongside Willie Ormond's widow, Margaret, and given an emotional reception as they were introduced to the crowd.

After years of not having bothered, all of this football-related activity seems to have set Bobby's mind thinking, and he soon decided to sell the key items of soccer memorabilia that he had accumulated throughout his career – at least those items that he hadn't given away! He told the press that he 'never looked at them, and they were gathering dust in the loft'. Bobby had never been too possessive about them, and one story vividly illustrates the point. One time, while out with a close friend, he had promised a football jersey to someone, who, on attending at Betty's house to collect, was told brusquely 'there's naebody takin' nae jerseys frae this hoose!' Seemingly Betty had a better eye for the importance of these things than Bobby did!

A collection such as Bobby's career possessions needed to be given professional attention. This involved detailed research and careful cataloguing, and ultimately it was Christie's of Glasgow, the world-renowned valuers and auctioneers, who handled the sale of Bobby's valuables in 1998. There were a large number of football lots, at the time the largest-ever auction of football memorabilia, which realised over £300,000 in total. Pre-sale estimates for Bobby's items alone were in the region of £10,500, but at the event auctioneers were stunned when the 28 items relating to Bobby's football career raised almost £23,000. The Scotland cap that Bobby received on his international debut in 1951, when he scored against England at Wembley, was sold for over £1,000. The shirt that Bobby had worn in Ireland when he played for Great Britain against The Rest of Europe in 1955 sold for £1,300 to a member of his own family. The silver plaque from the same game achieved almost four figures. Hibernian FC paid a considerable sum to retrieve the two Scottish League Championship medals handed to Bobby in the early 50s, but the main item, of course, was his 1956 FA Cup-winners' medal, which fetched £4,945, double its estimate, and a full reflection of the historic nature of Bobby's achievement more than 40 years previously.

By now Bobby had become a fairly active member of the Manchester City Former Players' Association, and had even been persuaded to start watching the Blues again. This was something he did two or three times a year, usually sitting alongside Ken Barnes... 'I used to look forward to him coming to the games. I used to tell him to come more often, but he'd say "what, to watch this rubbish!" I went up to Oldham once and met him up there in the boardroom, and he sat with us. He used to wonder why the crowd were getting all excited when they won a corner, or a defender booted it into the stand... "what are they all cheering about... what's it all about Ken?" Just because they'd stopped an attack or something. I knew what he was saying though. A player of his calibre, and he just wasn't happy with the way the game had gone. You know, there ain't no bloody Bobby Johnstones about in the game today; they don't try to beat players now...' The game had moved on dramatically since those days, and in many senses was unrecognisable – as was Bobby, if this example is anything to go by! On another visit to Maine Road, Bobby went into the Bobby Johnstone Bar underneath the Main Stand, where he ordered a pint for himself and Bert Lister...and playfully mentioned to the young lady behind the counter that the bar was named after him, but the reply was terse: 'Look, just stop messing about, that's £2.60!'

With his interest somewhat re-kindled, and perhaps a truer sense of his own place in the affections of those who love the game, Bobby had visited Boundary Park in November 1998, although by now he had been living back in Selkirk for some time. He had been invited to a Second Division fixture between the two English clubs for which he had played first-class soccer, Oldham Athletic and Manchester City. While Oldham were at the same level as when Bobby had retired, City were in the doldrums and playing third-tier soccer for the first time in their history. Bobby was welcomed on to the pitch to conduct the half-time draw, and he perhaps witnessed the very beginning of the turnaround in City's fortunes, as they triumphed 3–0. One of goals that day was a blistering 30-yard volley from a man who, ironically, would also be a catalyst in those changes at his new club, just as Bobby had been. This time the Scotsman's name was Andy Morrison.

At this stage of his life, Bobby seemed to have finally settled back in Selkirk, and was enjoying a life of leisure, mainly centred on the bowling club, the rugby club bar, and the friends he had there. Louise Ovens (née McEwen), who had been among the first to know about Bobby signing for Hibs all those years ago, occasionally bumped into him on the High Street... 'My daughter worked in the Conservative club, and she got to know Bobby when he came back home. He would ask after me, though I seldom saw him, other than just passing by.'

In September 1999 Bobby celebrated his 70th birthday with get-togethers both at Selkirk Bowling Club and also at home with his family and friends. Betty remembers how contented he seemed at this time, surrounded by his family, and seemingly in good health. 'He had two lovely cakes for his 70th. He took a lot of it down to Oldham for a short time, for his friends there.'

In 2000 he was back down in Oldham. Bobby gave up his rented accommodation on Withins Road at this point. He spent a short time living with Maureen in Chadderton, near Oldham, before the two of them left to go to Blackpool, where they lived for a short period.

While there, Bobby made a surprise call on Bert Lister, and he nearly caused an accident! At this time, Bert was living at a Blackpool hotel, and working as a part-time taxi-driver. The day Bobby arrived, completely unannounced, Bert was working up a ladder, and because of his precarious predicament, it took him a moment to grasp who it was... 'We'd always kept in contact, exchanging Christmas cards and things, and we'd seen each other at the odd Former Players' Association functions. But it was so out the blue, I was up a ladder, concentrating, I didn't recognise him at first and then I nearly fell off!'

By November 2000 Bobby was back in Selkirk – permanently as it turned out, and he was fairly settled now living with Betty.

Just before Christmas, on Friday 24 December 2000, Bobby was out celebrating and had called in on friends at the rugby club for a drink. Later, on his way home in icy conditions, Bobby had a fall, causing a serious head injury and a minor stroke. He was taken to a hospital near Galashiels, where he regained consciousness on the Sunday, after around 36 hours, but he was kept in hospital while a series of tests were carried out. After a few days Bobby was transferred to another hospital because the test results indicated that Bobby had suffered a brain injury, and he started to receive rehabilitation therapy as his speech had been affected, though only slightly.

By February Bobby was on the mend, and the *Oldham Evening Chronicle* reported that he was 'making good progress' after his fall. Over time it became clear that the fall was to have permanent, long-lasting effects though, and his regular visitors knew that he just wasn't himself. After several months in hospital, in May 2001 Bobby was discharged and Betty and Margaret arranged for them all to spend a week together at a holiday flat in Eyemouth, a few miles north of Berwick on the east coast. Margaret and Bobby went out for short walks, which he enjoyed immensely, and for drives out and about. A short while later it was discovered that Bobby had cancer, and he later died at home in Selkirk.

CHAPTER 11

Tributes to Bobby Johnstone

Bobby's career is still legendary and his skills and achievements are remembered. Bert Lister was clear; Bobby was the best player he ever played with… 'and as a centre-forward, without that supply, I'd have never have scored goals. It's alright for some of the others, their game's not relying on Bobby Johnstone and the likes!' Roy Cheetham, who first played in the City side in 1958 in a re-shuffle that saw Bobby dropped, said, 'He'll always be in the top ten, your team, yes. Actually, you might find there'd be no room for his type in the game these days. He'd certainly never be allowed to get forward as much today, particularly as he wasn't the fastest towards the end of his career – though he was as fast as he needed to be at that time, that was as fast as football was.'

Bill Spurdle felt that injuries had been the major barrier for Bobby, almost from the time he first joined City. He was adamant 'He wasn't even 80% fit at City, if he had been fully fit, he would have been world-class. In fact, out of this world. The way he played was so natural; when you went into open space, the ball was there. He could stroll through a game, he was an absolute master.'

One of the most famous of Former Players' Association members is Fred Eyre. He saw his first game in April 1949, and recalls three phases in his contact with Bobby. Firstly, even as a schoolboy 'I could not believe his skill'. He knew he'd seen something special when, stationed behind the goal, he saw Bobby score in a Blues versus Maroon pre-season game not long after he first came to Manchester. John Savage, the reserve-team goalkeeper, turned to the crowd behind the goal and told them that wasn't just the best goal he'd ever conceded – it was the best goal he'd ever seen! Fred later had trials with City while Johnstone was still at Maine Road, and technically he was a teammate for a short period, but Bobby had left for Scotland by the time Fred signed his apprenticeship forms in December 1959.

Their next meeting was as opposing players in the early 60s, by which time Bobby was at Oldham Athletic. Fred recalls playing at Boundary Park when 'Latics wore dark-blue and white halved shirts in a Northern Regional league game'. Fred describes Bobby as 'a little portly, and playing the game from memory by this time'. Once again Fred enjoyed watching him perform, but now at closer quarters. Bobby played around him in the first half, scored twice and laid on another '…his passing was like radar'. When Fred got into the dressing room, he felt himself the focus of everyone's attention, and his ill-judged response was telling: 'Don't blame me, I was nowhere near him!'

In Ken Barnes's opinion 'Then, football had six or seven different Champions every decade. These days it's all about the bloody money. Bobby was in the game at an early age, he had a great career though he never bragged about things, he just got on with it, he was quiet in many respects. We were very close, we'd have a laugh, take this piss, but he was a treat to play with. You know, I can see it now, the "weighted" pass… you don't break your stride when you're in full flight.'

The news of Bobby's death immediately generated a wealth of tributes, naturally led by those clubs for which he had played with such distinction. Hibernian Football Club released an official statement under headlines that read 'Hibs legend Johnstone dies. Famous Five forward passes away at 71'. The release went on to describe how '...he played for six highly-successful seasons until his transfer to Manchester City in 1955, where he further endeared himself to an entirely new set of fans. Hibs' chairman Malcolm McPherson today echoed the thoughts of all Hibs fans when he said, "It is a sad day at the club and for the supporters, but first and foremost our thoughts have to be with Bobby's family. The Famous Five are a significant part of our history, and are the heart and soul of the club; Bobby was a key part of that peerless forward line. We intend to precede Saturday's game with Celtic with a minute's silence as a mark of respect".'

Under the headline 'Death of a City Legend', the leading article within the sports pages of the *Manchester Evening News* described Bobby as one of City's greatest post-war players, too, and recalled how, on arriving in Manchester in March 1955, he had 'almost overnight been elevated to cult status by the appreciative Maine Road fans'. Manchester City secretary Bernard Halford said 'Bobby was a true City legend, and one of the finest players ever to play for the club. He was an absolute wizard on the ball, and a great exponent of the weighted pass. He was a personal friend, and I have got long, fond memories of him. It is a tragic loss, and he is a person who will always be remembered at this club. He was one of the greatest inside-forwards ever to play the game.'

Paul Hince, the ex-City player and then Manchester City correspondent for the *Manchester Evening News*, revealed that Bobby Johnstone had been the reason he became a 'blue' in the first place, having cried, aged 10, on the day City lost against Newcastle in the 1955 Cup Final. He was hooked that day on Manchester City in general, and Bobby Johnstone in particular. 'We used to call him Bobby Dazzler, because that was what he was... absolutely dazzling. He didn't look much like a professional footballer. He was small and rotund. He liked a drink. But you should have seen him with a ball at his feet. He was pure magic. How I wish he had been born 40 years later, and just starting his career today. He would have been a sensation. He could make the ball sit up and beg. He was as near to being a genius as it's possible for a footballer to be. Perhaps one of the tragedies of Bobby Johnstone's life is that he played his soccer when there was very little money in the game for the players themselves. Had he been playing today, with his amazing skills, he would have been a millionaire before reaching his 25th birthday. But Bobby Johnstone had something which money can't buy. He had the genuine and lasting affection of thousands of City fans privileged to have watched him in action. I was one of those lucky fans, and I bless his memory for that.'

Oldham Athletic chief executive Alan Hardy said 'The club is very saddened by the news. Bobby was revered and will be dearly missed by everyone who knew him.' The *Oldham Evening Chronicle*, in a full-page article, reported the sad news to friends and former colleagues in the Lancashire town where Bobby had lived for around half of his life. Bobby would be 'fondly remembered as Athletics' biggest-ever crowd puller and best-loved entertainer. He was the master-craftsman of his trade: clever on the ball, a supreme footballing artist, a talented exponent of the weighted pass, and a player who, with one sway of the hips, would often leave defenders literally going the wrong way.' To illustrate the point, the article was accompanied by a brilliantly evocative photograph of a poor Doncaster Rovers defender, who, in April 1961, had been left helpless, facing the wrong way, and almost looking back through his own legs at Bobby, who was racing away having 'sold him a dummy'. In Scotland, the *Edinburgh Evening News* supplemented their coverage with views from former playing colleagues. Joe Baker, who had broken Hibs' seasonal goalscoring record (with 42 League goals) the year Bobby returned to Easter Road – in spite of what had been, before his arrival, a poor start to the season – credited Bobby Johnstone as being the architect behind his feat, saying 'I played with the likes of Jimmy Greaves and Bobby Charlton, too, but Bobby Johnstone was the best of the lot, he stuck out a mile. He was always two moves ahead of you, he could pinpoint you with a pass, and if it hadn't been for him I doubt I'd have got anywhere near 42 goals that season.' Lawrie Reilly said 'Bobby was a great wee player, as good a player as you could get to play with. He had a great partnership with Gordon Smith. He was an easy guy to play with because he always put the ball where you wanted it. I roomed with Bobby when we were away with Scotland, and I got on well with him. It's very sad news to hear of his death.' Just a year earlier Lawrie had given his thoughts on some of the many memorable matches he had played in, and at that time he had recalled one of Bobby's finest hours: 'A special match that stands out for me was the 3–2 victory over Rangers in 1952 in the quarter-final at Ibrox. There was a huge crowd, and Bobby got the winner; after that we thought the Cup was ours, but once again it was not to be.'

Down in Colchester, John Gwynne was commentating on the Essex versus Lancashire match for GMR, and he heard about Bobby's death as the main news headlines were broadcast. He prefaced his next live update with a spontaneous tribute to Bobby, briefly telling listeners about Bobby's passing ability, and how upset he was at 'the saddest news I've heard in along time'. He still remembers seeing Bobby for the first time as an awestruck 12-year-old, shortly after his family had moved to Fallowfield, Manchester, from Shrewsbury, during the late 1950s. John still recalls how excited he felt at pointing out Bobby and then Bert Trautmann to three of his younger siblings at a pre-season match at Maine Road.

Bernard Halford was assistant club secretary at Oldham Athletic when he first met Bobby Johnstone in the early 1960s. He admitted that this had been the only time in his life when he felt professionally obliged to tell lies! 'He transformed the club, there's no doubt about that. On match days, the phone never stopped ringing, with people asking "is Johnstone playing?" Bobby might have been sitting in my office with his ankle in plaster, but I had to say he was playing, otherwise the fans wouldn't have turned up.'

Jimmy Frizzell, a fellow-Scot, came south to Oldham from the Scottish League in 1960, and the two played alongside each other many times. Unlike Bobby, Frizzell then had a long career as manager at both Oldham Athletic and Manchester City, and he speculated as to Bobby's likely transfer value in the modern game... 'What on earth would he have been worth today? He had great ability; he was a tremendous reader of the game with an astute footballing brain and superb touch.

I think his best days were probably at Hibs, but Latics fans will take a lot of convincing.'

Johnny Hart has graphic memories of Bobby and his seemingly continual struggle against injuries. 'I rated Bobby highly, but I suppose I most remember his knee injuries! That was what nearly did for him in the 1956 game. He played on until 1965, of course, but by then he was just walking around! He read the game, tactically, but he couldn't run like me, and obviously he passed the ball very well. I liked him as a fella, but we led different lives back then. I was married, coming back to Golborne every night, and though he was quiet, he lived a different life to me. Actually, I was lucky in one respect, I didn't going clubbing or owt like that, I got married in 1950. Paul was born in 1953, so when Bobby came down here, I was a family man. Really, Barnesy knew him best.'

All of the leading nationals and many regional and local newspapers carried fulsome obituaries, many of them including personal anecdotes from the leading sports correspondents of the post-war years. One article recalled the words of the great John Arlott, the cricket commentator, interviewed on the radio some years earlier. During a spell in Edinburgh, Arlott had watched some football, and he always claimed to have been left with five great memories of that beautiful city, 'Smith, Johnstone, Reilly, Turnbull and Ormond'. In a superb obituary in *The Times*, the much-respected Brian Glanville recalled his own first sighting during young Bobby's national service. Bobby played for the British Army at White Hart Lane, and Glanville recalled 'the impressive sight of his precocious skills as a teenager'. He was sad that Bobby had not gone to the 1954 World Cup in Switzerland, saying 'Had he done so, the Scots might not have suffered so badly.'

In *The Sunday Post*, Doug Baillie had a special reason to remember Bobby, ruefully recalling their meeting of October 1959. Baillie was playing centre-half for Airdrie that day, and Bobby had only just returned to Hibs from Manchester City: 'he didn't look in the best of condition, and the word in the home dressing room was "Don't worry about Johnstone, he's obviously past it."' The final score (Airdrie lost 1–11) revealed only half the story according to Baillie's recollection: 'Tammie Preston got four, Joe Baker three, Johnny McLeod two and Willie Ormond and Joe McLelland one apiece. Every goal had one thing in common – they were put on a plate for the scorers by Bobby Johnstone. What a player; what a great loss to everybody who knew him and played with or against him.'

The *Daily Mail* carried a tribute from Brian Scott, who talked of the Five having comprised arguably the best and most exciting forward line in the history of the Scottish club game. Bobby, the youngest, 'was a true craftsman; one who teased with his dainty dribbling and tormented with his rare ability to play the defence-splitting pass. Easter Road fans sensed the end of a marvellous era when the wee man with the big number eight on his back moved to Manchester City. Fair to say he wasn't long in making an impact with the Maine Road side.' Phil Gordon, the author and journalist, reminded us that all footballers of Bobby's generation bemoaned having missed the boat financially, but, as he reminded his readers, 'Johnstone had more cause to complain than most. There is no shortage of witnesses to the talent of the man who won two Scottish League Championships with Hibernian and scored in two successive FA Cup Finals with Manchester City;

attendance records at every club were broken, and Johnstone was one of the reasons why.'

Bobby's sister Sheila, who lives in Australia, discovered an article that showed that the news of Bobby's death had reached the far outposts of the footballing globe. The *Herald Sun* in Melbourne, Australia, carried a 200-word obituary listing Bobby's key career details, ending with a fulsome tribute to the style of the Famous Five. 'In the absence of video footage to preserve such talent, it is left to word of mouth to pass on any lasting footnote in football history. It was Hibs' brand of daring soccer, signified by five forwards, unheard of now, which prompted newspapers of the time to refer to Johnstone, Smith, Reilly, Turnbull and Willie Ormond as the Famous Five.' In the age of the internet, fans too get their chance to contribute within websites often dedicated to specific clubs. Martin Beckett, who described himself as one of 'a diminishing band of old blues' wrote that Bobby 'gave enjoyment to a whole generation, and I'll guarantee that his memories of having played in two Wembley Cup Finals lived more vividly with him than for the more recent brand of superstar. In 45 years will Liverpool fans remember the 2001 Cup Final in the way I remember squatting behind closed curtains watching a 12inch screen in 1956? I doubt it. It was a genuine great who could appear in, and score in, consecutive Cup Finals in the days when prizes were fewer. Thanks and RIP Bobby.'

On the following Saturday, the wider football world began their tributes, led by Selkirk FC. They faced an Ayrshire side, Girvan Amateurs, in a Scottish Qualifying Cup tie at their new Yarrow Park ground. The match was preceded by a minute's silence, and all home-team players wore black armbands in memory of the club's most famous player. Before Hibernian's home game against Celtic the same day, almost 15,000 fans in Easter Road fell silent in tribute before an early evening kick-off. Journalist Carl Marsden felt that, ironically, the whole scene had typified the sense of the winding down of a bygone football age. He wrote 'This fixture, pitching a nascent Hibernian side against a treble-winning Celtic, sported a 5.30pm kick-off due to the demands of the satellite paymasters. The Champions, given the go-ahead to begin talks to enter the English Premiership, fielded two Swedes, a Russian and defenders from Slovakia and the Ivory Coast. Both teams ditched their traditional colours in favour of replica strips, no doubt the focus of their latest marketing drive. It would all have seemed another world to the man who earned £20 for winning an FA Cup Final.'

Manchester City also played a home game that day, against Crewe Alexandra, although due to production schedules the match programme could not include mention of Bobby's death. More importantly, neither did the club hold a minute's silence specifically in remembrance of Bobby, because of a recently introduced, and controversial, policy. This policy deferred all such tributes until the last home game of each calendar year, at which homage is paid to all those associated with the club who have passed away. Thus City fans did not get chance to pay their tribute until the Boxing Day game against West Bromwich Albion, some four months after Bobby's funeral. The name Bobby Johnstone was recalled as part of a list of players and others whom fans were invited to reflect upon. This approach attracted criticism from some supporters, who felt that the likes of Bobby Johnstone deserved better than a generic tribute, but the club chairman, David Bernstein conceded in the autumn that 'the question of tributes to deceased players is a very difficult one. Bobby Johnstone was obviously a great player for the club, and it's a difficult issue because if you do it for one player, it's only right that you should do it for all players. It can be difficult to distinguish between a player who played one game and a player who played 100 games. We took the decision that we could not do it, but what we are going to do is stage a minute's silence before one of the Christmas fixtures to pay tribute to all of the players that have died through the last year. We think that this is the best way of reconciling these kind of sensitivities.' The recent innovative use of a minute's applause might prove a more appropriate and durable response to these circumstances.

Among the many reflections from those who had known Bobby, several have emerged about the early years of his football career, stories that in some cases have a ring of truth, but others that have proved not possible to substantiate. Craig Douglas told the *Border Telegraph* that he believed that, in 1946, while at Selkirk, Bobby had trialled for Hamilton Academical. 'He was rejected, and they asked him if he had a bigger brother to send.' More realistically, news of Bobby's death prompted Eddie Turnbull to recall that Willie McCartney had first picked Bobby up having seen him against 'Hibs B', the then Hibs third team, who played in the East of Scotland League along with Selkirk FC.

Lawrie Reilly recalled his 'favourite question' about Bobby 'Who were the opposition when Bobby played his first game at Easter Road?' Not too surprisingly, this is a 'trick', with the answer, Hibs, providing the justification for the question. Lawrie vividly recalls Bobby, on more than one occasion, having told him that he had once faced Hibs Reserves at Easter Road as a 15-year-old lad in 1944. Apparently he had played just that one game as a trialist for Stirling Albion reserves (under the pseudonym A.N.Other), and he had actually played against Lawrie, who at that time was a winger. Unfortunately, though I was privileged to spend a couple of hours alongside Lawrie, working through his own extensive collection of newspaper cuttings from that period, we were unable to authenticate the tale.

By coincidence, two of Bobby's former clubs, Oldham Athletic and Manchester City, had arranged to play in a friendly match at Boundary Park around this time. The game had originally been intended as a pre-season friendly, but the fates conspired to see it first postponed and then played just eight days after Bobby's funeral, on Tuesday 4 September. The match programme contained an article that had plainly been revised to accommodate news of Bobby's death, but nevertheless it served to honour his memory by stating 'the debate continues as to whether he is the club's greatest ever player'. In fact, that accolade had some time previously been given to Oldham's then manager, Andy Ritchie, who had been acclaimed as such in a poll conducted by the Football League. Unquestionably, Ritchie had played a key part in the Latics side that had brought Oldham Athletic to new heights when they reached the Premiership and played at Wembley several times. The other contender was Roger Palmer, who was Oldham's record goalscorer. The article went on to argue that, as the poll had been conducted some 36 years after Bobby Johnstone had last played for Latics, many voters simply could not have seen all contenders in the flesh. Judged on the player's whole career, Bobby Johnstone would win the argument 'hands down': he had been successful at the highest level, won two Championship medals at Hibernian, where he was a member of the 'all-international' Famous Five forward line, earning 17 caps in an age when internationals were far less frequent than today. He gained further silverware at Manchester City, and made history into the bargain. On the downside, his contribution for Latics, while an important one given its timing – they were at their lowest ebb – Ritchie and Palmer played at higher levels. The article concludes that Ritchie and Palmer cannot touch Bobby in terms of what they each achieved in their careers, so the article concluded that Bobby was Latics greatest-ever player. Ritchie and Palmer made major contributions for the Latics, and at a higher level. As Ritchie pips that one, he is deemed to be the greatest-ever Latics player, and the rationale is difficult to dispute.

Manchester City didn't get the opportunity to provide a written obituary for their supporters until their next home game, against Birmingham City on Saturday 15 September. City's leading historian, Gary James, paid rich tribute in an 'Obituary to a true blue hero', describing Bobby's key career details and the fact that he became only the second Manchester City player ever to be selected to represent Great Britain after the great Frank Swift. This wonderful full-page tribute contains two photographs, the first showing Roy Paul introducing Bobby to Prime Minister Harold MacMillan, and Prince Philip, HRH The Duke of Edinburgh, before the 1956 Final, the other is of his historic goal later in the day. 'He was an influential player in a team of stars, and should be remembered alongside the likes of Trautmann and Revie as one of the club's greatest players from that era' James concludes.

Bobby had been laid to rest and, quite naturally, the tributes began to subside. One of the last tributes to be published appeared in the popular fanzine *King of the Kippax*, and there John Gwynne paid his respects, speculating upon how supporters may have wanted to pay homage: 'They didn't sing it in his day, but "There's only one Bobby Johnstone" would have been wholly appropriate. The pint-sized, dark-haired, round-faced inside-forward had a deft and delicate touch, a wonderfully natural control and an instinctive capacity to play the perfect pass. The quintessential Scottish inside-forward if you like: brilliant on his day, frustratingly defective off it. Yes, he had his bad days, Bobby, but many a good one, too. When he played well, the team played well. It was as simple as that.'

Robbie Russell had spent some time with his Uncle Bobby in the period just before he had passed away, and he reflected upon the family's loss 'He had a bad knock, and I've always thought that if it hadn't have been for the fall, he'd be here now. I feel these things can trigger off other problems, and things deteriorate... it's frustrating. I'm disappointed that he didn't stay in football, too, coaching or something. Yet he wasn't a great lover of coaches, though, he just thought you should let people play. But there's some sense that he underachieved somehow, perhaps he should have been more famous. You know everyone knows Jim Baxter or Lawrie Reilly, yet at one point Bobby was considered the best inside-forward in Britain.'

CHAPTER 12

The Memory Lives On

Selkirk FC had been forced to move from Ettrick Park in 2000, their home since 1906, and the place where Bobby, his father and several of his uncles had played all those years ago. The new facility, Yarrow Park, lies further west along the banks of Ettrick Water, adjacent to the rugby union and cricket club grounds at Philiphaugh. Bobby was more than familiar with that location, of course, as these were the grounds where, as a young scrum half, he had enjoyed playing rugby, and also demonstrated his prowess as a cricketer – something he continued with even at the height of his professional football career. Once the club identified its new home, Bobby was pictured in the local press assisting with the formalities. He was seen holding the club crest with Graham Bateman as this was symbolically removed from the old site before being transported the short distance to the new ground.

Selkirk's original clubhouse, built in 1937, had been replaced in the mid-1970s, and the then manager of St Mirren FC Alex Ferguson brought his side to celebrate its construction. Selkirk FC now needed a new changing facility, and they began trying to raise funds in order to build one at Yarrow Park – rather a tall order for a side in the East of Scotland League. Ideally, funds would run to a quite substantial building, with both home and away dressing rooms and a room for match officials. There were plans for a larger room overlooking the pitch, for use by the club committee and their guests. Further areas would cater for the refreshment needs of the club's supporters, and there would be secure storage space to accommodate the ground's maintenance equipment. In August 2002, with the club still settling in, Manchester United sent a young reserve team to officially open the new ground, though this time Sir Alex Ferguson was not present, which was probably for the best as the changing facilities were still quite inadequate.

In 2003, under the chairmanship of Roger Arnold, the clubhouse plans came to fruition. Fittingly, it was announced that the new facility would be named in honour of the club's most famous player, and on 2 September Selkirk FC staged a match against a Manchester City XI to celebrate the grand opening of the Bobby Johnstone Pavilion. On the evening of the game a healthy crowd built up, and eventually more than 500 spectators turned out, raising around £2,000 for club funds. Before the game kicked-off there were several short speeches from dignitaries including Nicola Taylor, Bobby's daughter, and Bernard Halford, City's general secretary. Alongside Craig Douglas, the new chairman of Selkirk FC, they unveiled a commemorative plaque. Many others that had been associated with Bobby Johnstone's football career were present, too, and City were further officially represented by Ian Niven, Bert Lister and John Riley, the latter on behalf of the MCFC Former Players' Association. Hibernian FC were represented by chairman Mr Rod Petrie, and their club captain Grant Brebner, while Oldham

Athletic's chairman, Mr Alan Hardy, and his wife Vivienne represented Bobby's last senior club.

Bernard Halford is perhaps uniquely positioned to comment on Bobby, having seen many of his games at both City and Oldham after 1955, and in a marvellous speech he recalled Bobby playing for Oldham Athletic in the early 1960s when he was club secretary there. Of his 40-year career on the administrative side of the game, he said 'You see good players, you see a few great players, but tonight we're here to honour a genius of a player. I can honestly say that he was the greatest player I have ever seen with the ball at his feet.' Bobby's daughter Nicola said 'It is a great honour to be invited to Selkirk, and I'm sure that my Dad would have appreciated the efforts of everyone involved. This really is a most thoughtful gesture.'

Bobby's granddaughter Caroline Taylor was City's mascot for the night, and she led the team out just before the early evening kick-off time, ensuring that the fixture could be completed in daylight. The match itself, which was almost literally men against boys, was conducted in a sporting manner, and it was the boys from Manchester that won 4–1 against a team of spirited and competitive amateurs. The Selkirk players gave the impression of being proud to be part of the occasion, and later Ian Niven summed the event up for the *Border Telegraph*, saying 'Selkirk is beautiful and a wonderful setting for a special night like this. It has been a wonderful occasion, and a fitting tribute to Bobby Johnstone. For me, he was one of the two greatest players to have played for City alongside Denis Law.' Selkirk Football Club's chairman rounded off the formalities by thanking those who had attended on a memorable evening for the club, and, in closing, said 'Bobby's skills were respected all over the world; it is only fitting that we named our new pavilion after him'. The following day's *Border Telegraph* reported the occasion with a full match report and several pictures of the speakers, the unveiling ceremony and both teams, all of whom had been brought together because of Bobby Johnstone... 'without doubt the best footballer and all-round sportsman Selkirk has ever seen, or is ever likely to see'.

Records for Posterity

	Scottish League/ Football League		Scottish Cup/ FA Cup		Scottish League Cup/ League Cup		Total	
	Apps	Gls	Apps	Gls	Apps	Gls	Apps	Gls
Hibernian								
1948–49	2	0	0	0	0	0	2	0
1949–50	26	9	1	0	1	1	28	10
1950–51	29	12	5	3	*12	8	46	23
1951–52	27	23	3	0	6	3	36	26
1952–53	30	16	5	1	5	5	40	22
1953–54	30	11	3	3	9	8	42	22
1954–55	20	12	1	0	4	2	25	14
Total	164	83	18	7	*37	27	219	117

*Includes abandoned match v. Dundee that was never replayed

	Apps	Gls	Apps	Gls	Apps	Gls	Apps	Gls
Manchester City								
1954–55	8	2	2	1			10	3
1955–56	31	12	7	4			38	16
1956–57	31	16	2	3			33	19
1957–58	33	7	1	0			34	7
1958–59	18	4	2	1			20	5
1959–60	3	1	0	0			3	1
Total	124	42	14	9			138	51
Hibernian								
1959–60	30	17	3	2	0	0	33	19
1960–61	1	0	0	0	3	2	4	2
Total	31	17	3	2	3	2	37	21
Total for Hibs	195	100	21	9	40	29	256	138
Oldham Athletic								
1960–61	30	11	3	1	1	0	34	12
1961–62	40	10	5	2	1	0	46	12
1962–63	28	5	1	0	1	0	30	5
1963–64	34	9	3	0	0	0	37	9
1964–65	11	0	0	0	0	0	11	0
Total	143	35	12	3	3	0	158	38
Grand Total	462	177	47	21	43	29	552	227

Retired from professional football in May 1965

	Scottish Internationals		Scottish League Representative Games		Total	
	Apps	Gls	Apps	Gls	Apps	Gls
1950–51	3	1	1	0	4	1
1951–52	2	2	2	0	4	2
1952–53	2	1	2	0	4	1
1953–54	4	2	1	0	5	2
1954–55	3	2	0	0	3	2
1955–56	3	2	0	0	3	2

Scottish League Representative Honours

1950–51	League of Ireland	Glasgow, Parkhead	7–0
1951–52	Football League	Sheffield, Hillsborough	1–2
	Irish League	Glasgow, Ibrox Stadium	3–0
1952–53	League of Ireland	Glasgow	5–1*
	Football League	Glasgow	1–0
1953–54	League of Ireland	Dublin, Dalymount Park	3–1

* The match in which all but Turnbull of the Famous Five played

Other Senior Appearances

Played and scored for Great Britain versus Rest of Europe (August 1955) in a 1–4 defeat
Played 3 times in St Mungo Cup tournament in 1951–52, scoring 3 goals
Played 4 times in Coronation Cup tournament in 1952–53, scoring 1 goal

Scottish International Caps

Season	Date	Venue	Opponents	Competition	Result
1950–51	14 Apr	Wembley	England	Home Int	3–2 (goal)
	12 May	Hampden Park	Denmark	Friendly	3–1
	16 May	Hampden Park	France	Friendly	1–0
1951–52	6 Oct	Windsor Park	Northern Ireland	Home Int	3–0 (2 goals)
	5 Apr	Hampden Park	England	Home Int	1–2
1952–53	18 Apr	Wembley	England	Home Int	2–2
	6 May	Hampden Park	Sweden	Friendly	1–2 (goal)
1953–54	4 Nov	Hampden Park	Wales	World Cup Q	3–3 (goal)
	3 Apr	Hampden Park	England	World Cup Q	2–4
	5 May	Hampden Park	Norway	Friendly	1–0
	25 May	Helsinki	Finland	Friendly	2–1 (goal)
1954–55	3 Nov	Hampden Park	Northern Ireland	Home Int	2–2 (goal)
	8 Dec	Hampden Park	Hungary	Friendly	2–4 (goal)
	2 Apr	Wembley	England	Home Int	2–7
1955–56	8 Oct	Windsor Park	Northern Ireland	Home Int	1–2
	9 Nov	Hampden Park	Wales	Home Int	2–0 (2 goals)
	14 Apr	Hampden Park	England	Home Int	1–1

Among the dozen or so players that have scored more goals for the Scottish international team are some great names such as Dalglish, Denis Law and Lawrie Reilly, and more recently Ally McCoist and John Collins, the latter also an ex-Hibee. Almost invariably, these players had international careers that spanned a decade or more, while Bobby's international career lasted just five years. Maurice Johnston (14 goals from 38 caps) and Alan Gilzean (12 goals from 22 caps) had international careers spanning between seven and eight years, but Andrew Wilson (Dunfermline Athletic and Middlesbrough) managed his 12 goals in the 12 appearances he made between 1920 and April 1923. All of Bobby's international goals came from 'open play' – in later years Bobby would remark that he was Scotland's penalty-taker throughout his international career, but as they didn't get any he never missed any!

Career Goals
Hibernian

Season	Date	Goals	Opponents	Competition	Venue	Result
1949–50	17 Sep	1	Partick Thistle	SLC	Firhill Park	2–4
	12 Nov	1	Motherwell	SLA	Fir Park	3–1
	19 Nov	2	East Fife	SLA	Easter Road	4–1
	26 Nov	1	Third Lanark	SLA	Cathkin Park	2–0

Season	Date	Goals	Opponents	Competition	Venue	Result
	10 Dec	1	Falkirk	SLA	Easter Road	5–1
	24 Dec	1	Raith Rovers	SLA	Easter Road	4–2
	25 Feb	1	East Fife	SLA	Bayview Park	1–1
	11 Mar	1	Dundee	SLA	Easter Road	4–2
	8 Apr	1	Clyde	SLA	Easter Road	6–3
1950–51	12 Aug	1	Dundee	SLC	Easter Road	2–0
	15 Aug	2	St Mirren	SLC	Love Street	6–0
	2 Sep	1	Falkirk	SLC	Easter Road	4–0
	16 Sep	1	Aberdeen	SLC	Pittodrie	1–4
	20 Sep	1	Aberdeen	SLC	Easter Road	4–1
	3 Oct	2	Aberdeen (2nd Play-off)	SLC	Hampden Park	5–1
	14 Oct	2	Motherwell	SLA	Fir Park	6–2
	25 Nov	1	Airdrie	SLA	Easter Road	5–0
	23 Dec	1	Falkirk	SLA	Brockville Park	5–1
	2 Jan	2	Aberdeen	SLA	Easter Road	6–2
	6 Jan	1	Raith Rovers	SLA	Stark's Park	3–1
	20 Jan	1	Partick Thistle	SLA	Easter Road	1–1
	31 Jan	2	St Mirren	SC1R	Easter Road	5–0
	10 Feb	1	Rangers	SC2	Ibrox Park	3–2
	3 Mar	1	Airdrie	SLA	Broomfield Park	1–2
	17 Mar	1	Third Lanark	SLA	Easter Road	3–1
	24 Mar	1	St Mirren	SLA	Love Street	1–0
	14 Apr	1	England		Wembley	3–2
	28 Apr	1	Rangers	SLA	Easter Road	4–1
1951–52	14 Jul	2	Third Lanark	St Mungo	Easter Road	3–1
	21 Jul	1	Motherwell	St Mungo	Parkhead	3–1
	18 Aug	1	Stirling Albion	SLC	Easter Road	4–2
	25 Aug	2	Partick Thistle	SLC	Easter Road	5–1
	8 Sep	1	Raith Rovers	SLA	Starks Park	2–0
	15 Sep	2	Aberdeen	SLA	Easter Road	4–4
	29 Sep	2	Third Lanark	SLA	Easter Road	5–2
	6 Oct	2	Northern Ireland		Windsor Park	3–0
	20 Oct	2	Partick Thistle	SLA	Easter Road	5–0
	17 Nov	1	East Fife	SLA	Easter Road	4–2
	24 Nov	1	Airdrie	SLA	Broomfield Park	2–0
	1 Dec	2	Dundee	SLA	Dens Park	4–1
	8 Dec	2	Queen of the South	SLA	Easter Road	5–0
	15 Dec	2	St Mirren	SLA	Love Street	4–0
	22 Dec	2	Raith Rovers	SLA	Easter Road	5–0
	29 Dec	1	Motherwell	SLA	Fir Park	1–3
	2 Jan	1	Third Lanark	SLA	Cathkin Park	5–0
	12 Jan	1	Aberdeen	SLA	Pittodrie	2–1
	2 Feb	1	Celtic	SLA	Easter Road	3–1
	1 Mar	1	Airdrie	SLA	Easter Road	4–0
	15 Mar	1	Queen of the South	SLA	Palmerston Park	2–5
1952–53	27 Aug	1	St Mirren	SLC	Love Street	1–3
	13 Sep	2	Morton	SLC	Cappielow Park	6–0
	17 Sep	2	Morton	SLC	Easter Road	6–3
	27 Sep	2	Motherwell	SLA	Fir Park	7–3
	25 Oct	2	Clyde	SLA	Shawfield Park	3–2
	15 Nov	1	Dundee	SLA	Easter Road	3–0
	24 Jan	1	Stenhousemuir	SC1	Easter Road	8–1

Season	Date	Goals	Opponents	Competition	Venue	Result
	28 Feb	2	Airdrie	SLA	Broomfield Park	7–3
	21 Mar	1	St Mirren	SLA	Love Street	2–2
	28 Mar	2	Celtic	SLA	Parkhead	3–1
	20 Apr	1	East Fife	SLA	Easter Road	2–1
	25 Apr	3	Third Lanark	SLA	Easter Road	7–1
	29 Apr	2	Raith Rovers	SLA	Easter Road	4–1
	6 May	1	Sweden		Hampden	1–2
	16 May	1	Newcastle United	Coro Cup	Ibrox Park	4–0
1953–54	12 Aug	1	Falkirk	SLC	Easter Road	4–1
	26 Aug	1	Falkirk	SLC	Brockville Park	2–1
	29 Aug	2	St Mirren	SLC	Easter Road	3–2
	12 Sep	3	Third Lanark	SLC	Cathkin Park	4–0
	16 Sep	1	Third Lanark	SLC	Easter Road	4–0
	26 Sep	2	Hamilton Academical	SLA	Easter Road	4–1
	4 Nov	1	Wales		Hampden	3–3
	14 Nov	2	St Mirren	SLA	Love Street	3–3
	2 Jan	1	Hamilton Academical	SLA	Douglas Park	6–2
	16 Jan	1	Aberdeen	SLA	Pittodrie	3–1
	6 Feb	3	Clyde	SLA	Shawfield Park	6–3
	13 Feb	2	Clyde	SC2	Easter Road	7–0
	27 Feb	1	Aberdeen	SC3	Easter Road	1–3
	13 Mar	1	East Fife	SLA	Bayview Park	3–1
	20 Mar	1	Dundee	SLA	Easter Road	2–0
	25 May	1	Finland		Olympic Stdm	2–1
1954–55	4 Sep	2	Queen of the South	SLC	Palmerston Park	5–3
	18 Sep	1	Heart of Midlothian	SLA	Easter Road	2–3
	25 Sep	1	Aberdeen	SLA	Pittodrie	3–1
	23 Oct	2	Clyde	SLA	Shawfield Park	3–6
	3 Nov	1	Northern Ireland		Hampden	2–2
	6 Nov	2	Stirling Albion	SLA	Annfield Park	4–2
	13 Nov	1	Motherwell	SLA	Easter Road	4–1
	27 Nov	3	East Fife	SLA	Bayview Park	5–1
	8 Dec	1	Hungary		Hampden	2–4
	1 Jan	1	Heart of Midlothian	SLA	Tynecastle	1–5
	8 Jan	1	Falkirk	SLA	Brockville Park	1–3
	15 Jan	3*	Queen of the South	Aband	Easter Road	3–0

Manchester City

Season	Date	Goals	Opponents	Competition	Venue	Result
1954–55	8 Apr	1	West Bromwich Albion	Div 1	Maine Road	4–0
	16 Apr	1	Charlton Athletic	Div 1	The Valley	1–1
	7 May	1	Newcastle United	FACF	Wembley	1–3
1955–56	10 Sep	1	Cardiff City	Div 1	Maine Road	3–1
	17 Sep	1	Huddersfield Town	Div 1	Leeds Road	3–3
	24 Sep	1	Blackpool	Div 1	Maine Road	2–0
	9 Nov	2	Wales		Hampden Park	2–0
	2 Jan	3	Portsmouth	Div 1	Maine Road	4–1
	11 Jan	1	Blackpool	FAC3	Maine Road	2–1
	14 Jan	1	Cardiff City	Div 1	Ninian Park	1–4
	25 Feb	2	Preston North End	Div 1	Deepdale	3–0
	3 Mar	1	Everton	FAC6	Maine Road	2–1
	7 Mar	1	Everton	Div 1	Maine Road	3–0

Season	Date	Goals	Opponents	Competition	Venue	Result
	10 Mar	2	West Bromwich Albion	Div 1	The Hawthorns	4–0
	17 Mar	1	Tottenham Hotspur	FACs-f	Villa Park	1–0
	5 May	1	Birmingham City	FACF	Wembley	3–1
1956–57	29 Aug	1	Tottenham Hotspur (pen)	Div 1	White Hart Lane	2–3
	20 Oct	1	Newcastle United	Div 1	St James' Park	3–0
	27 Oct	1	Sheffield Wednesday (pen)	Div 1	Maine Road	4–2
	10 Nov	2	Birmingham City	Div 1	Maine Road	3–1
	24 Nov	1	Portsmouth	Div 1	Maine Road	5–1
	8 Dec	3	Chelsea	Div 1	Maine Road	5–4
	15 Dec	2	Wolverhampton W	Div 1	Maine Road	2–3
	5 Jan	1	Newcastle United	FAC3	Maine Road	1–1
	9 Jan	2	Newcastle United	FAC3R	Maine Road	4–5
	19 Jan	1	Charlton Athletic	Div 1	Maine Road	5–1
	9 Feb	1	Blackpool	Div 1	Bloomfield Road	1–4
	16 Mar	3	Cardiff City	Div 1	Maine Road	4–1
1957–58	14 Sep	1	Portsmouth	Div 1	Maine Road	2–1
	28 Sep	2	Tottenham Hotspur	Div 1	Maine Road	5–1
	21 Dec	1	Sheffield Wednesday	Div 1	Hillsborough	5–4
	11 Jan	1	Nottingham Forest	Div 1	Maine Road	1–1
	22 Feb	2	Leicester City	Div 1	Filbert Street	4–8
1958–59	23 Aug	2	Burnley	Div 1	Turf Moor	4–3
	17 Sep	1	Luton Town	Div 1	Kenilworth Road	1–5
	24 Jan	1	Grimsby Town	FAC3R	Maine Road	1–2
	14 Feb	1	Manchester United	Div 1	Old Trafford	1–4
1959–60	22 Aug	1	Nottingham Forest	Div 1	Maine Road	2–1

Hibernian

Season	Date	Goals	Opponents	Competition	Venue	Result
1959–60	31 Oct	1	Celtic	SL1	Easter Road	3–3
	7 Nov	1	St Mirren	SL1	Love Street	3–2
	21 Nov	2	Dundee	SL1	Easter Road	4–2
	28 Nov	1	Stirling Albion	SL1	Easter Road	3–1
	12 Dec	2	Ayr United (1 pen)	SL1	Easter Road	5–1
	26 Dec	2	Aberdeen (1 pen)	SL1	Pittodrie	4–6
	1 Jan	1	Heart of Midlothian	SL1	Easter Road	1–5
	23 Jan	2	Clyde	SL1	Easter Road	5–5
	29 Feb	1	Dundee	SC2	Easter Road	3–0
	12 Mar	1	Rangers (pen)	SC4	Ibrox Park	2–3
	16 Mar	1	St Mirren	SL1	Easter Road	1–3
	26 Mar	1	Dundee	SL1	Dens Park	3–6
	30 Mar	2	Airdrie (1 pen)	SL1	Easter Road	3–3
	2 Apr	1	Stirling Albion	SL1	Annfield Park	3–2
1960–61	13 Aug	1	Kilmarnock (1 pen)	SLC	Rugby Park	2–4
	20 Aug	1	Airdrie	SLC	Easter Road	6–1

Oldham Athletic

Season	Date	Goals	Opponents	Competition	Venue	Result
1960–61	15 Oct	1	Exeter City	Div 4	Boundary Park	5–2
	29 Oct	1	Southport	Div 4	Boundary Park	3–2
	26 Nov	1	Chesterfield	FAC2	Saltergate	4–4
	3 Dec	1	Wrexham	Div 4	Racecourse Grd.	2–2
	31 Dec	1	Bradford Park Avenue	Div 4	Boundary Park	4–0

Season	Date	Goals	Opponents	Competition	Venue	Result
	14 Jan	2	Gillingham	Div 4	Priestfield	3–2
	25 Feb	1	Stockport County	Div 4	Boundary Park	3–0
	25 Mar	1	Darlington	Div 4	Boundary Park	3–3
	31 Mar	1	Mansfield Town	Div 4	Boundary Park	3–1
	3 Apr	2	Mansfield Town	Div 4	Field Mill	2–1
1961–62	21 Aug	1	Hartlepools United	Div 4	Victoria Ground	1–1
	26 Aug	1	Colchester United	Div 4	Boundary Park	2–2
	30 Aug	1	Hartlepools United	Div 4	Boundary Park	5–2
	9 Sep	1	Bradford City	Div 4	Boundary Park	1–1
	7 Oct	1	Barrow	Div 4	Holker Street	1–3
	28 Oct	1	Exeter City	Div 4	Boundary Park	1–1
	4 Nov	1	Shildon	FAC1	Boundary Park	5–2
	29 Nov	1	Chesterfield	FAC2	Boundary Park	4–2
	16 Dec	1	Chester	Div 4	Boundary Park	1–1
	30 Dec	1	Southport	Div 4	Haig Avenue	5–0
	13 Jan	1	Carlisle United (pen)	Div 4	Boundary Park	5–0
	3 Mar	1	Rochdale	Div 4	Spotland	1–3
1962–63	25 Aug	1	Tranmere Rovers	Div 4	Prenton Park	2–1
	8 Sep	1	Lincoln City (pen)	Div 4	Sincil Bank	2–1
	22 Sep	1	Barrow	Div 4	Boundary Park	2–1
	26 Sep	1	Oxford United	Div 4	Boundary Park	2–0
	1 Dec	1	York City	Div 4	Boundary Park	3–2
1963–64	14 Sep	1	Peterborough United	Div 3	Boundary Park	4–2
	2 Oct	1	Wrexham (pen)	Div 3	Boundary Park	3–2
	2 Nov	2	Reading	Div 3	Boundary Park	3–1
	30 Nov	1	Brentford (pen)	Div 3	Boundary Park	4–1
	14 Dec	1	Queen's Park Rangers (pen)	Div 3	Loftus Road	2–3
	21 Dec	2	Bristol Rovers (2 pens)	Div 3	Boundary Park	2–2
	4 Apr	1	Mansfield Town	Div 3	Boundary Park	1–0

A Brief History of Selkirk FC 1880 to 1939

Selkirk's terrain, with hills rising from its position on the Ettrick valley floor, is not ideal for games such as association football, and so the town's sportsmen have generally sought accommodation along the banks of Ettrick Water, which flows just to the north of the town. The numerous tweed and woollen mills that sprang up during the early Victorian era were in competition for that same land, however, and later further pressure was felt by the arrival of a railway branch line. As a result, Selkirk Football Club often lacked the security of tenure enjoyed by more senior clubs. The Mill Haugh, their initial home, was ideally located for river, road and railway connections with the town of Galashiels, and as the industrial landscape changed, superior claims upon the available space saw the footballers moved on. The Mill Haugh became occupied partially by the railway station yard, and then, later, by other commercial users.

Increasing numbers of working men were free of the week's work by Saturday lunchtime, and in most parts of Scotland football was establishing itself as the dominant leisure-time pursuit. According to Robert Crampsey, 'The game appealed to the Scottish worker. Unlike cricket, it was independent of the weather, needed little equipment and the playing pitch did not require the expensive cosseting of the cricket square.' Yet football struggled to establish itself as the prime force in the Borders, and authoritative sources at least partially trace this back to a decision taken in the earliest years of organised association football. Then Queen's Park FC, the renowned amateur club from Glasgow, were invited to take part in the English FA Cup and given exemption to the semi-final stage. In taking up their invitation to travel to London, a projected tour to the Tweed valley was cancelled, and their club funds (some £4) were used to travel south instead. Thus, plans to introduce soccer to the Borderers were shelved and this may have been a mistake. Having drawn 0–0 with Wanderers, Queen's Park found themselves unable to fund an extended stay in London, and they were forced to return home and scratch from the competition. Meanwhile, Rugby Union advanced over the border from northern England, and to this day the Borders area of south-east Scotland is the one area of the kingdom where rugby union has supremacy over the round-ball game.

In October 1880 Selkirk became the first town in the Borders area to make serious attempts to form an Association Football Club. Responding to a public notice in the *Southern Reporter*, volunteers came forward in numbers sufficient to allow the formation of a committee, and a date was fixed for the inaugural match. This was to be against Edinburgh's Hibernian, and such distinguished visitors warranted a special effort, so instead of continuing to use the Mill Haugh, arrangements were made for the temporary use of the superior facility upstream at the cricket ground. Eventually, the great day arrived, and in March 1881 the adventure really began. Although history records a 0–14 result, it was the beginning of close links between the infant club and their mighty neighbours, and some 65 years later Hibernian were to reap a rich dividend from having established those early links with Selkirk.

The football club remained in residence at the cricket ground for the next decade. The fields there had been the site of the historic Battle of Philiphaugh in 1645, during a savage religious war between the Marquis of Montrose and Sir David Leslie. Hundreds were murdered on and around this ground, with more slain further up the valley; Selkirk Cricket Club's crest contains two swords crossed, the symbol used in Ordnance Survey maps to depict a battle site.

In 1891 the club moved again, to the Angle Field on a short-term lease. During their short stay there, Queen's Park finally did pay a visit, winning a friendly match by 4–1 in front of a large crowd. Selkirk FC were soon on the move again, this time to Linglie Haugh, having been granted a lease by the owner, a farmer named McCombe. With association football becoming more popular in the Borders, a new trophy, the Association Border Counties Challenge Cup competition, was established that year, and the Souters promptly won it, beating Hawick 4–3 in the Final. Thus, they collected their first trophy, and a key player in those early days of Selkirk FC and indeed one of the goalscorers in the Final was Geordie Johnstone. He was one of a number of Johnstones who would help shape the destiny of the club over the next half a century, and he was Bobby Johnstone's great-uncle.

The pioneers of the club were justifiably proud. On the field of play, the club had taken on and proved the match of all-comers, and Selkirk remained undefeated by any Borders side for seven years. In 1892–93 Selkirk FC were accepted into the Border League, which was established that year under the auspices of the Scottish Football Association, now itself 20 years old. Along with Vale of Gala, Vale of Leithen, Duns, Earlston, Kelso and Hawick Rangers, they formed an eight-strong League. The next year, 1894, saw Selkirk travel to Kirkcaldy for a Scottish Cup tie against Raith Rovers, but they were soundly beaten 8–1.

From 1895 new arrangements for the Scottish Cup applied to junior clubs, specifically the Scottish Association Qualifying Cup. Though Selkirk were surprisingly beaten in their inaugural tie, by 2nd Black Watch, they remained the top side in the Borders, collecting the Borders Cup three times between 1894 and the end of the century and losing the Final on two further occasions. They claimed the Border League Championship too, in 1897, after a play-off with Peebles Rovers. This game finished 4–0 in front of a large crowd, including some 500 who made the journey on specially laid-on trains.

Being somewhat isolated geographically, Selkirk was insulated to a degree from two particular impacts upon Scottish football as the Victorian era drew to a close. Firstly, the Scottish administrators were somewhat compelled by the fact that, in 1885, professionalism had been legalised in England. '...many Scots came south to England and particularly clubs such as Blackburn Rovers, Preston North End, Aston Villa and West Bromwich Albion. Then, players would be paid to play, but be found work too, within their trade. This drain 'forced' professionalism upon the Scottish game, which even then could only be expected to thrive in the Forth/Clyde valley.' The railway network meant that travel around the central lowland belt, and in particular between Glasgow and Edinburgh, was much more quick and reliable. Football crowds now began to flock to the major centres, within the heavily industrialised areas along the Clyde, or the mining towns in Fife and Lanarkshire. Selkirk, some 40 miles from the beaten track, was in a geographical position that was less advantageous, if that is the correct interpretation, and so their true amateur status was never in doubt.

However, Selkirk did indeed begin to find life becoming a bit harder. Many new clubs had been formed since their birth in 1880, and often these rivals, particularly where they were located nearer to the capital, benefitted from the fall-out from the professional game. The club's leading position came under attack from new clubs, and Vale of Leithen, less than a decade after their formation, became a particular threat. In 1899 the Border Cup Final between the two clubs became a marathon. After an initial 3–3 draw at neutral Melrose, the Selkirk Silver Jubilee Band lent support at the replay, which was also a draw, 1–1, in front of a crowd of over 2,000. For the second replay, Vale replied with the Innerleithen Pipe Band, and to compound this setback Selkirk then conceded an 'o.g.' through Geordie Johnstone, still a key member of the side. Vale went on to win the Cup in extra-time.

Off the field, Selkirk's residence at Linglie Haugh was coming to an end, and the club needed to look for a new site. Achieving this would remove at least one recurring problem – the occasional loss of valuable leather footballs! In one instance Duns were severely criticised for 'kicking the ball too strongly when playing at the bottom end of the field'. On that occasion, two balls were lost to the Ettrick – indeed, it was recorded that one of those was nearly new!

By 1900 Selkirk FC were homeless. Away games were possible, of course, and several were played, but support for the football team fell away badly. After a couple of temporary moves, the chance to return to the cricket field was taken up. In 1901 further progress came when two Leagues were fashioned. The Southern Division was formed principally by Berwick Rangers, who had been playing for 15 years in the Northumberland League, along with Kelso, Duns, Coldstream and Tweedmouth. The Northern Division involved Selkirk, Vale of Leithen, Selkirk Woodburn, Peebles Rovers and a couple of Galashiels sides. Back at the cricket field, the Souters lost no footballs but did lose the Borders Cup Final to Vale of Leithen. Happily, they avenged that defeat with a 4–1 League win though, a major factor in the Souter's successful retention of the Border League title.

A list of the players and club officials around this time illustrates the great commitment made by several families, often the key to the survival of clubs engaged in regional football. The McBains provided at least four players in the early years of the club, and there were two Batemans in the 1903–04 Cup-winning side. The captain, Willie Bateman, was presented with the Cup after the Final against Peebles Rovers, and he brought it back by train from Innerleithen, where the team, also containing his brother John, was greeted by a large crowd and given a hero's welcome.

In August 1906, after an uneasy period domiciled at the cricket pitch – there were tensions around the overlapping of the respective seasons – the football club found itself a home further along Ettrick Water at the Under Haugh. For a rent of £10 per annum, payable to the local council, Selkirk FC moved to their new home, which they named Ettrick Park. The deal was not without it's problems, as there was competition from at least one farmer who wanted the land for grazing, and some of the Council officials had other concerns, as it had come to their attention that some spectators had a tendency to 'unruly behaviour'. The lease was granted on the condition that policemen would be employed to preserve order. Thus Selkirk FC moved into what would be their home for almost a century, and a home pitch that would witness one of Scottish football's true greats, a lad who would hone his skills there in preparation for a career within the upper echelons of the game.

The first game at Ettrick Park was against the Royal Garrison Artillery (Leith), a first-round match in the East of Scotland Qualifying Cup. Although the pitch was rather undulating, for now the game was on, and the considerable attention the pitch required would have to wait. George Kemp become the first to score at their new home, Selkirk winning 2–1. A small pavilion was erected adjacent to the main gate at Ettrick Park. The home team enjoyed a large changing room, and while the visitors enjoyed facilities of a lesser standard, nonetheless this was a vast improvement on previous days at the cricket field. Then both teams would have to make their way to a local hotel to clean up after a game. Here, at least, there was shelter and a plentiful supply of cold water for the buckets, usually drawn from the nearby Ettrick. There was even a small 'doo-cot' provided for the referee, but this could barely be described as largesse.

The following year, 1907, Selkirk Rugby Union Football Club erected a grandstand at Philiphaugh cricket field, quite a setback because some at the more sensitive end of the football-supporting market now deserted soccer to watch some sport under cover, a comparative luxury. From this time, at least until the end of World War One, the Johnstone family had no lads to play; Hopey Johnstone, Geordie's nephew, who was born in 1904, and his brothers were still too young.

Sixteen members of the club perished in World War One, after which the new generation began to make their contribution. At this time the soccer men were starting to struggle as rugby was gaining an even firmer foothold. Fortunately, friends in high places saw a series of lucrative friendly matches keep the club afloat, teams such as Queen of the South, Glasgow's Celtic, and the two Edinburgh giants, Hibernian and Hearts, all visited, and often declined their due share of any gate money.

By the start of 1928–29 Selkirk FC were making reasonable progress in the East of Scotland League, and brothers Tom and George (Hopey) Johnstone were making their presence felt. A couple of years later, Selkirk claimed the Borders Cup once again, and a special celebration dinner at a local hostelry, the Cross Keys, was attended by Sam Douglas, with 28 years playing experience behind him, and Geordie Johnstone, who had accumulated an incredible six Border Cup-winning medals.

The Johnstones

While the Selkirk FC records show the achievements of Hopey and Tom Johnstone, a third brother, Alec, also served Selkirk, although he was unable to compete as a player. As a young man, he had got an infection, which meant him having a leg amputated. Instead, he gave sterling service as a committee member, the club president and, for a time, chairman of the club. Margaret, Bobby's eldest sister, knew all about Geordie from her father, Hopey, but 'There are many Johnstones that we never knew. We only knew the younger ones really, Tom, Alec and Jim. My father was one of 11, the others being Robert and Willy, who both emigrated to Australia, Walter, who was killed in World War One, and then Elizabeth, Janet, Mary and Margaret.'

Jim ('Chic') Johnstone was killed in World War Two, while he was based at Greenlaw in Berwickshire, with the Kings Own Scottish Borderers, almost at the end of the war. It is believed that a German plane, on its way home after a bombing raid, was looking for a target, spotted a light and actually dropped a landmine on the billet where Jim was resting.

In 1932 the Borders Cup was retained, adding more medals to the Johnstone family collection, and the Heart of Midlothian manager Willie McCartney was present as an honoured guest at the celebrations, this time held at the County Hotel. Mr McCartney had earlier brought his Hearts team to Selkirk for a pre-season friendly, which ended in a 4–4 draw, and he had sensibly established good working relations with the Borders club. This would stand him in good stead in future years. In 1946, by then as manager of Hibernian, McCartney would return to Selkirk and reap a rich dividend by signing Hopey's only son, Robert 'Bobby' Johnstone.

The Borders Cup double was the clearest indication that the game in Selkirk was booming, and attendances frequently topped 1,000, and were seldom fewer than 500. The two full-backs, Hopey Johnstone and Jock Buckham, both over six foot, the tallest players in the League, were attracting considerable attention, and both had trials for senior clubs. In 1933 both played in a 3–0 win against Bo'ness in a Scottish Cup tie. By 1937 the original 'Black-house' pavilion was showing serious signs of deterioration; it was replaced with a newer, more substantial structure, better reflecting the clubs status. Much more impressive than its predecessor, in addition to changing facilities, of course, it boasted a committee room, and even had curtains at the windows!

The final Borders Cup win for Selkirk, in 1939, seemingly heralded the end of an era, as it appeared that an attempt by the Berwickshire clubs (including Berwick Rangers) to reduce the size of the League, and thus their travelling expenses, would see off the Selkirkshire pair of Selkirk and Gala Fairydean. But the Eastern-based teams reckoned with the resilience of the Selkirk chairman, Bob Lindsay secured the *status quo* for the start of the 1939–40 season. By now aged 10, young Bobby Johnstone will no doubt have heard his father talking about how old Bob Lindsay's efforts had been to no avail anyway – not too long after the season kicked-off, World War Two broke out, and all clubs under the direction of the Scottish FA were instructed to cease playing organised football until further notice.

Bibliography

Adams, A. *Fifty Years of Sports Report* Collins Willow, London, 1997.

Barnes, K. *This Simple Game* Empire, Manchester, 2005.

Barrett, N. *Daily Telegraph Football Chronicle*, Sevenoaks, London, 2004.

Bateman, G. *Century of Soccer in Selkirk* Selkirk AF & RC, 1990.

Beckett, S. *The Team From a Town of Chimneys* CAS, Manchester, *c.*1983.

Buchan, C. *Football Monthly April 1956* Buchan's Publications.

Butler, B. *Official Illustrated History of the FA Cup* Headline, London, 1996.

Clayton, D. *Everything Under the Blue Moon* Mainstream, Edinburgh, 2002.

Correspondent Ltd DVD – *The Famous Five* Correspondent, 2003.

Crampsey, R. *The Scottish Footballer* Blackwood, Edinburgh, 1978.

Crampsey, R. *The Scottish Football League – First 100 Years* The SFL, Glasgow, 1990.

Deards F. & F. Geddes *Daily Worker Football Annual 1948–49* Peoples Press, 1949.

Durham, S. *Workington AFC 1884–1984*, Durham, Workington, 1984.

Dykes, G. *Oldham Athletic Complete Record 1899–1988* Breedon Books, Derby, 1988.

Eade P. *Images of Sport (Workington AFC)* Tempus, Stroud, 2003.

Eyre, F. *Kicked Into Touch*, Pomona, West Yorks, 2005.

Gardner P. *Manchester City Football Book* Stanley Paul, London, 1979.

Goble, R. *Manchester City – A Complete Record 1887–1987* Breedon Books, Derby, 1987.

James, G. *Farewell to Maine Road* Polar, Leicester, 2002.

James, G. *Manchester – The Greatest City* Polar, Leicester, 2003.

James, G. *Manchester City – A Complete Record*, Breedon, Derby, 2006

Litster, J. CD – *Post-war Scottish League Players* Programme Monthly.

Mccartney, I. *Duncan Edwards – The Full Report* Britespot, West Midlands, 2004.

Mackay, J. *The Hibees*, Donald, Edinburgh, 1987.

Maddox Saffer Robins *Manchester City – Cup Kings 1956*, Over T Moon, Liverpool, 1999.

Mourant, A. *Revie – Portrait of a Football Legend*, Mainstream, Edinburgh, 2003.

Nannestad, I. *Soccer History Magazine 2, 8 and 12* Soccer History Ltd, Birmingham.

Pia, S. *Sunshine On Leith* Mainstream, Edinburgh, 1995.

Penney, I. *Blue Heaven – Manchester City Greatest Games* Mainstream, Edinburgh, 1996.

Penney, I. *Legends of Manchester City* Breedon Books, Derby, 2002.

Rafferty, J. *100 Years of Scottish Football* Pan, London, 1993.

Robinson, M. *Football League Tables 1888–2005* Soccer Books, 2005.

Robotham, R. *Waverley Route – Post-war Years* Ian Allan, Shepperton, 1999.

Rowlands, A. *Trautmann – The Biography* Breedon, Derby, 1990.

Saffer, D. *Images of Sport (MCFC)* Tempus, Stroud 2000.

Sharp, I. and D. Jack *Empire News & Sunday Chronicle Annual* Empire, Manchester, 1957.

Soar, P. & M. Tyler *Encyclopaedia of British Football* Collins Willow, London, 1983.

Thornton, E. *Meredith To Mercer and the FA Cup* Hale, London, 1969.

Waldon, A. & D. Saffer *Manchester City – The Finest Matches* Tempus, Stroud, 2001.

Whittell, I. *Manchester City Greats* Donald, Edinburgh, 1994.

Young, A. *Old Selkirk* Stenlake, Ayrshire, 2005.